Our Stories

"Oh, mother, people get run over by trucks every day. Why can't something like that happen to Uncle Elwood?"
    —*Myrtle Mae Simmons, in* Harvey, *starring James Stewart*

Our Stories

ESSAYS ON LIFE, DEATH, AND FREE WILL

John Martin Fischer

OXFORD
UNIVERSITY PRESS

OXFORD

UNIVERSITY PRESS

Oxford University Press, Inc., publishes works that further
Oxford University's objective of excellence
in research, scholarship, and education.

Oxford   New York
Auckland   Cape Town   Dar es Salaam   Hong Kong   Karachi
Kuala Lumpur   Madrid   Melbourne   Mexico City   Nairobi
New Delhi   Shanghai   Taipei   Toronto

With offices in
Argentina   Austria   Brazil   Chile   Czech Republic   France   Greece
Guatemala   Hungary   Italy   Japan   Poland   Portugal   Singapore
South Korea   Switzerland   Thailand   Turkey   Ukraine   Vietnam

Published by Oxford University Press, Inc.
198 Madison Avenue, New York, New York 10016

www.oup.com

Oxford is a registered trademark of Oxford University Press.

Library of Congress Cataloging-in-Publication Data
Fischer, John Martin, 1952-
Our stories : essays on life, death, and free will /
John Martin Fischer.
   p. cm.
ISBN 978-0-19-537495-6 (hardcover)
ISBN 978-0-19-976723-6 (pbk)
1. Metaphysics.   2. Death.   3. Life.
4. Free will and determinism.   I. Title.

BD95.F57 2009
113'.8—dc22   2008040481

Printed in the United States of America
on acid-free paper

Contents

Acknowledgments

I am very grateful to Neal Tognazzini and Patrick Todd for their excellent assistance in preparing this book for publication.

Permission to reprint the following articles is hereby acknowledged:

John Martin Fischer and Anthony Brueckner, "Why Is Death Bad?" *Philosophical Studies* 50 (1986), pp. 213–21.

"Death, Badness, and the Impossibility of Experience," *Journal of Ethics* 1 (1997), pp. 341–53.

John Martin Fischer and Daniel Speak, "Death and the Psychological Conception of Personal Identity," *Midwest Studies in Philosophy* 24 (2000), pp. 84–93.

John Martin Fischer, "Earlier and Later Birth: Symmetry Through Thick and Thin," Richard Feldman, Kris McDaniel, and Jason R. Raibley (eds.), *The Good, the Right, Life and Death* (Aldershot, England: Ashgate Publishing, 2006), pp. 189–202.

John Martin Fischer, "Why Immortality Is Not So Bad," *International Journal of Philosophical Studies* 2 (1994), pp. 257–70.

John Martin Fischer and Ruth Curl, "Philosophical Models of Immortality in Science Fiction," George Slusser, Gary Westfahl, and Eric S Rabkin, eds., *Immortal Engines: Life Extension and Immortality in Science Fiction and Fantasy* (Athens, Ga.: University of Georgia Press, 1996), pp. 3–12.

John Martin Fischer, "Epicureanism About Death and Immortality," *Journal of Ethics* 10 (2006), pp. 355–81.

John Martin Fischer, "Stories," *Midwest Studies in Philosophy* 20 (1996), pp. 1–14.

John Martin Fischer, "Free Will, Death, and Immortality: The Role of Narrative," *Philosophical Papers* 34 (2005), pp. 379–404.

John Martin Fischer, "Stories and the Meaning of Life", revised and expanded version of "A Reply to Pereboom, Zimmerman, and Smith," part of a book symposium on John Martin Fischer, *My Way: Essays on Moral Responsibility, Philosophical Books* (2006), pp. 235–44; forthcoming in *Philosophic Exchange*.

Our Stories

1

Introduction: Meaning in Life and Death

All around me are familiar faces
Worn out places, worn out faces
Bright and early for their daily races
Going nowhere, going nowhere
Their tears are filling up their glasses
No expression, no expression
Hide my head I want to drown my sorrow
No tomorrow, no tomorrow
And I find it kinda funny
I find it kinda sad
The dreams in which I'm dying
Are the best I've ever had
I find it hard to tell you
I find it hard to take
When people run in circles
It's a very, very mad world mad world
　　"Mad World," as sung by Gary Jules

Let us hope, however, that there is a method to the madness—or at least some philosophical insights that can help to structure the insanity. I shall begin by laying out in the barest bones my overall view on the badness of death, the possible goodness of immortality, and the meaning of life. I believe that the notions of "narrative" (stories) and free will play key roles in understanding these deep and mysterious phenomena, and I shall seek to sketch some of the connections between free will, stories, and the meaning of life. In this introductory essay, I only give the briefest overview of issues I explore in more detail in the essays in the book. Also, I go on to offer some ruminations on the nature and (possible) implications of these views, including suggestions for future directions in thinking about this web of fundamental existential issues.

I. AN OVERVIEW

Let me begin this essay by distinguishing the phenomena picked out by "dying," "death," and "being dead." Dying is part of life—the last part, and it is not too mysterious how it can be bad for the individual who dies (insofar as it can involve pain and suffering).[1] Sometimes death is taken to be the "transition," as it were, between the last part of life and the first part of being dead; metaphorically, death might be thought of as (e.g.) the crossing of the River Styx. But I shall lump together the referents of "death" and "being dead," taking them to be (roughly speaking) the state of permanent nonexistence after being alive.[2]

Now one can ask how death can be bad for the individual who dies. Again, as it is relatively clear that pain and suffering can be bad for an individual, it is not terribly mysterious how the death of one person can be a bad thing for another (living) person. But how can the death of an individual be bad for that very individual? If one believes in an "afterlife" with conscious episodes or something akin to conscious episodes, then it would be fairly straightforward that death could be bad for an individual—it could involve the pain and suffering of Hell. And I certainly don't *know* that there isn't a Hell (i.e., a Hell apart from our actual lives[3]). But here we will simply put the possibility of an afterlife to the side and assume, simply for the sake of the argument, that there is no "afterlife." That is, we assume that death is an experiential blank. Now how can it be that an experiential blank can be bad for an individual? Worse yet, how can it be that this sort of state can be bad for the individual, given that the individual has gone out of existence?

The followers of Epicurus and Lucretius argue that despite the commonsense view that death can indeed be bad for the individual who dies, we can see, upon more careful consideration, that death cannot be bad for the individual who dies. The Epicurean view is that our ordinary belief death is (or at least can be) bad for the very individual who dies is based on a set of confusions. After all, the Epicurean reminds us, badness or misfortune typically involves unpleasant experiences, and presumably it always requires a *subject*. But death is an experiential blank, and it even robs us of a subject. Given that there is no subject when death takes place, when exactly does the harm, badness, or misfortune of death occur? Given these difficulties, death cannot be bad for the individual who dies, according to the Epicurean. The commonsense view is based on a failure to think carefully about the philosophical issues, and perhaps a conflation of the "body" (that does, lamentably, molder in the grave or otherwise decay) and the person.

Lucretius adds a fascinating and important argument to the arsenal provided by Epicurus. Lucretius points out that, on the view according to which death is nonexistence and an experiential blank, it is the "mirror image" of the time before we were born (or perhaps conceived). Prenatal and posthumous nonexistence seem to have relevantly similar features; but since we are indifferent to prenatal nonexistence, we should be indifferent to posthumous nonexistence. Put in other words, since we don't regret that we were born when we were born rather than significantly earlier, we should not think that it is a bad thing that we will die when we actually die, rather than later. Lucretius challenges us to say what the relevant difference is between prenatal and posthumous nonexistence.

I attempt to defend the commonsense view that death can (although it need not be) a bad thing for the individual who dies.[4] First, I take on the challenges posed by Epicurus and his followers. I claim, following Thomas Nagel, that death can be a bad thing for the individual who dies insofar as it is a *deprivation* of the goods of life; a bit more carefully, the view is that death is a bad thing for the individual who dies, when it is in fact a bad thing, insofar as it deprives him of what would be on balance a good life (or at least a life minimally worth living).[5] So the badness of death (when it is indeed bad) does not consist in anything "positive," as it were; it consists entirely in being a deprivation of certain sorts of goods—goods involved in the continuation of a worthwhile life. (Of course, not any old deprivation of goods will be a misfortune of the relevant sort: the fact that I didn't win the California Lottery today constitutes a deprivation of certain goods, but it presumably does not thereby count as a misfortune or bad thing for me.) Insofar as the badness of death consists entirely in its being a certain sort of deprivation, it is compatible with there being no unpleasant experiences. I thus need to defend the thesis that some things can genuinely be bad for an individual without involving *any* unpleasant experiences at all.

In "Why Is Death Bad?" (chapter 2), I (together with my coauthor, Anthony Brueckner) begin a defense of the examples provided by Nagel; that is, we defend his conclusion that some things can be bad for an individual *without* involving *any* unpleasant experiences.[6] Nagel's first example is of a man who is (apparently) "betrayed" by his so-called friends behind his back. That is, we can suppose that a person's acquaintances and even relatives regularly get together without the individual's ever finding out about these meetings, or experiencing *anything* as a result of these meetings.[7] At the meetings, the people excoriate their "friend," impugning all his work, contending that he cheats on his wife, that he is disloyal to his family, and that he is a cowardly and creepy pervert. Nagel argues that the man is indeed betrayed, and that he has been wronged; it is not simply that the people have behaved badly, but a bad thing has happened to the individual himself (although, admittedly, this is not a bad that is experienced as such).

I agree with Nagel. Consider, also, an example provided by Robert Nozick.[8] Nozick asks us to imagine that someone has secretly placed a camera in your bedroom and is videotaping all the goings-on. You (reasonably) believe that you have privacy in your bedroom, but your activities are beamed by satellite to movie theaters in Outer Mongolia. We can, as with Nagel's example, stipulate that you are causally isolated from Outer Mongolia, and that there are *no* consequences for you (including unpleasant experiences) as a result of the camera in your bedroom.

Nevertheless, Nozick argues that you have been wronged by the placement of the camera in your bedroom; it is not simply that someone has acted badly; *your right to privacy has been violated*. I agree with Nozick: a bad thing has happened to you, even though you are unaware of it.

Now in both Nagel's case of the man betrayed behind his back and Nozick's case of the violation of privacy, it might be thought that at least it is *possible* (in some sense) that the individuals find out about the relevant activities; further, it might be thought that it is this *possibility*, with the attendant possibility of unpleasant experiences, that explains the badness in both cases (if indeed there is badness for the individuals in question). Nagel, however, has an insightful response:

> Loss, betrayal, deception, and ridicule are on this view bad because people suffer when they learn of them. But it should be asked how our ideas of human value would have to be constituted to accommodate these cases directly instead. One advantage of such an account might be that it would enable us to explain *why* the discovery of these misfortunes causes suffering—in a way that makes it reasonable. For the natural view is that the discovery of betrayal makes us unhappy because it is bad to be betrayed—not that betrayal is bad because its discovery makes us unhappy.[9]

Given this sort of worry (to which Nagel seeks to respond), however, it might be helpful to have examples in which we would be inclined to say that an individual has been harmed (or that a bad thing has happened to the individual), even though he *cannot* experience anything unpleasant as a result of the thing. It seems to me that Nagel has provided an additional example of precisely the required kind. Nagel asks us to imagine that an intelligent adult receives a brain injury (perhaps as a result of an accident or stroke) which leaves him in the "mental condition of a contented infant, and that such desires as remain to him can be satisfied by a custodian, so that he is free from care."[10] It would seem that, after the brain injury, it is both true that the individual does not have any unpleasant experiences (as a result of the injury) and also *cannot* have any such experiences; but, intuitively, he has been harmed by the stroke or accident—a bad thing has happened to him, although he has no experiential access to the badness.

Consider, similarly, my revision of Nagel's betrayal-behind-one's back example, which I present in "Death, Badness, and the Impossibility of Experience," (chapter 3). Here I employ the resources of "Frankfurt-cases"—examples provided by Harry Frankfurt which purport to impugn the Principle of Alternative Possibilities (PAP), according to which moral responsibility for performing some action requires genuine metaphysical access to an alternative possibility in which one does otherwise.[11] I thus seek to forge a connection between central issues in the free will/moral responsibility debates and the debates about the metaphysics of death.[12] It will be helpful to have a version of a Frankfurt-case before us:

> Black is a basically nice, but admittedly also slightly naughty, neurosurgeon. He has secretly inserted a chip in Jones's brain which enables Black to monitor and control Jones's brain activities. Black can exercise this control through a sophisticated computer which he has programmed so that, among other things, it monitors Jones's voting behavior. Black is a committed Democrat, and he has yet again signed up with the Democratic Party to be of service. (Black lives in Chicago, where worse things happen, and, as he says, "It is the least I can do to help.") If Jones were to show any inclination to vote for McCain (or, let us say, anyone other than Obama), then the computer, through the chip in Jones's brain, would intervene to assure that he actually decides to vote for Obama and does so vote. But if Jones decides on his own to vote for Obama (as Black, the old progressive, would prefer), the computer does nothing but continue to monitor—without affecting—the goings-on in Jones's head.
>
> Now suppose that Jones decides to vote for Obama on his own, just as he would have if Black had not inserted the chip in his head. It seems, upon first thinking about this case, that Jones can be held morally responsible for this choice and act of voting for Obama, although he could not have chosen otherwise and he could not have done otherwise.[13]

Return to Nagel's betrayal-behind-one's back example, but now add a Frankfurt-style "counterfactual intervener," White.[14] White is, like Frankfurt's Black, a strictly *counterfactual* intervener. That is, White plays no role in how the story actually unfolds, because he doesn't need to. But we suppose that he can effectively prevent you from ever finding out about the secret meetings and the betrayals that take place at those unfortunate meetings. So, for example, if someone were about to call you to inform you of these meetings, White can prevent him from making the connection; perhaps White can snip the telephone wire, or White can temporarily paralyze the person, or whatever. We suppose that White stands by, like Black, disposed to intervene to prevent you from finding out about the betrayals; given that White is envisaged as having the power to prevent you from ever finding out anything about the meetings, you *cannot* have any unpleasant experiences as a result of those meetings. And yet it seems that you are harmed by the activities at those meetings—you have been betrayed, even though you have no experiential access to the betrayals.

The revised betrayal example and the brain-injury example seem to be cases in which something bad has happened to an individual and yet that individual *cannot* experience anything unpleasant as a result. Consider, also, an example due to Jeff McMahon.[15] In this example, your daughter is trekking in the Himalayas and tragically dies in an accident. Before you can possibly find out about this tragedy—say five minutes after the death—you (independently) die of a sudden heart attack. (This was not a good day for you.) It seems to me that the death of your daughter is a bad thing for you; your interests are intertwined with hers in such a way that her death is a deeply bad thing for you. And yet, given the circumstances, you *cannot* (in any relevant sense) experience anything unpleasant as a result of her death. For the last five minutes of your life, you have been harmed, although you have no experiential access to the harm (or its etiology).

So, arguably, there are cases in which something bad happens to an individual, and yet the individual cannot experience anything unpleasant as a consequence. In this respect, death—construed as a permanent experiential blank—could be assimilated to these examples. But there is still an arguably crucial difference between death and the examples in question: death robs us of a subject, whereas the subject persists in all of the examples. Thus, we cannot *straightforwardly* extrapolate from the apparent badness in the three examples (the brain-injury case, the revised betrayal case, and the trekking case) to the badness of death.

I nevertheless think that, upon reflection, we should conclude that death is *relevantly similar* to the examples under consideration. In developing my defense of this contention, I discuss the signature structure of what I have called "Dialectical Stalemates," and I draw additional comparisons between the debates about free will and moral responsibility, on the one hand, and the debates about death, on the other (see chapter 7). I argue that, whereas we have here an argumentative Black Hole (Dialectical Stalemate) similar to those encountered in the free will debates (and, indeed, other philosophical contexts such as discussions of epistemological skepticism), our philosophical response to the Stalemates here should be different. Although I argue for a *restructuring* of the debates about free will and moral responsibility, I argue for a different approach to the debates about the putative badness of death.[16]

I have thus sought to reply to the objections raised by Epicurus to the commonsense view that death can be bad for the individual who dies. But what about Lucretius' Mirror-Image Argument? Nagel says that the asymmetry in our attitudes toward our own past and future nonexistence is "the most perplexing feature of our attitude toward death."[17] I (with my coauthor, Anthony Brueckner), have addressed this deeply puzzling characteristic of our ordinary attitudes.[18] Our claim (following Parfit) here is that human beings have asymmetric attitudes toward pleasures and pains; holding other things fixed, and assuming that we are situated at a particular point in time, we prefer our own pleasures in the future and pains in the past. The crucial point for us in this context pertains to *pleasures* (or experiences of a positive nature), not pains;

insofar as death deprives us of future pleasures, there is a reason to be particularly concerned about death, as opposed to prenatal nonexistence. That is, we argue that the ordinary asymmetry in our attitudes toward prenatal and posthumous nonexistence is a special case of a more general asymmetry in our attitudes toward past and future pleasures; we prefer our pleasures in the future, holding other things fixed, and we are relatively indifferent to past pleasures.

Note that this explanation makes some progress insofar as it exhibits the asymmetry in our attitudes toward prenatal and posthumous nonexistence as a special case of a more general asymmetry; but a full explanation would establish the rationality (or appropriateness) of the more general asymmetry. I discuss this difficult issue in "Earlier Birth and Later Death: Symmetry Through Thick and Thin" (chapter 5). Also, there is further discussion of the Brueckner/Fischer approach to addressing the asymmetry in our attitudes toward prenatal and posthumous nonexistence, including a defense of this strategy against alternative strategies in John Martin Fischer and Daniel Speak, "Death and the Psychological Conception of Personal Identity" (chapter 4) and "Earlier Birth and Later Death: Symmetry Through Thick and Thin" (chapter 5).

I have, then, charted out an overall strategy of response to some of the major concerns about commonsense views about death raised by Epicurus and Lucretius. I have defended the deprivation account of death's badness, and I (together with Brueckner) have shown how our asymmetric attitudes toward prenatal and posthumous nonexistence follow from a more general asymmetry (that is arguably defensible). Now if death can be a bad thing for the individual who dies, it might seem that we should wish for immortality (that is, eternal life in some sort of embodied form). Again, it is arguably a part of ordinary thinking that immortality would in fact be desirable, given the right circumstances. I have again attempted to defend common sense against the more curmudgeonly view of many philosophers (such as Heidegger and Bernard Williams) to the effect that immortality would *necessarily* be unattractive (if coherent at all). I argue against the immortality curmudgeons in "Why Immortality Is Not So Bad" (chapter 6), "Epicureanism About Death and Immortality" (chapter 7), and "Free Will, Death, and Immortality: The Role of Narrative" (chapter 9).

Return to the Frankfurt-case sketched above. Recall that in the example, Jones chooses to vote for Obama and does vote for Obama "on his own" (and without the intervention of Black). The actual sequence that issues in Jones's choice and action flows exactly as it would have, had there been no Black (or other "counterfactual intervener"). In various places, I have argued that we can learn important lessons from the Frankfurt cases.[19] I have argued that the cases are part of an overall package of considerations that render it plausible that an agent can act freely and be morally responsible for his actions, even though he lacks genuine metaphysical access to alternative possibilities. Given that there can be moral responsibility without the sort of control that involves access to alternative possibilities, the *value* of acting so as to be morally responsible—what we care about in caring about moral responsibility—cannot be explicated in terms of the value of metaphysical access to alternative possibilities ("freedom to choose and do otherwise"). More specifically, I contend that the value of acting so as to be morally responsible is *not* the value of "making a difference," but of "making a statement" (of a certain sort).[20] More specifically, my contention is that the value of acting so as to be morally responsible is a species of the value of self-expression.

Of course, I do not think that the value of acting so as to be morally responsible trumps all other sort of value in all circumstances; nor do I suppose that the value of self-expression is hegemonic. My contention is simply that the value of acting so as to be morally responsible—what we care about in caring about being morally responsible agents—is the value, whatever that is, of a certain distinctive kind of self-expression.

But what is this kind of self-expression? In a nutshell, my view is that it is a species of artistic or aesthetic self-expression. When we act freely (and thus exhibit the kind of control that grounds moral responsibility), we are, to put it metaphorically, writing a sentence in the stories of our lives. More specifically, in exhibiting the distinctive control involved in moral responsibility, we make it the case that our lives have a certain dimension of value: narrative value. Insofar as having an irreducible narrative dimension of value presupposes that our lives are indeed narratives or "stories," strictly speaking, we are properly thought of as the authors of the stories of our lives. As such, we are engaging in a species of aesthetic activity. Note that, although our free actions are a species of artistic or aesthetic self-expression, the *value* we place on such self-expression is not necessarily a specifically *aesthetic* form of value. My claim is that the *nature* of the activity involved in free action is aesthetic self-expression; further, I contend that its *value* is the value—whatever kind of value it is—that we place on this specific sort of aesthetic activity. Note that the value in question might be "moral" or "ethical" in a broad sense, or value from the perspective of living a good life; in addition to leaving the *kind* of value open, I also mean to leave open the *amount* of the value in question. For further discussion, see "Stories and the Meaning of Life" (chapter 10).

The above claims employ notions that need considerable attention, even if they cannot be given complete reductive analyses. First, what exactly is a "narrative" or "story," strictly speaking, and what is the putatively irreducible "narrative dimension of value"? Here my work builds on some of the important work of David Velleman, although I depart from Velleman in some crucial ways.[21]

What exactly is a narrative or—in the strict sense—a story? After all, we can write the "story"—in a loose sense—of just about anything. We can, for instance, write the story of the table on which my laptop computer currently sits, or the laptop itself, or the rocks around the beautiful tree outside my window—or, for that matter, the tree or the window or... But arguably these would not be "stories, strictly speaking"; instead we can call them mere chronicles. What turns a chronicle into a narrative or story, strictly speaking? To mimic Wittgenstein's famous question about what needs to be added to mere behavior to get *action*, what ingredient needs to be added to a chronicle to get something more than a *mere* chronicle: a full-blooded story?

The answer, according to Velleman, is that a full-blooded story or narrative is a chronicle that is apt to produce (presumably in a certain audience) a certain sort of understanding, including a distinctively *affective* or *emotional* component. A story, as opposed to a mere chronicle, is apt (in a certain audience) to produce not just an "aha-moment," but an emotionally suffused aha-moment. Arguably, then, a narrative or story provides a certain sort of understanding or explanation—one that allows the audience to "comprehend" something in some sense "as a whole," and where this comprehension is in part affective (or affectively underwritten). A narrative or story, in a strict sense, is a chronicle with emotional hooks, as it were.

This view about narrativity has various interesting implications. It resonates with Martha Nussbaum's view that reading fiction is necessary in order to gain the kind of insight that is required for deep moral insight and understanding. On Nussbaum's view, it is precisely because stories, strictly speaking, elicit and engage the emotions that they are crucial to moral understanding. I discuss Nussbaum's views, and the role of stories (and hypothetical examples) in moral understanding, in "Stories" (chapter 8). It is also sometimes claimed that, insofar as our lives are stories (in a strict sense) or narratives, they must have a beginning, middle, and (most importantly), an end. That is, some have claimed that, if we model our lives on narratives, we will have to say that immortality is incoherent. I explore and (not surprisingly) reject this suggestion in "Free Will, Death, and Immortality: The Role of Narrative" (chapter 9).

Given that we have some sort of grasp of what it would be for our lives to be narratives, what does it mean that our lives have an irreducible narrative dimension of value? This is admittedly a difficult and delicate issue, but I think it can be given a tolerably clear explication. Velleman argues that we have a dimension of value that cannot be reduced to considerations of "welfare" or "utility" experienced at certain times (or during certain durations); that is, this dimension is not to be understood in terms of a function that combines such welfare or utility in *any* way.[22] Rather, it is a matter of our lives having certain structural features, or perhaps it is a matter of the *relationships* between various parts of our lives. More specifically, we score higher on this dimension insofar as the various parts of our lives *fit together* in certain ways—ways arguably characteristic of certain (but *not all*) deeply resonant stories, and not capturable solely in terms of utility information.

Unfortunately, Velleman does not give a general account of the relevant sort of relationships between parts of our lives, in virtue of which we have greater value along the narrative dimension; and I do not think that I can provide such an account. It is perhaps helpful, however, to have before us some examples of the sorts of relationship in question. Velleman offers the following sorts of examples. Arguably, we prefer a life in which we thrive as a result of learning from our mistakes rather than from mere accident, or a life in which we flourish as a result of conscientiousness and hard work, rather than a mere windfall (such as winning the lottery). A life in which we complete projects or fulfill commitments seems to be preferable to a more fragmented, unconnected life, even holding fixed the sum total of aggregate utility (welfare) or even the profile of utility (welfare) over time. Although the examples are perhaps less plentiful than desirable, and the analysis at best highly sketchy, I believe that there is something important in Velleman's contention: we do seem to care not just about utility (combined and weighted in various possible ways), but we also care about how the parts of our lives hang together, as it were. More specifically, we seem to care about certain relationships that can reasonably be dubbed "narrative" in character, where this rubric groups together a congeries of different elements of what we can recognize as stories of lives that in some sense go well.

Despite the somewhat unsatisfactory lack of completeness in Velleman's (and my) presentation, I maintain that it is at least plausible to suppose that our lives have an irreducible dimension of value that can be described as "narrative." Note that this notion of narrative value is crucially different from the notion that is relevant to (say) a reader of a story or a literary critic (insofar as such critics actually read stories any longer!); that is, a story can be "good in the telling," but not score high along the narrative dimension of value identified above. We can recognize certain chronicles as stories, strictly speaking, at least in part in virtue of their tendency to elicit a certain emotional response. So, for example, if I tell you about a man who tries so hard to succeed that he thwarts his own efforts, you may well recognize this as a story, strictly speaking, and not as a mere chronicle. It might not however yet be a story that's good in the telling; this depends crucially on *how* the story is told. Finally, such a story might pass both the test of *being a story, strictly speaking*, and being a story *good in the telling*, but *not* score high along the narrative dimension of value.

Above, I warned against inferring from the nature of our free actions as aesthetic activity to the conclusion that the *value* of such activity is properly considered *aesthetic*. Additionally, it is extremely important not to conflate the notion of *good in the telling* with a higher score along the narrative dimension of value. A story of one's life can be rather boring, from the perspective of (say) a literary critic or potential "reader," but score high marks along the narrative dimension of value. It is important to note that I do *not* in any way wish to suggest that we pattern our lives on good stories (in the sense of good in the telling), or that we employ primarily aesthetic considerations (in the sense of "good in the telling") in our practical reasoning. These views might be defended by other philosophers, but they are no part of my views.[23] For further discussion, see "Stories and the Meaning of Life" (chapter 10).

I *do* contend that it is specifically by our acting freely—our exercise of the distinctive kind of control involved in moral responsibility—that we make it the case our lives have an irreducibly narrative dimension of value: "Free Will, Death, and Immortality: The Role of Narrative" (chapter 9). Although it is hard to *prove* this thesis, it does seem to me correct. Imagine, for example, a man who has learned (painfully) from many years of failure in relationships; perhaps he has engaged in difficult (and expensive!) psycho-dynamically informed psychotherapy, and he combines these hard-earned insights with hard work in his new relationship. Although it is not straightforward or easy for him, he builds a healthy, satisfying new relationship, and he finds great satisfaction in it. Contrast this man with one who is equally frustrated in a series of failed relationships, but engages in no attempt to learn from them and no subsequent efforts to change his behavior. Rather, his brain is secretly manipulated (perhaps the neurosurgeon Black, bored with his role as a purely counterfactual intervener in the Frankfurt-cases, has run amok) to induce precisely the sorts of change in behavior that come "the old-fashioned way" for the first man. I think we would all say that the first man's life has more value than the second man's, even though the utility-information may well be the same in both lives. Further, note that the behavior is the same in both lives; the only difference is that the first man's is free, whereas (after the relevant point) the second man's is not. More specifically, I think it is plausible that the first man's life has (or scores more highly on) the irreducible narrative dimension of value, whereas the second man's lacks this dimension entirely (after the point of external intervention and manipulation).

More generally, consider scenarios in which individuals are secretly manipulated in such a way that it would be indisputable that they were not acting freely. Stipulate that the manipulation is clandestine and inaccessible to the conscious awareness. Now, presumably, we can think about various life-histories involving learning from mistakes, thriving as a result of hard work and conscientious efforts (rather than sudden windfalls), and so forth. In all of these cases, I contend that the fact that the stretches of the lives instantiate the relevant relationships—the relationships in virtue of which we would (apart form the manipulation) say that the lives score higher on the narrative dimension of value—is entirely *irrelevant* to the overall value of the lives. That is, when the kind of control associated with moral responsibility is lacking, I do *not* have any intuition that it *matters* that (say) someone has succeeded as a result of hard work, rather than winning the lottery; that fact does not matter apart from the underwriting provided by the relevant kind of free will. And yet in general we *do* think it matters that our lives (or stretches of them) instantiate the relationships in question. I conclude that it is in virtue of our exercising our capacity for free will—more specifically, our acting freely—that we are the kinds of creatures whose lives have an irreducible narrative dimension of value. I contend that by exercising a distinctive kind of control, we endow our lives with this additional dimension of value, and we thus become the authors of our life-stories. (Of course, it does *not* follow, as I have emphasized above, that in writing the story we should be guided exclusively or primarily by aesthetic considerations or factors that make for a better story *in the telling*. Nor does it follow that I should seek to *experience* my life as a narrative, to interpret it as a narrative, and so forth.)

II. CONTINUITY

Followers of Epicurus typically point to the *differences* between death and what might be called (perhaps somewhat tendentiously) "standard" evils (misfortunes or "bad things"). As discussed above, death (construed as an experiential blank) differs from standard evils insofar as it does not involve unpleasant experiences. Also, death robs us of a subject, so that the "existence requirement" (the claim that all evils require a contemporaneous subject) is not met. Finally, standard evils are "comparative" in nature; to the extent that something is bad for an individual, it makes the individual worse off than he otherwise would be. Typically, then, we would compare an individual's situation in the scenario in which he is affected by the purportedly bad thing with the situation of that very individual in relevant alternative scenarios in which he is not so affected. But death makes such comparisons impossible. The Epicurean tends to focus on what are deemed paradigmatic or standard evils, note these salient differences, and conclude that death cannot be an evil (or bad thing) for the individual who dies.

But there is another way of looking at these matters.[24] Common sense presumably has it that if *anything* is (typically or at least often) a bad thing for an individual, it is death; that is, death is arguably a *paradigmatic* harm (or bad thing). So whatever other harms there are, our philosophical theorizing should accommodate death's being a harm (or evil or bad thing). Perhaps then we should divide the class of evils (or bad things) into standard and non-standard subclasses. On this way of proceeding, the standard evils involve unpleasant experiences, satisfy the existence requirement, and are comparative in nature. In contrast, nonstandard evils (including death) would not meet (all of) these criteria. A defender of the common sense view here might insist that the claim that death can be a bad thing for the individual who dies is on firmer footing than the alleged requirements that evil requires a subject, that it involves unpleasant experiences, and that it is essentially comparative.

How can this debate be resolved? That is, what is the route past the relevant Dialectical Stalemates? I have suggested what I take to be a promising path (chapter 7). Here, I simply wish to note that there might be something to be said for the kind of "continuity" that appears to underwrite the commonsense view that death can indeed be a bad thing for the individual who dies. This, roughly speaking, is what I have in mind. Think of various indisputable and unproblematic harms, such as pain. If I twist your arm for thirty seconds, thus causing you pain during this period, I thereby cause you harm. As we ratchet up the level of pain and/or its duration, presumably we also increase the level or severity of the harm. If we add tissue damage or damage to the functioning of the body and/or mind, we again increase the severity of the harm. Rape, dismemberment, mutilation, and torture are clearly among the most severe evils one can undergo. Now suppose that (say) torture is so severe that it issues in the individual's death. It would seem natural that this would make the harm of the torture *even worse*. It seems to follow that there is a kind of *continuity* in the nature of harm.

Let me try to say a little more about this notion of continuity. There are certain features—call them "Level One Features"—that appear to be arranged on a spectrum of increasing intensity or significance. In the examples, these features include pain, suffering, and various kinds of impairment and damage. Further, it is natural to suppose that the "Level Two Feature" of evil (badness or misfortune) in some sense *supervenes* on the Level One Features. At least it seems that as the Level One Features become more and more significant—that is, as we move along the spectrum of Level One Features—this is reflected at Level Two in greater severity of harm. But the Epicurean must say that when we get to death, there is a radical *discontinuity*; although death would appear to be at the far end of the Level One spectrum, this is *not* reflected continuously at Level Two. Put slightly differently, as the features that intuitively underwrite harm-attributions get more and more significant, this is reflected in greater harm *until we get to death*, where there is suddenly no harm at all.

Now I believe that in general we should aim for philosophical understanding of various phenomena that meets certain desiderata, including (but, of course, not limited to) elegance and comprehensiveness. I also have a preference for such features as *symmetry* and *continuity*. (Note that, on this approach, the equilibrium or default position is symmetry, but *explained* asymmetry [as with our asymmetric attitudes toward prenatal and posthumous nonexistence] is perfectly acceptable.) Granted, the preference is somewhat weak, and can be defeated or outweighed by other considerations. But there is something to be said for continuity.

Of course, the Epicurean might well point to continuity as one of the factors that *confuses* us. That is, he might grant that philosophical homeostasis tends toward such features as symmetry and continuity, and we thus get lulled into thinking that death is just straightforwardly at the end of the Level Two spectrum that supervenes on the Level One harm-relevant features. But the Epicurean will insist that this is a mistake, and that upon more careful reflection, we should resist the underlying picture that favors continuity. I do not have a knockdown response to the Epicurean here, but I simply commend the beauty and appeal of the framework that embodies continuity. Given that the Epicurean presumably has no knockdown argument for the framework within which we consider death *outside* the set of harms rather than a *nonstandard harm*, I suggest that the appeal of continuity (understood and applied as above) might constitute at least a small consideration on behalf of the ordinary view that death can indeed be a bad thing for the individual who dies.

Perhaps it is also noteworthy that my approach to immortality embraces a *similar* kind of continuity. I argue that immortality can be (although it need not be) a good thing for the individual who is immortal. Start with an indisputably rich, attractive, and meaningful human life—filled with pleasant experiences, relationships, and significant accomplishments. Suppose that the individual dies at 70. Surely we can get an even *more attractive* life by adding more pleasant experiences, more or deeper relationships, and/or more significant accomplishments. And presumably, we can get an even more attractive life by adding (say) two years; wouldn't it be better if the life ended at 72 (other things equal) than 70? And wouldn't it be even better if it ended at 75? And so forth.

Presumably, there are features at Level One—such as pleasant experiences, relationships, and accomplishments—that intuitively are the basis of Level Two properties of lives, such as desirability. Again, as above, it seems natural to suppose that the Level One features are (or can be) arranged along a spectrum of increasing significance. Further, it is extremely plausible to think that there is a supervenience relation such that as we move along the Level One spectrum, this is reflected at Level Two. That is, it is intuitively appealing to think that as the Level One features become more and more significant, the relevant

Level Two features, such as desirability or goodness become greater. (I have argued that we must be careful to think of moving along the Level One spectrum in a way that is sensitive to various factors, including the nature and *distribution* of the various features.) In contrast, the skeptics about immortality—the immorality curmudgeons—appear to be committed to a *radical discontinuity*; they will concede that our lives get better and better as they are more pleasant and increasingly filled with meaningful relationships and accomplishments—but suddenly they cannot be good at all when they become *infinitely long*. As with death, I find this discontinuity at least a bit jarring and disconcerting. I prefer continuity.

Now, as above, the immortality curmudgeon will insist that our general preference for continuity has perhaps lulled us into a mistaken complacency about immortality. It has, according to the curmudgeons, inclined us not to focus on the *fundamental differences* between very long but finite life and *immortal life*. And, again, I do not have a knockdown argument against this view. Rather, I simply report that I do not see exactly why the indisputable differences between very long but finite life and immortal life would *make a difference* as regards desirability. I consider this one of the most difficult and challenging issues surrounding immortality. I have argued that, properly understood, immortal life would involve a mix of activities that could propel us into the future with genuine engagement; and I do not see exactly why this engagement would disappear as we move from a very long finite life to an immoral life. But perhaps this simply reflects my cognitive limitations or lack of imagination.

In any case, I take it that, absent a decisive argument on either side, there is something to be said for continuity. Indeed, I prefer a picture of the possible badness of death and the possible goodness of immorality that employs a framework that embraces the relevant sort of continuity. Indeed, perhaps it is a consideration in favor of my overall view that it is *symmetrically continuous*, as it were; the continuities in the considerations pertinent to death and immortality turn out to be isomorphic. At the very least, I hope that invocation of the notion of continuity can help to structure and illuminate key aspects of the debates about the (possible) badness of death and (possible) goodness of immortality; the proponents of common sense tend to be driven by certain sorts of continuities, whereas the skeptics are driven by salient discontinuities.

III. SELF-EXPRESSION: SOME SPECULATIONS

III.1. Close Calls Versus Clear Cases

In this section, I take the liberty of offering a few suggestions that are (if this is possible!) even more speculative, and less tightly argued for, than those of the previous sections. I hope that, even if they are not entirely persuasive, they will be to some extent both illuminating and suggestive. The ideas all pertain—in some way or another—to the central notion of self-expression.

I have argued that the "value" of acting so as to be morally responsible—what we care about in caring about moral responsibility—is making a statement (of a certain sort), not making a difference (of a certain sort). Here I rely to some extent on what I take to be the moral of the Frankfurt stories—that there can be cases of moral responsibility in which the relevant agent lacks genuine metaphysical access to the appropriate kind of alternative possibilities.[25] Given that what we care about in caring about moral responsibility is present in such cases, we cannot construe this as involving the importance of making a difference. Rather, upon reflection, I believe that it is plausible that the value of acting so as to be morally responsible can be understood as a species of the value—whatever that is—of artistic self-expression. After all, in acting freely, we are writing a sentence in the book of our lives—we are so acting that our lives have an irreducibly narrative dimension of value (a dimension that presupposes that our lives are indeed stories, strictly speaking).

I suggest that this explanation of the value of acting so as to be morally responsible might illuminate an extremely puzzling disagreement among philosophers who have written about free will and moral responsibility. Some philosophers *anchor* free will and moral responsibility in contexts in which "reason" (presumably, practical reason) does *not* clearly dictate a correct path. Of course, there are various such contexts, but the key is that the agent's reasons for action do not clearly or obviously recommend one course of action over others apparently available to the agent. Perhaps these cases involve conflicts between morality and prudence, or conflicts internal to morality or prudence; maybe in these contexts reasons are comparable but "close" or maybe the reasons are incommensurable. In any case, in Close Calls practical reason does not commend a unique choice and action. The proponents of Close Calls as anchoring free will and moral responsibility point to such contexts as the fundamental or basic locus of free will and moral responsibility; they sometimes claim that it is only in such contexts that an agent exhibits "true freedom" and moral responsibility, and they typically wish to "trace" all genuine instances of free will and moral responsibility back to Close Calls.

On the other hand, other philosophers find this view highly implausible; they think of Close Calls as contexts characterized by *arbitrariness*, which they take to be antithetical to the sort of *control* that is involved in free will and moral responsibility. The proponents of Clear Cases as anchoring free will and moral responsibility contend that it is only when practical reason clearly dictates a unique path that we are truly free and morally responsible; typically, such philosophers will claim that all cases of genuine free will and moral responsibility must be traceable back to Clear Cases.

It has long been puzzling to me how to explain the debate between proponents of Close-Call freedom and Clear-Case freedom. It has seemed to me that the differences in views must be based on a difference at a deeper, more fundamental level. It might be suggested that the proponents of Close-Call freedom must be implicitly adopting the "make-a-difference" view about the value of acting so as to be morally responsible, whereas the proponents of Clear-Case freedom must be implicitly adopting the "make-a-statement" view. The "make-a-difference" view may in fact motivate some proponents of Close-Call freedom. But I believe that a proponent of Close-Call freedom would wish to accommodate the moral of the Frankfurt stories; that is, nothing in the view that Close-Call freedom is the anchor of free will and moral responsibility requires that the relevant agent have genuine metaphysical access to alternative possibilities (and thus the power to make a difference of the relevant kind). That is, the main point emphasized by the proponent of Close-Call freedom is that agents are truly free when they make a choice that is not uniquely dictated by practical reason; this point is completely compatible with the relevant agent's not having freedom to choose and do otherwise. (Note that it is thus a mistake to assimilate Close-Call freedom to the traditional doctrine of the *liberty of indifference* or to assimilate the debate between the proponents of Close-Call freedom and Clear-Case freedom to the debate between the proponents of liberty of indifference and the proponents of liberty of spontaneity.)

Consider the possibility that the more fundamental idea is that the value of acting so as to be morally responsible is the value of a certain distinctive kind of self-expression. If this is correct, we can perhaps illuminate the debate between the proponents of Close-Call freedom and the proponents of Clear-Case freedom. Perhaps the proponents of Close-Call freedom are emphasizing the "creativity" component of self-expression; here the idea is that nothing external to the agent, including the configuration of practical reasons—*requires* any particular decision or action. Rather, the decision comes entirely from the *unconstrained creative activity of the agent*. In contrast, it might be that the proponent of Clear-Case freedom emphasizes a different aspect of self-expression— the idea of "endorsement." Sometimes self-expression involves rational endorsement or agreement with what one takes to be the course of action or policy dictated by reason.

Although I have only given the bare bones of my suggestion here, I have broached the idea that we can explain the apparently intractable debates between proponents of Close-Call freedom and proponents of Clear-Case freedom by invoking a deeper agreement on the value of self-expression. Both parties to the dispute might be understood as adopting the fundamental value of self-expression. But the disagreement issues from an emphasis on two different elements or "faces" of self-expression: pure creativity and reflective endorsement. My own view is that we should look to *neither* Close-Call contexts *nor* Clear-Case contexts as the anchors of free will and moral responsibility. I believe that it is a mistake to suppose that either of these sorts of contexts is the home of true freedom, or that we must trace back to such contexts to anchor our subsequent attributions of freedom and moral responsibility. Perhaps a consideration in my favor here issues precisely from acceptance of the very idea under discussion that what we value in acting so as to be morally responsible is self-expression of a signature sort. If this is correct, one will find unsatisfactory any view that flows from only a *part* or *element* of the relevant sort of self-expression; and it is clear that neither pure creativity nor reflective endorsement captures the entirety of the notion of self-expression.

Further, I believe that, whereas pure creativity and reflective endorsement capture notions that are importantly *related* to the relevant elements of self-expression, each actually is a *distortion* of the basic notion of self-expression that is involved in moral responsibility. The problem with pure, unconstrained creativity is that it is hard to see how this differs from mere arbitrariness, and it is also hard to see how such activity flows from the *agent* (the agent's values and reasons) in the right way. The problem with reflective endorsement is that we sometimes act freely *without* reflective endorsement; that is, we sometimes freely do what we do *not* believe to be normatively defensible. Weakness of the will is a fact of life, and it presents a devastating problem for reflective endorsement accounts. For example, it seems to me to be the basis of a decisive objection to the "normative" approach to moral responsibility pioneered by Gary Watson—an objection I do not believe Watson or his followers have ever adequately addressed.[26]

III.2. Authorship, God, and Freedom

Some of the proponents of irreducible Agent-Causation have contended that our distinctive agency consists (in part) in a Godlike power to create *ex nihilo*. But the problems with irreducible agent-causation (causation by an agent that is not reducible to causation by agent-involving events) and divine creation *ex nihilo* can be seen to be similar, at least insofar as the notions are taken to play a certain theoretical role. If a God who can create *ex nihilo* is posited as part of a Cosmological Argument—an argument according to which ordinary attributions of causation or perhaps ordinary explanation can only be defensible if there is an uncaused cause (or unexplained explainer)—it is natural to respond that such a God is merely the *label* for a desideratum. That is, it might seem that the only way we can defend our ordinary attributions of causation or our ordinary explanations is if there were an entity with certain properties; but, even if this were true, it would only point to the *desirability* of the existence of such an entity. It would *not* thereby provide any independent evidence that this sort of entity actually exists. On this view, then, "God" (construed as purporting to refer to a first cause or unexplained explainer) is the name of a solution to a problem, not the solution itself.

Exactly the same sorts of consideration apply to irreducible agent-causation. It might seem that the only way to make sense of the ideas that our choices are not *causally determined* by previous events (together with the laws of nature) and yet that we are *in control* of our choices is to posit irreducible agent-causation. But, as with God as First Cause, this power is then simply the *label for a solution* to the problem of explaining the relevant sort of control, but we do not yet have any independent evidence of its existence (independent, that is, of our wishful thinking).[27]

Roderick Chisholm contends that our agency can be patterned after God's capacity for creation *ex nihilo*.[28] I would suggest that we think of ourselves as "in God's image" in a different way. Perhaps it would be illuminating to think of being similar to God in being an "author," but *not* in the sense of creator *ex nihilo*. My claim is that the relevant similarity is authorship, although divine and human authorship (of the relevant kind) is interestingly different. I have suggested that we think of ourselves as authors in the sense that we freely endow our lives with a special sort of meaning: an irreducible narrative dimension of meaning. Recently, Velleman has argued for an even more robust connection between our free action and authorship. Velleman has argued that we can fruitfully think of ourselves as the authors of improvisational dramas in which we are the protagonists.[29]

Here, I wish to focus (very briefly) on God's side of the equation. If God is an author, he is an author of a story in which *we* are characters. It might be helpful to think of our relationship to God as analogous to the relationship between an author and the characters in his novel. More specifically, this model might be at least of some help in conceptualizing important features of the great traditional problem of the relationship between God's omniscience and human freedom. We wish to capture God's sovereignty while at the same time endowing human beings with some degree of autonomy. Perhaps we can here invoke an analogy with the relationship between an author and his characters, at least on a certain interpretation of this relationship.

Although there is perhaps a clear sense in which an author has sovereignty, many authors have emphasized the constraints imposed by their characters. For example, some authors (most notably, perhaps, Stephen King) have emphasized that, especially as the stories unfold, the traits of the characters impose certain limits on the directions in which the story can plausibly go.[30] The issues here are very nuanced and complex, but perhaps it would be worth considering the idea that the characters impose certain constraints on the authors that flow (in some difficult-to-characterize way) from the developing story. At least I wish to suggest—in a very tentative and provisional way—that it might be fruitful to explore the contention that our relationship to an omniscient God (if such a God exists) could be modeled on the relationship between an author and his characters. After all, arguably the authors have a certain autonomy that is nevertheless compatible with the sovereignty of the author. This suggestion is not entirely new, nor have I developed it in any detail here; I hope to give it further development in future work. Here I wish simply to highlight an alternative conception of our creativity and authorship—a conception that fits well with my contention that in exercising our freedom, we are engaging in a distinctive kind of artistic self-expression. This suggests a way—very different from Chisholm's suggestion—in which we are arguably created in God's image, or at the least, have properties importantly similar to those attributed to God in the Judeo-Christian tradition.

NOTES

1. Presumably, pain and suffering is intrinsically bad, but they may not be the *only* intrinsic bads; nor is it obvious that states of affairs involving pain and/or suffering need be all-thing-considered or on-balance bad. These are all difficult and contentious issues.

2. For an interesting exploration of some of the complexities involved in defining "death," see Fred Feldman, *Confrontations with the Reaper* (New York: Oxford University Press, 1992).

3. See Bad Religion's album, *How Could Hell Be Any Worse?*

4. Death is not necessarily bad for the individual who dies. An individual in terrible pain or significant disability may welcome death under certain circumstances, and we might think that death would not be a bad thing for the individual in such circumstances.

5. For Nagel's classic treatment of these issues, see Thomas Nagel, "Death," in his *Mortal Questions* (Cambridge, U.K.: Cambridge University Press, 1979), pp. 1–10; reprinted in John Martin Fischer, ed., *The Metaphysics of Death* (Stanford, Calif.: Stanford University Press, 1993), pp. 61–9. (Subsequent references to the Nagel piece will be to the reprinted version.)

6. For further discussion of these examples, see "Death, Badness, and the Impossibility of Experience" (chapter 3) and "Epicureanism About Death and Immortality" (chapter 7).

7. Further, we can assume that the individual does not fail to get some good he otherwise would have got, but for the meetings.

8. Robert Nozick, "On the Randian Argument," in *Socratic Paradoxes* (Cambridge, Mass.: Harvard University Press, 1999), pp. 249–64.

9. Nagel, "Death," p. 65.

10. *Ibid.*

11. The original presentation is in Harry Frankfurt, "Alternate Possibilities and Moral Responsibility," *Journal of Philosophy* 66 (1969), pp. 829–39. The literature on such examples is huge, but we need not delve into it in any detail here. For some preliminary discussion, see John Martin Fischer, "Recent Work on Moral Responsibility," *Ethics* 110 (1999), pp. 93–139; also, see David Widerker and Michael McKenna, *Moral Responsibility and Alternative Possibilities: Essays on the Importance of Alternative Possibilities* (Aldershot, U.K.: Ashgate, 2003).

12. For additional connections, see chapter 7.

13. This is a slightly updated version of a Frankfurt-case I presented originally in John Martin Fischer, "Responsibility and Control," *Journal of Philosophy* 79 (1982), pp. 24–40.

14. See chapter 3; for further reflections, see chapter 6.

15. Jeff McMahan, "Death and the Value of Life," *Ethics* 99 (1988), pp. 32–61; reprinted in Fischer, ed., *The Metaphysics of Death*, pp. 233–66.

16. For my argument that we should restructure the debates about free will and moral responsibility, see Fischer, *The Metaphysics of Free Will*.

17. Thomas Nagel, *The View from Nowhere* (New York: Oxford University Press, 1989), p. 228.

18. Anthony Brueckner and John Martin Fischer, "Why Is Death Bad?," chapter 2; for additional discussions, see Anthony Brueckner and John Martin Fischer, "The Asymmetry of Early Death and Late Birth," *Philosophical Studies* 71 (1993), pp. 327–31; and "Death's Badness," *Pacific Philosophical Quarterly* 74 (1993), pp. 37–45.

19. See, for instance, John Martin Fischer, *The Metaphysics of Free Will: An Essay on Control* (Oxford: Blackwell Publishers, 1994); John Martin Fischer and Mark Ravizza, *Responsibility and Control: A Theory of Moral Responsibility* (New York: Cambridge University Press, 1998); and John Martin Fischer, *My Way: Essays on Moral Responsibility* (New York: Oxford University Press, 2006).

20. See John Martin Fischer, "Responsibility and Self-Expression," *Journal of Ethics* 3 (1999), pp. 277–97; reprinted in Fischer, *My Way: Essays on Moral Responsibility*, chapter 5, pp. 106–23.

21. J. David Velleman, "Well-Being and Time," *Pacific Philosophical Quarterly* 72 (1991), pp. 48–77; reprinted in Fischer, ed., *The Metaphysics of Death*, pp. 327–57; and "Narrative Explanation," *Philosophical Review* 112 (2003), pp. 1–26.

22. *Ibid.*

23. In his review of the photography exhibit, "Making It New: The Art and Style of Sara & Gerald Murphy" at the Williams College Museum of Art in *The New Yorker* (August 6, 2007), pp. 74–5. Peter Schjeldal says:

> The most revelatory and moving item in the show for me is a letter from Zelda Fitzgerald, following Scott's death, in 1940. She writes that Scott's love of the Murphy's reflected a "devotion to those that he felt were contributing to the aesthetic and spiritual purposes of life." There is a world of excitement and woe in that conflation of the aesthetic and the spiritual. It's a madness, which life will punish. (p. 75)

I have warned of similar conflations. In the epigram to this introductory essay, Gary Jules reminds us of the world's madness. We will no doubt be punished for our various kinds of madness, even if we avoid certain errors of conflation.

24. For further discussion, see John Martin Fischer, "Introduction: Death, Metaphysics, and Morality," in Fischer, ed., *The Metaphysics of Death*, pp. 3–30, esp. pp. 23–4.

25. I believe that the Frankfurt-cases are just one "route" to the conclusion that moral responsibility does not require the kind of control that involves freedom to choose and do otherwise. There are also paths that follow the work of Peter Strawson and Daniel Dennett to get to the same conclusion; Peter Strawson, "Freedom and Resentment," *Proceedings of the Aristotelian Society* 48 (1962), pp. 1–25; Daniel Dennett, *Elbow Room* (Cambridge: MIT Press, 1984); and *Freedom Evolves*. There is a sustained development of a Strawsonian critique of the Principle of Alternative Possibilities (PAP) in R. Jay Wallace, *Responsibility and the Moral Sentiments* (Cambridge, Mass.: Harvard University Press, 1994)

So there is more than one way to reject PAP. Further, they seem to me to be entirely compatible and mutually reinforcing. The situation here thus may be a bit different from that of a man described by my wife. The man came to her Buddhist temple near Pasadena, California. He was elderly and concerned about death, and he was engaging in the preparations for death prescribed by *various* of the major religions: Christianity, Judaism, Hinduism, Buddhism, and so forth. Better safe than sorry, I suppose, but…

26. Gary Watson, "Free Agency," *Journal of Philosophy* 72 (1975), pp. 205–20. For additional important work by Watson, see Gary Watson, *Agency and Answerability* (Oxford; Clarendon Press, 2004).

27. Gary Watson makes this point in "Free Will and Free Action," *Mind* 96 (1987), pp. 145–72.

28. Roderick Chilshom, "Human Freedom and the Self," reprinted in Gary Watson, ed., *Oxford Readings in Philosophy: Free Will* (Second Edition), (New York: Oxford University Press, 2003), pp. 26–37.

29. David Velleman, *How We Get Along*, forthcoming, Cambridge University Press; a model for what Velleman has in mind might be Larry David's HBO television show, *Curb Your Enthusiasm*, in which Larry David plays himself (and the script is not fully written out in advance, so the actors improvise, at least within certain constraints).

30. Stephen King develops an account of authorship which emphasizes the autonomy of his characters in *On Writing* (New York: Pocket Books, 2002). The mystery writer, Barbara Seranella, the sister of a close friend of mine, once told me that she always starts with a corpse and a bunch of characters. She then figures out "who dunnit" (personal conversation, 2006) This is clearly an even more "extreme" version of the model described by Stephen King. Sadly, Seranella died at a tragically young age in 2007, awaiting a liver transplant that never came.

Seranella was the author of the "Munch Mancini" mystery series, culminating in *An Unacceptable Death*. The "About Barbara" part of "Barabara Seranella's Webpage," accessed Monday, January 22, 2007 says:

> Seranella was born in Santa Monica, California and grew up in Pacific Palisades. After a restless childhood that included running away from home at 14, joining a hippie commune in the Haight, and riding with outlaw motorcycle clubs, she decided to settle down and do something normal so she became an auto mechanic.
>
> She worked at an Arco station in Sherman Oaks for five years and then a Texaco station in Brentwood for another twelve. At the Texaco station she

rose to the rank of service manager and then married her boss. Figuring she had taken her automotive career as far as it was going to carry her, she retired in 1993 to pursue the writing life.

Seranella's books have been hailed for their "gritty realism, smart plotting, taut suspense, and [their] highly original heroine."

A *Booklist* review of An Unacceptable Death says:

Mancini herself has crawled up from the streets. As an ex-abuse victim, ex-prostitute, ex-biker old lady, ex-drug addict, she is both forever conscious of how lucky she is to be one of the few to escape and how unlucky the many others are who never do; this perspective, plus street smarts, enables her to go undercover convincingly.

In Fall 2006, Barbara Seranella won the Dennis Lynch Memorial Award for Social Consciousness in Crime Fiction.

2

Why Is Death Bad?

Anthony L. Brueckner and John Martin Fischer

I find this in my diary, written twenty and more years ago:
People say of death, 'There's nothing to be frightened of.' They say it quickly, casually.
Now let's say it again, slowly, with re-emphasis. 'There's NOTHING to be frightened
of.' Jules Renard. 'The word that is most true, most exact, most filled with meaning,
is the word "nothing".

Julian Barnes, Nothing To Be Frightened Of

I. WHY IS DEATH BAD?

It seems that, whereas a person's death needn't be a bad thing for him, it *can* be. In some circumstances, death isn't a "bad thing" or an "evil" for a person. For instance, if a person has a terminal and very painful disease, he might rationally regard his own death as a good thing for him, or at least, he may regard it as something whose prospective occurrence shouldn't be regretted. But the attitude of a "normal" and healthy human being—adult or child—toward the prospect of his death is different; it is *not* unreasonable in certain cases to regard one's own death as a bad thing for oneself.[1] If this is so, then the question arises as to *why* death is bad, in those cases in which it is bad.

If one believes in an afterlife, one could explain how death (conceived of roughly as the cessation of bodily functioning) can be bad insofar as it can involve eternal torment—an indefinitely long sequence of (highly) unpleasant experiences. Of course, on this sort of account, death *needn't* be bad, even for a normal and healthy human being, since he may experience eternal bliss in the afterlife. If there is an afterlife, and for some it includes unpleasant experiences, then this would explain how death can be a bad thing, but it is controversial whether there is an afterlife. Since it is quite possible to deny the controversial assumption that there is an afterlife and yet regard death as a bad thing, it would be desirable to produce an explanation of death's badness which doesn't presuppose that there are experiences after death. Many have thought that such an explanation can be given.

If death can be a bad thing for a person, though not in virtue of including unpleasant experiences of that person, then death is a bad thing for a person in a way that is different from the way in which, say, *pain* is a bad thing for a person. That is, some things which are bad (or evil) for a person (such as pain) are "experienced as bad by the person," whereas other things which are bad for a person (such as death) are not (ever) experienced as bad by the person.[2] Death, then, is assimilated to such bads as betrayal by a friend behind one's back, which, though never experienced as bad (one never finds out and suffers no bad consequences), are nevertheless bad for a person.[3]

Let's suppose that some things which are never experienced as bad by a person are nevertheless bad for the person. Death could then be an *experiential blank* and still be a bad thing for an individual. And one plausible explanation of why this is so is that death (though an experiential blank) is a *deprivation* of the good things of life. That is, when life is, on balance, good, then death is bad insofar as it robs one of this good: if one had died later than one actually did, then one would have had more of the good things in life. This is the sort of explanation of death's badness which is adopted by Thomas Nagel.[4]

But a problem emerges. We intuitively think that it is appropriate to have *asymmetric* attitudes toward prenatal nonexistence and death. We think that it is reasonable to regard death as a bad thing in a way in which prenatal nonexistence is not. If death involves bad experiences in an afterlife, then this asymmetry could be explained. But we are assuming here that death's badness is *not* experienced as bad by the individual who dies. If this is so, how can we explain the intuitive asymmetry between prenatal and posthumous nonexistence? Both periods are, after all, experiential blanks. And it seems that prenatal nonexistence constitutes a deprivation in a sense analogous to that in which death is a deprivation: if a person had been born earlier than he actually was born, then he would have had more of the good things in life. (When it is supposed that one is born earlier here, we hold fixed the date of one's death. Similarly, when it is supposed above that one dies later, we hold fixed the date of one's birth.) Being born at the time at which one was born (rather than earlier) is a deprivation in the same sense as dying at the time when one dies (rather than later). Both Epicurus and Lucretius argued that our ordinary asymmetric attitudes are irrational and since we don't regret prenatal nonexistence, we ought not regard death as a bad thing. If death is a bad insofar as it is a deprivation, the challenge posed by Epicurus and Lucretius is pressing: why should we treat prenatal and posthumous nonexistence asymmetrically?

One way to respond to the challenge (and thus defend the Nagelian explanation of death's badness) is to say that, whereas one could (logically) have lived longer, it is logically impossible that one should have been born much earlier. Further, the claim is that it is irrational (or impossible) to regret that a proposition which is necessarily false isn't true.[5] This response is unsatisfying. It is not clear that it is logically impossible that an individual should have been born substantially earlier than he actually was. It is not at all clear, for instance, that Socrates—the very same Socrates—couldn't (logically) have come into being ten years earlier than he in fact did. Why exactly should (roughly) the actual time of one's birth be an essential property of a person? Given that the essentiality of the actual time of birth is a *controversial* metaphysical claim, it is unsatisfying to use it as part of an explanation of the intuitive asymmetry.[6] The explanation will not be acceptable to anyone who denies the assumption.[7] If it is at least logically possible that one should have been born much earlier (and no reason has been offered to rule this out), then we still need to develop a response to the challenge raised by Epicurus and Lucretius (insofar as we cling to the explanation of death's badness in terms of deprivation).

Recently, Derek Parfit has suggested another response.[8] His position could be put as follows:

> We have a (not irrational) bias toward the future to the extent that there are cases where we are indifferent toward (or care substantially less about) our own past suffering but *not* indifferent toward our own future suffering. Since there are such cases, and the attitudes therein seem rational, the general principle that it is always rational to have symmetric attitudes toward (comparable) past and future bads is false, and so it might be true that it isn't irrational to have asymmetric attitudes toward our own past and future nonexistence (where such periods of nonexistence are taken to be *bads*). Thus, death could be considered a bad thing for us, and yet we needn't assume symmetric attitudes toward death and prenatal nonexistence.

Consider Parfit's example:

> I am in some hospital, to have some kind of surgery. This kind of surgery is completely safe, and always successful. Since I know this, I have no fears about the effects. The surgery may be brief, or it may instead take a long time. Because I have to co-operate with the surgeon, I cannot have anaesthetics. I have had this surgery once before, and I can remember how painful it is. Under a new policy, because the operation is so painful, patients are now afterwards made to forget it. Some drug removes their memories of the last few hours.
>
> I have just woken up. I cannot remember going to sleep. I ask my nurse if it has been decided when my operation is to be, and how

long it must take. She says that she knows the facts about both me and another patient, but that she cannot remember which facts apply to whom. She can tell me only that the following is true. I may be the patient who had his operation yesterday. In that case, my operation was the longest ever performed, lasting ten hours. I may instead be the patient who is to have a short operation later today. It is either true that I did suffer for ten hours, or true that I shall suffer for one hour.

I ask the nurse to find out which is true. While she is away, it is clear to me which I prefer to be true. If I learn that the first is true, I shall be greatly relieved.[9]

Parfit's claim is that it seems to be a deep-seated feature of us that we regard our own past and future sufferings asymmetrically. He doesn't explicitly defend the rationality of this sort of asymmetry, but he has pointed to a class of examples involving bads *other than death* in which it doesn't appear obviously unreasonable to hold asymmetric attitudes.[10]

Let us grant, for the sake of argument, that Parfit is correct about his example. The problem is that it cannot be extended to the case of death. The reason is that Parfit's case involves a bad for a person which is *experienced as bad by the person*. One's own pain is perhaps paradigmatic of such bads. But death is not a bad of this kind; indeed, the entire problem of justifying our intuitive asymmetric attitudes arises precisely because death is a bad for a person which is *not* experienced as bad by the person. Further, it seems that it is plausible to suppose that Parfit's conclusion will *only* apply to cases involving bads experienced as bad by the person. Cases which are structurally similar to Parfit's except involving bads *not* experienced as bad by the person yield *symmetric* attitudes.

Suppose, for instance, that you know that either some friends of yours have betrayed you behind your back nine times in the past or some friend will betray you behind your back once in the future. Here, it seems that you should prefer the one betrayal in the future (given that the betrayals are comparable, etc.). It also appears that, given a choice between being mocked once behind your back in the past and being similarly treated once in the future, you should be *indifferent*. (Of course, we assume here that you know that you can have no effect on the future events).[11] These cases suggest that Parfit's point only applies to the class of bads experienced as bad by the person, and *not* to the class of bads (like death) which are *not* experienced as bad by the person.

Note that there are two different kinds of cases within the class of things which a particular person might reasonably regret (or wish wouldn't happen or take to be bad), but which he himself doesn't experience as bad. One kind contains things which no person experiences as bad (such as death). Another kind contains things which are experienced as bad by *another* person (such as another's pain). If it is reasonable to take temporally symmetric attitudes toward regrettable things which we don't experience as bad and which *no one* experiences as bad, then it shouldn't be surprising that we take temporally symmetric attitudes toward regrettable things which are experienced as bad *by others*. And Parfit has produced just such an example:

> I am an exile from some country, where I have left my widowed mother. Though I am deeply concerned about her, I very seldom get news. I have known for some time that she is fatally ill, and cannot live long. I am now told something new. My mother's illness has become very painful, in a way that drugs cannot relieve. For the next few months, before she dies, she faces a terrible ordeal. That she will soon die I already knew. But I am deeply distressed to learn of the suffering that she must endure.
>
> A day later I am told that I had been partly misinformed. The facts were right, but not the timing. My mother did have many months of suffering, but she is now dead.[12]

Parfit claims, about this example, that the new piece of information—that my mother's suffering is in the past—should *not* have a crucial impact on my attitude. Concerning the suffering of others it is rational to have temporally symmetric attitudes. This is precisely what one should expect in the light of the foregoing discussion of the appropriateness of temporally symmetric attitudes toward certain bads not experienced as bad by the person—those not experienced by *anyone*. The difference between our symmetric attitudes toward another's past and future suffering and our asymmetric attitudes toward our own past and future suffering is a special case of the difference between our attitudes toward bads not experienced by us and bads experienced by us. If this is correct, it is appropriate to have temporally symmetric attitudes toward the class of regrettable things experienced by others, even if it is appropriate to have temporally asymmetric attitudes toward the class of regrettable things experienced by us.[13] Thus Parfit's own example highlights the inadequacy of the present response to the challenge posed by Epicurus and Lucretius, namely the response suggested by Parfit's examples of temporally asymmetric attitudes toward experienced bads.

It might seem appealing to suggest that what makes death a bad thing for a person is that it is the deprivation of good things *already had* by the person. On this account, the asymmetry between our attitudes toward prenatal and posthumous nonexistence is due to the fact that the time before our birth cannot be conceived as a deprivation of good things we have *already had*, whereas the time after our death clearly can be so conceived. But why exactly should we care especially about the lack of good things we already have had, in comparison with the lack of good things which we could have had, had we been born earlier?

The plausibility of the suggestion may come from a psychological truth which says that, in general, if a person has experienced a good thing and then been deprived of it, he tends to lament its absence (to "miss it") in a way in which a person who has never experienced the good *doesn't*. If a person has regularly drunk fine wines with dinner, he regrets the lack of a fine wine at tonight's dinner more than someone who has never had a fine wine with dinner.

But why would one regret the absence of something good to which one has grown accustomed? Presumably, because one tends to be *frustrated* by the lack of such goods—their absence causes *unpleasant experiences*. When a person accustomed to fine wines must do without, he is likely to have unpleasant experiences caused by the (partially involuntary) comparison of his present quite ordinary wine with his past delightful wines. In general, it *is* true that, when one is accustomed to a good thing, its absence causes unpleasant experiences and is therefore especially regrettable.

But clearly this principle is not applicable to death, since death deprives a person of goods *without* causing *any* experiences at all (according to our supposition). The psychological principle may apply to bads which are experienced as bad by a person (or which *cause* unpleasant experiences had by the person), but it doesn't apply to death, since it is *not* such a bad. So this explanation of our asymmetric attitudes suffers from the same problem as the above strategy. Suppose, on the other hand, that we do not appeal to the psychological principle and instead conceive of death as a bad which is *not* experienced. Then, insofar as it is held that in regretting the prospect of death we regret the future deprivation of goods we have already had, it would be equally reasonable to regret the prenatal deprivation of such goods, goods which, we *now* know, could have graced our life had it begun earlier.

If death is taken to be a bad thing for a person, and it is appropriate to take symmetric attitudes toward past and future bads that are not experienced as bad by the person, then either we ought radically to revise our attitudes toward prenatal nonexistence, or we haven't explained why death is a bad thing for a person. In *Annie Hall*, Woody Allen says, "We have two complaints about life. First, life is terrible. And second, life is too short." If life is terrible, it is—in the typical case—because of bad experiences. But if life is too short, why?

II. WHY DEATH IS BAD

Imagine that you are in some hospital to test a drug. The drug induces intense pleasure for an hour followed by amnesia. You awaken and ask the nurse about your situation. She says that either you tried the drug yesterday (and had an hour of pleasure) or you will try the drug tomorrow (and will have an hour of pleasure). While she checks on your status, it is clear that you prefer to have the pleasure tomorrow. There is a temporal asymmetry in our attitudes to "experienced goods" which is parallel to the asymmetry in our attitudes to experienced bads: we are indifferent to past pleasures and look forward to future pleasures.

Perhaps it is this temporal asymmetry in our attitudes toward certain goods, and not the asymmetry in our attitudes toward bads, which explains our asymmetric attitudes toward prenatal and posthumous nonexistence. Death is a bad insofar as it is a deprivation of the good things in life (some of which, let us suppose, are "experienced as good" by the individual). If death occurs in the future, then it is a deprivation of something to which we look forward and about which we care—*future* experienced goods. But prenatal nonexistence is a deprivation of *past* experienced goods, goods to which we are indifferent. Death deprives us of something we care about, whereas prenatal nonexistence deprives us of something to which we are indifferent.

Thus we can defend Nagel's account of the badness of death by explaining the asymmetry in our attitudes toward prenatal and posthumous nonexistence. This explanation makes use of a principle clearly related to (but different from) Parfit's principle concerning the asymmetry in our attitudes toward past and future experienced bads. If we have asymmetric attitudes toward past and future experienced goods, then death is a bad thing in a way in which prenatal nonexistence is not.[14]

Let us end with a fanciful example that illustrates the present point. It is now 1985 and you will live eighty years in any case. Suppose you are given the following choice. Either you were born in 1915 and will die in 1995, or you were born in 1925 and will die in 2005. In each case, we will suppose, your life contains the same amount of pleasure and pain, distributed evenly through time. It is quite clear that you would prefer the second option—you want your good experiences in the future. Note that the periods before 1915 and after 2005 involve "experiential blanks" *in any case*. However, on the first option there is an "extra" blank between 1995 and 2005, and on the second option this extra blank is placed between 1915 and 1925. If one focuses simply on this experiential blank of ten years and asks whether it would be better to have the blank in the past or the future, it seems that one shouldn't care. That is, as argued above, it is rational for a person to have temporally symmetric attitudes toward bads not experienced by him. Thus, our preference for the second option—living more in the future—cannot be explained directly by an alleged asymmetry in our attitudes toward experiential blanks. Rather, it is crucial that the placement of the "extra" experiential blank of ten years *determines* the temporal distribution of experienced goods, since we do have temporally asymmetric attitudes toward experienced goods.

Nagel is correct to assimilate death to a bad such as betrayal by a friend behind one's back—both bads do not involve unpleasant experiences. But the two sorts of bads are interestingly different. If death occurs later than it actually does, we will have a stream of good experiences in the future. The *alternative* to death is good experiences, whereas (in the typical case, at least) the alternative to a future betrayal behind one's back is *not* good experiences. Thus prenatal and posthumous nonexistence deprives us of things to which we have temporally asymmetric attitudes, whereas past and future betrayals do not. Death's badness is similar to the badness of betrayal behind one's back, but different in a way which explains why death is rationally regarded as worse than prenatal nonexistence.[15]

NOTES

1. This does not imply that it is rational to *preoccupy* oneself with one's own death or to focus one's attention upon it constantly, etc.

2. Something is "experienced as bad by a person" roughly speaking insofar as that thing causes unpleasant experiential episodes in the person (and perhaps, the person believes that the thing is causing such experiences).

3. Thomas Nagel discusses such bads in: "Death," reprinted in Thomas Nagel, *Mortal Questions* (Cambridge: Cambridge University Press, 1979), pp. 1–10. Also, Robert Nozick discusses similar examples in: "On the Randian Argument," in Jeffrey Paul (ed.), *Reading Nozick* (Totowa, N.J.: Rowman & Littlefield, 1981), pp. 218–222.

4. Nagel, *Ibid.*

5. *Ibid.*, pp. 7–8.

6. Even if one—controversially—held that generation from such and such gametes is an essential property of an individual, this would not commit one to the further essentialist claim in the text.

7. Nagel himself is unsatisfied with this response. (Nagel, *Ibid.* fn. 3, pp. 8–9). He points out that "it is too sophisticated to explain the simple difference between our attitudes toward prenatal and posthumous nonexistence." (*Ibid.*) To explain his doubts, he presents an example (attributed to Robert Nozick) in which it is granted that it *is* logically possible that an individual be born years before he is actually born (by prematurely "hatching" the spore from which one develops), and yet it seems that even here the intuitive asymmetry is justified. Thus, the logical impossibility of being born earlier cannot *explain* the asymmetry in our attitudes.

8. Derek Parfit, *Reasons and Persons* (Oxford: Oxford University Press, 1984), pp. 165–185, esp. p. 175.

9. *Ibid.*, pp. 165–166.

10. Nagel seems to have been aware of some version of Parfit's claim. Given his worries about the view that it is logically impossible that one should have been born much earlier than one actually was, Nagel admits that "Lucretius' argument still awaits an answer." He continues (*Ibid.*, fn. 3, p. 9): "I suspect that it might require a general treatment of the difference between past and future in our attitudes toward our own lives. Our attitudes toward past and future pain are very different, for example. Derek Parfit's unpublished writings on this topic have revealed its difficulty to me."

11. So a *symmetric* attitude towards past and future betrayals involves *preference* for one betrayal over several comparable ones regardless of when they occur and *indifference* between two comparable betrayals regardless of when they occur.

12. *Ibid.*, p. 181.

13. Parfit (*Ibid.*, p. 182), says: "My own examples reveal a surprising asymmetry in our concern about our own and other people's pasts. I would not be distressed at all if I was reminded that I myself once had to endure several months of suffering. But I would be greatly distressed if I learnt that, before she died, my mother had to endure such an ordeal."

This asymmetry is not the same as the asymmetry between my attitudes toward my own past and my own future, yet the two asymmetries are connected as follows. The first asymmetry consists in my indifference to my own past suffering paired with my concern for another's past suffering. Given my concern for my own future suffering, it follows that I have asymmetric attitudes toward my own past suffering and my own future suffering. Given my concern for another's future suffering, it follows that I have symmetric attitudes toward another's past suffering and another's future suffering. Thus the contrast between temporally asymmetric attitudes regarding my own suffering and temporally symmetric attitudes regarding another's suffering stems from the "surprising" asymmetry Parfit notes in the above-quoted passage. But the contrast in question, which arises from the "surprising" asymmetry, is precisely what one should expect given the discussion in the text: the contrast matches up with the contrast between bads which one experiences and bads which one does not.

14. Though Parfit focuses upon examples involving temporally asymmetric attitudes towards pain, he speaks of our "bias toward the future" with respect to experienced goods such as pleasure as well. So he would endorse the principle about temporally asymmetric attitudes toward experienced goods, which grounds the foregoing explanation of the asymmetry in our attitudes toward prenatal and posthumous nonexistence. Though this explanation is *consistent* with Parfit's remarks in the passages surrounding his discussion of Epicurus on death, that discussion itself does not indicate that he had the explanation in mind: "Epicurus's argument fails for a different reason: we are biased towards the future. Because we have this bias, the bare knowledge that we once suffered may not now disturb us. But our equanimity does not show that our past suffering was not bad. The same could be true of our past nonexistence. Epicurus's argument therefore has force only for those people who lack the bias towards the future, and do not regret their past non-existence. There are no such people. So the argument has force for no one." (*Ibid.*, p. 175)

In any case, it is crucial to see that only the principle about temporally asymmetric attitudes toward experienced *goods* such as pleasure will afford an explanation of why death is bad. The principle about experienced *bads* which is suggested by Parfit's examples, it has been argued, will not generate such an explanation.

15. We would like to thank Phillip Bricker for helping us to arrive at the foregoing explanation of why death is bad.

3

Death, Badness, and the Impossibility of Experience

John Martin Fischer

Dying
Is an art, like everything else.
I do it exceptionally well.
I do it so it feels like hell.
I do it so it feels real.
I guess you could say I've a call,…
    Sylvia Plath, "Lady Lazarus"

Few Fallacies depressed me more than the line, "I don't mind being dead; it's just like
being asleep. It's the dying I can't face." Nothing seemed clearer to me in my nocturnal
terrors than that death bore no resemblance to sleep. I wouldn't mind dying at all,
I thought, as long as I didn't end up Dead at the end of it.
                    Julian Barnes, Metroland[1]

I. NAGEL AND THE CRITIQUE OF EPICURUS

It is a perennial philosophical puzzle how death can be bad for the individual who dies. Insofar as death is construed as an experiential blank, some have argued (following Epicurus) that one's own death (as opposed to one's dying) cannot be bad for one; after all, one does not experience death as bad or have any unpleasant experiences as a result of it. As the saying goes, "What you don't know can't hurt you."

But is the view expressed by this saying correct? Thomas Nagel has argued that it is not.[2] Nagel argues that an individual can be harmed by something which does not result in any unpleasant experiences for that individual.[3] He employs the following example in support of his position:

> It (the view that what you don't know can't hurt you) means that even if a man is betrayed by his friends, ridiculed behind his back, and despised by people who treat him politely to his face, none of it can be counted as a misfortune for him so long as he does not suffer as a result.[4]

Let us call Nagel's example the "betrayal-behind-one's-back" example (or the "betrayal" example). Other philosophers have presented similar examples in support of the view that what one does not know can indeed hurt (or at least harm or be bad for) one.[5]

But various philosophers have replied to Nagel. In order to develop the approach of Nagel's critics, it is helpful to distinguish two principles:

> Experience Requirement I (ER I): An individual can be harmed by something only if he has an unpleasant experience as a result of it (either directly or indirectly).

> Experience Requirement II (ER II): An individual can be harmed by something only if it is possible for him to have an unpleasant experience as a result of it (either directly or indirectly).

The critics have noted that Nagel's betrayal-behind-one's back example only impugns ER I, and not ER II. After all, it is presumably *possible* (in some appropriate sense) for the individual in Nagel's example to find out about the betrayal and thus have unpleasant experiences, even if he actually does not. Further, these philosophers have emphasized that ER II appears to imply that death—construed as an experiential blank—is not bad for the individual who dies: death rules out even the possibility of experience. Thus, it is alleged that Nagel's example falls short of establishing that death can be bad for an individual. What is needed (according to these philosophers), and what has not been provided, is a counterexample to ER II rather than simply to ER I; that is, what is required is a non-question-begging example in which an individual *cannot* have unpleasant experiences as a result of something and yet we would say that that thing is bad for the individual.[6]

It will be useful to have some examples of this criticism of Nagel before us. Harry Silverstein says:

> …Nagel's argument has force only against the strongest and least plausible version of VCF [the "Values Connect with Feelings" view], the version that requires that the value-recipient *actually have* the appropriate feeling. It has no force against more plausible versions, e.g., a version according to which x can intelligibly be said to have a certain A-relative value provided merely that it be possible, or possible under certain conditions, for A to have the appropriate feeling as a result of x. For A's suffering from, e.g., undetected betrayal is possible in the sense that he may later discover the betrayal and suffer as a result—indeed, he may then suffer, not merely from the fact that he was betrayed but from the fact that the betrayal was undetected until that time. Thus, Nagel's examples are quite consistent with, and therefore constitute no argument against, this weaker version of VCF…

Hence, Nagel's argument by counterexample is insufficient.[7]

Following Silverstein on this point, Stephen Rosenbaum says:

Thomas Nagel argues that what a person does not know may well be bad for the person. Nagel seems thereby to object to premise (A) [A state of affairs is bad for person P only if P can experience it at some time]. He gives plausible cases in which something can be bad for a person even if the person is unaware of it. Unknown betrayal by friends and destruction of one's reputation by vile, false rumors of which one is unaware are examples of evils which a person might not consciously experience. Strictly, however, such cases are logically compatible with (A) [ER II] and hence do not refute (A) [ER II], since all (A) [ER II] requires for something to be bad for a person is that the person *can* experience it (perhaps not consciously) at some time, not that he actually experience it consciously. We can grant that what one *does not* consciously experience can hurt one without granting that what one *cannot* experience can hurt one.[8]

II. A DEFENSE OF NAGEL: NAGEL MEETS FRANKFURT

I concede that Nagel's betrayal-behind-one's-back example does not, as it stands, decisively establish the falsity of ER II. But I believe it can be modified so that it can indeed establish the falsity of ER II. The problem with the example is that, although you do not actually have bad experiences as a result of the betrayal, you nevertheless *can* (in some suitable sense) have such experiences. (It is thus open to the proponent of ER II to admit that you are harmed, but say that this is in virtue of your *ability* to have unpleasant experiences.) Now it seems to me that there are various ways in which Nagel's example could be modified so that you *cannot* (in some natural sense) have any bad experiences as a result of the betrayal. One such way employs the idea of a "counterfactual intervener"—an agent who does not play any role in the actual course of events, but stands ready to intervene under certain (counterfactual) circumstances.[9]

Imagine first that the example is as described by Nagel. You are betrayed behind your back by people who you thought were good friends, and you never actually find out about this or have any bad experiences as a result of the betrayal. But now suppose that these friends were (very) worried that you might find out about the betrayal. In order to guard against this possibility, they arrange for White to watch over you. His task is to prevent you ever from finding out about the betrayal. So, for example, if one of the individuals who betrayed you should decide to tell you about it, White can prevent him from succeeding: White can do whatever is required to prevent the information from getting to you. Or if you should begin to seek out one of the friends, White could prevent you from succeeding in making contact. I simply stipulate that White is in a position to thwart any attempt by you or your friends to inform you of what happened.[10]

In this Frankfurt-style version of Nagel's betrayal example, I further stipulate that everything (plausibly thought to be relevant) that actually happens among your friends and to you (and your family) is exactly the same as in the original version of the example; we could "subtract" the existence of White and this would make *no relevant difference* to what actually happens among your friends and to you (and your family) for the rest of your life. The *only* difference between the original case and the modified case is that your friends have so arranged things that White is poised to intervene at any point in your life where there would be a chance that you would discover what happened; it turns out that intervention is never actually necessary, and thus the actual sequence of events in the modified example is in relevant respects precisely like that of the original example. White serves as a fail-safe mechanism; his intervention is never triggered, but his presence ensures that you will never find out about the betrayal.

I claim that this modified version of Nagel's example is one in which it is plausible to say that something happens that is bad for you—the betrayal—and yet it is *not possible* for you to have any bad experiences as a result of it. If this is correct, then we do indeed have a counter-example to ER II.

I suppose that someone could concede that in the modified example you cannot have any bad experience as a result of the betrayal but insist that *precisely this* makes it the case that the betrayal is *not* bad for you. Whereas this position is certainly open to one, it results in the extremely implausible differentiation of the original betrayal case and the modified betrayal case: one must say that you are harmed by the betrayal in the original case but *not* in the modified case. But although you are harmed (according to this view) only in the original case, everything that happens among your friends and to you (and your family) is in all relevant respects the same in both cases.[11] It then seems very implausible to say that you are harmed in the original case but not in the modified case.

I thus claim that the modified example is precisely the sort of example demanded by philosophers such as Silverstein and Rosenbaum in order to establish that ER II is to be rejected: an example in which something is bad for an individual and yet it is not even possible for him to have unpleasant experiences as a result of it. The existence of such an example should not be surprising, given certain insights of Nagel. Consider again the original betrayal-behind-one's-back example. Reflecting on this example, it is natural to think that it is not merely the *actual* lack of unpleasant experiences that is relevant; the example suggests that even the *possibility* of unpleasant experiences is not what makes the betrayal bad. And Nagel provides some theoretical resources that could be developed to bring out this point more explicitly.

After laying out the original version of the example, Nagel says:

> Someone who holds that all goods and evils must be temporally assignable states of the person may of course try to bring difficult cases into line by pointing to the pleasure or pain that more complicated goods and evils cause. Loss, betrayal, deception, and ridicule are on this view bad because people suffer when they learn of them. But it should be asked how our ideas of human value would have to be constituted to accommodate these cases directly instead. One advantage of such an account might be that it would enable us to explain *why* the discovery of these misfortunes causes suffering—in a way that makes it reasonable. For the natural view is that the discovery of betrayal makes us unhappy because it is bad to be betrayed—not that betrayal is bad because its discovery makes us unhappy.[12]

Nagel is here discussing whether future *actual* discovery of the betrayal, with its attendant unpleasant experiences, is what would make the betrayal bad. But his Euthyphro-type point could be adapted to the issue of whether the *possibility* of discovery and attendant unpleasant experiences is what makes the betrayal bad. For it is natural to say that it is not the possibility of bad experiences that makes betrayal bad, but rather the badness of betrayal that explains why one would have unpleasant experiences given the possible circumstance of discovery of the betrayal. If this sort of analysis of the order of explanation is correct, then it is not surprising that there should be examples in which something is bad for an individual and yet there is not even the possibility that the individual have bad experiences as a result.

III. CLARIFICATION: TWO KINDS OF POSSIBILITY

Notoriously, the notion of "possibility" is vague. And of course this notion plays a crucial role in ER II and my counterexample to it. It will be useful to make a distinction between a broader and a narrower notion of possibility. The broad notion is "metaphysical possibility in the broad sense." This is the sort of possibility that is (very roughly) compatibility with the laws of logic, the analytic or conceptual truths, and the propositions entailed by basic metaphysical truths (including truths about the essences of things). According to this broad notion of possibility, it *would* be possible for you to have bad experiences as a result of the betrayal even in the modified betrayal example. This is because it is compatible with the laws of logic (and the basic metaphysical truths) that White not succeed in performing his task (for whatever reason).

But broad possibility is very broad indeed. Suppose that you are chained to your chair by very heavy chains which you cannot break, and also imagine that there is no way that you can get anyone else to help you remove the chains (within, say, an hour). Given certain plausible ancillary assumptions, it follows that you cannot get out of the chair within an hour, in the sense of "can" typically thought to be relevant (in some way or another) to moral responsibility. Note, however, that your breaking the chains is compatible with the laws of logic (and the relevant metaphysical truths), and thus your getting out of the chair is possible in the broad sense.

Let us say that the sort of possibility that corresponds to the freedom typically associated (in some way or another) with moral responsibility is "narrow possibility." This sort of possibility implies that the relevant agent have a general ability to do the thing in question and also the opportunity to exercise the ability. Of course, it would be too daunting a task for me to attempt to provide an analysis of the relevant sort of freedom. Here I simply associate the narrower sort of possibility with this freedom (however it is analyzed, if it is analyzed at all). Possibility in the narrow sense implies that a certain course of action is genuinely accessible to or open to an agent. It is not genuinely open to you in the modified betrayal example to discover that you have been betrayed.[13]

Note that, if the broad notion of possibility is employed in ER II, then the modified betrayal example is no counterexample. But I would contend that it is the narrow notion of possibility that is relevant to ER II. Surely, if one is concerned to connect badness (or harm) with the possibility of experience, it is not plausible to employ the broad notion of possibility. Consider, as an example, an individual who has been reduced to a persistent vegetative state as a result of a stroke. Physicians reliably diagnose this person as terminally comatose. Presumably, in the sense of possibility relevant to the issue of whether this individual can be harmed by (say) a betrayal, it is *impossible* for the individual to have unpleasant experiences. But if this is correct, then the relevant notion of possibility cannot be the broad notion, for it is possible in the broad sense for the individual to have unpleasant experiences (as a result, say, of a miraculous recovery of the capacity for consciousness). I contend then that it is the narrow notion of possibility that is appropriately employed in ER II, and that the modified betrayal example constitutes a counterexample to ER II thus interpreted.[14]

IV. IMPLICATION: DEATH'S BADNESS

One implication of this result is to vindicate the Nagelian critique of Epicurus' argument that death is not bad for the individual who dies. In the paper cited above (and others), Rosenbaum has sought to give a reconstruction of Epicurus' argument which withstands Nagel's assault.[15] His main point is that Epicurus relies upon ER II rather than ER I, and thus Nagel's original case does not undermine Epicurus' argument. But if I am correct and the modified betrayal example shows the inadequacy of ER II, it follows that Rosenbaum's attempt to provide a defense of Epicurus must fail.

It is interesting to note how Rosenbaum attempts to argue for ER II:

> Suppose that a person P cannot hear and never will hear. Then the egregious performance of a Mozart symphony cannot causally affect P at any time, supposing that what makes the performance bad is merely awful sound, detectable only through normal hearing, and supposing further that the performance does not initiate uncommon causal sequences that can affect the person. It is clear that the person cannot experience the bad performance, auditorily or otherwise. Furthermore, it seems clear that the performance cannot be bad for the person in any way. It cannot affect the person in any way. The reason why it is not bad for him is that he is not able to experience it.... Similarly, a person born without a sense of smell cannot be causally affected by, and thus cannot experience, the stench of a smoldering cheroot. The stench cannot be an olfactory negativity for her. We could imagine indefinitely many more such cases.
>
> Since I see nothing eccentric about these cases, I believe that we are entitled to generalize and claim that our judgments about these cases are explained by the principle that if a person cannot experience a state of affairs at some time, then the state of affairs is not bad for the person.[16]

Certainly, there is nothing so "eccentric" as a counterfactual intervener (such as White) in the cases envisaged by Rosenbaum. Nevertheless, I contend that his examples are indeed eccentric in the sense of being an inappropriate sample on the basis of which to generalize. To explain, the question at issue in this dialectic is whether there are some things that are bad for someone and yet cannot result in unpleasant experiences for the individual. Now Rosenbaum invokes a number of examples in which the thing in question typically causes unpleasant experiences: an "egregious performance of a Mozart symphony," and "the stench of a smoldering cheroot." Such things, by their very nature, would be bad for an individual precisely by causally affecting him and producing unpleasant experiences. This is because in these cases the badness could only be (or be the result of) *sensory* unpleasantness. It is surely uncontroversial that in this class of cases an individual cannot be harmed by the thing in question, if he cannot be causally affected by it.

But the critic of Epicurus will point out that this class is *only a proper subclass* of all the relevant cases. There are other cases in which it is alleged that there is something which is bad for an individual even though it does not (and cannot) causally affect the individual. In these cases, the alleged badness would not be a *sensory* badness (i.e., an unpleasant experience coming from some offensive sensory stimulus). Now of course it is contentious whether this allegation is true; but all I wish to point out is that it surely is dialectically unfair to point to the "sensory subclass" of cases and then generalize on the basis of this subclass to the conclusion that badness requires the possibility of experience. And of course, the betrayal examples (both the original version and the modified version) are precisely examples which are *not* in the sensory subclass. Here the badness is supposed to be something like the undetected ruining of one's reputation; if the example works as it is supposed to, the mechanism of harm would not be sensory. It is an example of a very different sort.

Let me highlight the—admittedly quite delicate—dialectical situation. The class of putative bad things can be partitioned into various proper subclasses (in various different ways). On one way of making the partition, one proper subclass contains putative bad things which involve—by their very nature—unpleasant sensory stimuli; in virtue of this fact, it seems to be true of such putative bads that they could not be bad for an individual who is unable to experience the sensory stimuli. A quite different proper subclass of putative bads does not contain members which involve unpleasant sensory stimuli; if these are indeed bad for individuals, they could be bad for individuals who are incapable of experiencing them as bad. Given the existence of this second subclass, it is clearly inappropriate to generalize from the first subclass to a conclusion such as ER II. Of course, this does *not* imply that the mere existence of the second subclass (of *putative* bads) decisively establishes that there are indeed things that are bad for individuals who cannot experience them as bad (or have unpleasant experiences as a result of them); rather, it simply shows that one cannot precipitously generalize from the existence of the first subclass to ER II.

Finally, a defender of Epicurus might wish to take a slightly different tack. Rather than focusing on the experience requirement, he may put forward some sort of existence requirement. According to this sort of requirement, an individual cannot be harmed by the occurrence of something at a time T if the individual does not exist at T. Clearly, my argument above does not in itself refute the existence requirement. But it is unclear why one would wish to insist on an existence requirement *apart from an experience requirement*. This is because the most natural reason (or at least a very salient reason) to require existence is that existence is necessary for experience. That is, if one gives up the experience requirement for badness (or harm), why exactly would one cling to the existence requirement? Perhaps there is reason to maintain an existence requirement without an experience requirement, and if so, my argument does not address this position. But my argument clearly has force against the proponent of an existence requirement who *bases it upon an experience requirement*. And it seems to shift the argumentative burden to a proponent of the existence requirement to explain its basis, if it is not the experience requirement.[17]

V. CONCLUSION

Nagel's "betrayal" example is a case in which it seems that the betrayal is *directly* bad for someone—bad for someone quite apart from the individual's experiencing anything unpleasant as a result of the betrayal. It seems intuitively that actual or even possible experience is *not* what makes the betrayal bad. Further, Nagel's "Euthyphro-type" point (about the order of explanation of the badness of betrayal) provides some theoretical backing for the intuitive notion that experiential considerations are not the basis of the view that the betrayal is bad. Nagel's example and theoretical insight then show that in principle, there should be examples in which something is bad for an agent even though he *cannot* have bad experiences as a result. The "Frankfurt-type" version of Nagel's original betrayal case is precisely this sort of example. And if so, then ER II, together with the most powerful reconstruction of the Epicurean argument against death's badness, must be rejected.

Note, also, that if ER II is rejected, then so also must an intriguing recent argument by Walter Glannon.[18] Lucretius argued that posthumous and prenatal nonexistence should be treated *symmetrically*, and that, since we do not think of prenatal nonexistence as a bad thing, we should also not think of death as a bad thing. Various philosophers have responded, insisting on the commonsense *asymmetry*: prenatal nonexistence is not a bad thing, but death is.[19] Glannon has employed ER II to argue for precisely the *opposite* asymmetry: since we can (while we are alive) have unpleasant experiences as a result of things that happen in the prenatal environment, but we cannot have bad experiences after we are dead, Glannon argues that prenatal nonexistence can be bad for an individual, but death is not. However, it is clear that if ER II is rejected, then there is no basis for Glannon's asymmetry.

I wish to end with an even more fanciful example and some speculative reflections on its implications. Imagine that your spouse and your best friend are on a space colony orbiting Mars, which is now on the opposite side of the Sun from Earth. Hence, it will take a few minutes for light waves to travel from Mars to the village on the Alaskan coast where you reside. They betray you. It turns out, however, that a gargantuan earthquake-induced tidal wave is going to kill you in fewer than the number of minutes it takes for light to travel from Mars to Earth.[20]

Here it is impossible (in a very strong sense) for you to experience something bad as a result of the betrayal. And yet it seems that you have been harmed. Certainly, if you are harmed by the betrayal in the Frankfurt-type betrayal example, then you are harmed by the betrayal in the Mars example. But it is impossible (short of a violation of the laws of physics) that you experience anything bad as a result of the betrayal in the Mars example.

It seems to me that it is correct to say that there is an interesting analogy between space and time with respect to death's badness. Just as one can be harmed by a spatially distant event, one can also be harmed by a temporally distant event.[21] The Mars example drives this point home: one can be harmed by something that is spatially remote and from which one is causally isolated (barring violations of the laws of physics). But if this is so, then it is plausible to say that one can be harmed by temporally distant events (from which one is causally isolated). If you are harmed by the betrayal in the Mars case, why not also say you can be harmed by your death, even though the death occurs after you cease to exist?

These reflections, then, suggest simple answers to some of the most perplexing puzzles pertaining to the badness of death. Death is bad in virtue of being a *deprivation* of the good things in life. The subject of the misfortune of death is *you* (the individual who dies). The time of the misfortune is the *time during which you are dead*.[22] Just as some misfortunes occur at a spatial distance and are causally isolated from you, other misfortunes occur at a temporal distance (and are causally isolated from you).[23]

NOTES

1. I am indebted to G. Dworkin for bringing this passage to my attention. In "Death," T. Nagel expresses a similar view: "It is sometimes suggested that what we really mind is the process of dying. But I should not really object to dying if it were not followed by death" [T. Nagel, *Mortal Questions* (Cambridge, UK: Cambridge University Press, 1979), pp. 1–10; reprinted in J.M. Fischer (ed.), *The Metaphysics of Death* (Stanford: Stanford University Press, 1993), pp. 61–69].

2. T. Nagel, *Mortal Questions* (1979), pp. 1–10.

3. If the individual has unpleasant experiences simply as a result of discovering or recognizing that a certain event has taken place, this is a relatively "direct" way in which that event results in unpleasant experiences. If, however, the event has consequences (other than mere recognition by the individual) that then cause unpleasant experiences in the individual, this would be a relatively "indirect" way in which the event results in unpleasant experiences. For a similar distinction, see J. McMahan, "Death and the Value of Life," *Ethics* 99 (1988), pp. 32–61, esp. pp. 32–34; this essay is reprinted in Fischer (ed.), pp. 233–266. I mean to include both direct and indirect ways of resulting in unpleasant experiences in my discussion in this essay.

4. Nagel, p. 4.

5. See J. Feinberg, *Harm to Others* (Oxford: Oxford University Press, 1984), pp. 86–87; and R. Nozick, "On the Randian Argument," in J. Paul (ed.), *Reading Nozick* (Totowa, N.J.: Rowman & Littlefield, 1981), p. 221.

6. For the purposes of this discussion, I will not distinguish between something's being bad for an individual and that thing's harming the individual.

7. H.S. Silverstein, "The Evil of Death," *Journal of Philosophy* 77 (1980), pp. 414–415; reprinted in Fischer (ed.), pp. 95–110.

8. S.E. Rosenbaum, "How to Be Dead and Not Care: A Defense of Epicurus," *American Philosophical Quarterly* 23 (1986), p. 221; the essay reprinted in Fischer (ed.), 119–134. Another proponent of ER II is W. Glannon, who appears to base much of his view of death's badness on something like it. In his article, "Temporal Asymmetry, Life, and Death," *American Philosophical Quarterly* 31 (1994), pp. 235–244, Glannon is not always careful to distinguish ER I from ER II. For example, the following suggests that Glannon is a proponent of ER I:

> ... it is irrational to care now about the goods of which we allegedly will be deprived by death. For it is rational to be concerned about the pleasure and pain, the happiness and suffering, that we *actually* experience as persons. Yet we cannot experience anything after we die (p. 238) [emphasis added].

But I believe that Glannon's considered view is ER II. He says:

> We care about future experienced goods to the extent that we can anticipate actually experiencing them in the lived future. By contrast, in the postmortem future there are no goods that we *can* actually experience, and so there is no reason to be concerned now about the non-actual goods of which death purportedly deprives us (p. 238) [emphasis added].

Also, Glannon says:

> On the intuitively plausible assumption that the value of our lives is a function of what we *can* experience, something is intrinsically good or bad for us only if it is possible for us actually to experience it as such (p. 238).... Even if death is bad in the extrinsic sense of depriving the deceased of the goods they would have experienced if they had continued to live, it does not follow that it is rational to be concerned about death. For what makes our concern about a state of affairs rational is the *possibility* of our experiencing it as intrinsically good or bad, and we cannot experience anything in the state of postmortem nonexistence (p. 241) [emphasis added].

9. The "Principle of Alternative Possibilities" states that an agent can be morally responsible for what he has done only if he could have done otherwise. In "Frankfurt-style" counterexamples to this principle, an agent acts "on his own" in just the way we believe an agent typically acts when we hold him morally responsible, and yet some counterfactual intervener is associated with the agent in such a manner as to render it plausible that the agent cannot do other than what he actually does. The version of Nagel's example I develop in the text takes its cue from Frankfurt-type counterexamples to the Principle of Alternative Possibilities: H.G. Frankfurt, "Alternate Possibilities and Moral Responsibility," *Journal of Philosophy* 66 (1969), pp. 828–839; and "Freedom of the Will and the Concept of a Person," *Journal of Philosophy* 68 (1971), pp. 5–20.

10. The presence of White, so described, appears to rule out the possibility of the betrayal's directly resulting in unpleasant experiences. Although this makes the example a bit less elegant, I also stipulate that White is in a position to prevent indirect unpleasant experiences.

11. Of course, in the modified case, your friends arrange for White's presence, but I assume that this in itself (and absent any interventions by White) cannot be a relevant difference.

12. Nagel, p. 5.

13. I do not here suppose that there is some interesting connection between the issues related to moral responsibility and those related to death; rather, I am simply attempting to identify the notion of possibility that is relevant to ER II. Alternatively, one could simply say that it corresponds to Austin's "all-in" notion of possibility (or "can"): J.L. Austin, "Ifs and Cans," in his *Philosophical Papers* (London: Oxford University Press, 1961). That is, "narrow possibility"—having a pathway genuinely accessible to one—is picked out by Austin's "all-in" sense of "can."

14. I do not deny that someone could dig in his heels and simply insist that I have not "proved" that narrow possibility is the relevant notion of possibility. I concede this, but I think it is clear that if one bases value on the possibility of experience, it is not plausible to adopt the broader notion of possibility. The intuitive motivation for connecting value with the possibility of experience does not sit well with employing the broad notion of possibility.

15. Rosenbaum, "How To Be Dead and Not Care: A Defense of Epicurus," and "Epicurus and Annihilation," *The Philosophical Quarterly* 39 (1989), pp. 81–90. The latter essay is reprinted in Fischer (ed.), pp. 293–304.

16. Rosenbaum, "How To Be Dead and Not Care: A Defense of Epicurus," p. 219.

17. Suppose one sought to defend the existence requirement by basing it on some sort of requirement of the possibility of "being affected." On this approach, something could not be bad for one, if it were impossible for one to be affected by it (quite apart from experiencing it). It seems to me that the Frankfurt-style counterexample employed above against ER II would also work against this sort of approach.

18. Glannon, "Temporal Asymmetry, Life, and Death."

19. See, for example, Brueckner and Fischer, chapter 2. See also, F. Kamm, *Morality, Mortality*, Vol. One (New York: Oxford University Press, 1993).

20. I am grateful to M. Otsuka for this example.

21. For these points, see Silverstein. Silverstein believed that in order to sustain his analogy between space and time, he had to argue that the future "exists atemporally." But I wish to employ the analogy with space and time *without* making this further argument. I do not believe that one *needs* to establish the additional (highly contentious) fact about the future, in order to employ the analogy. For criticism of Silverstein here, and one alternative picture of the ontological status of future events, see: P. Yourgrau, "The Dead," *Journal of Philosophy* 86 (1987), pp. 84–101; reprinted in Fischer (ed.), pp. 137–156. T. Nagel also suggests the analogy between time and space in the context of death, saying "For certain purposes it is possible to regard time as just another type of distance." (Nagel, p. 6)

22. Thus, the conclusion I draw from the analogy between space and time in the context of death is different from the respective conclusions of Silverstein and Nagel. Silverstein believes that one is *atemporally* harmed by one's death. I believe that Nagel holds that the time of the harm of death is *indeterminate*.

In contrast, I believe that the time of the harm is the time during which one is dead. (Of course, I am thereby committed to the view that one can be harmed during a time at which one does not exist.)

23. I thank M. Otsuka, D. Copp, H. Silverstein, A. Brueckner, and D. Zimmerman for their help. My work on this essay has been supported by a Fellowship for Independent Study and Research from the National Endowment for the Humanities (let us hope that the NEH does *not* die!). I read a version of this essay at the Western Washington State University Philosophy Conference, Bellingham, Washington in March, 1996. I benefited greatly from the stimulating discussion at this conference.

4

Death and the Psychological Conception of Personal Identity

John Martin Fischer and Daniel Speak

The way I see it, being dead is not terribly far off from being on a cruise ship. Most of your time is spent lying on your back. The brain has shut down. The flesh begins to soften. Nothing much new happens, and nothing is expected of you.
                    Mary Roach, Stiff; The Curious Lives of Human Cadavers

I. THE PROBLEM: OUR ASYMMETRIC ATTITUDES

It is frequently claimed in the literature on the metaphysics of death that human beings have asymmetric attitudes toward death and pre-natal nonexistence. The claim is that we tend to consider the prospects of our future deaths as bad or unfortunate for us, whereas we do not regret the fact that we were born when we actually were born, rather than earlier. This is not to say that we would think of *any* future death as bad; if we are asked to consider that we might be in the end stages of a very painful, debilitating, and terminal disease, we might well look at death in such circumstances as a welcome relief. However, when it is assumed that life is still good, we tend to consider death (but not failure to be born earlier) a bad thing for the individual in question.

This alleged datum—the asymmetry in our attitudes toward prena-tal and posthumous nonexistence—poses a problem for an appealing account of death's badness. On the assumption that death is a period of nonexistence that is an experiential blank, then it is tempting to say that death is bad for the individual who dies insofar as it deprives the individual of the goods (whatever they are thought to be) of life. We find this "deprivation account" of death's badness highly plausible.[1] But if the deprivation account of death's badness is correct, then it would appear to imply that we should also consider the fact that we were born when we actually were, rather than earlier, a bad thing. It seems that the time of our birth deprives us of time during which we could enjoy the goods of life in just the way in which the time of our death deprives us of such goods.

51

One could of course address this apparent problem in various ways. One approach would be to stick with the deprivation account and accept the conclusion that we should indeed have symmetric attitudes toward prenatal and posthumous nonexistence. There are various different versions of this approach. One possibility would be to contend that we should regret *both* the fact that we do not die later and the fact that we are not born earlier. Another possibility would be to regret *neither* fact.

An alternative way of responding to the problem is to continue to embrace the deprivation account of death's badness but to argue that (despite the initial appearance) it does not entail that we should have symmetric attitudes toward prenatal and posthumous nonexistence. A salient version of this strategy contends that whereas a person could live longer than he actually lives, he *could not* have been born earlier than he actually was born. Thus, since deprivation requires the relevant possibility, death can deprive the person of the goods of life, but the time of his birth—the fact that he was born when he actually was born—cannot deprive him of such goods.

Thomas Nagel presented this way of defending the deprivation account in "Death," although he confessed to some doubts about its adequacy.[2] Why exactly is it not possible for an individual person to have been born considerably earlier than he actually was born? It is not clear why this would be impossible (in some broad metaphysical sense). If it is suggested that it is a necessary condition of an individual's being the individual he actually is that he come from a particular sperm and egg, then why is it impossible that that sperm and egg have existed considerably earlier than they actually existed? Of course, the particular sperm and egg came from the individual's parents, but why exactly is it impossible (in some appropriately broad metaphysical sense) for the parents to have lived considerably earlier?[3]

II. THE PSYCHOLOGICAL CONCEPTION OF THE PERSON

Recently Frederik Kaufman has proposed a different way of arguing that an individual could not have been born earlier.[4] In brief, Kaufman argues that when an individual is concerned about his own death, he is concerned about the death of a "psychologically thick" person—an individual with a particular history and thus a particular set of memories, desires, beliefs, values, personality traits, and so forth. But, Kaufman argues, such an individual could not have existed earlier; an individual existing (considerably earlier) would necessarily have been some other particular individual (construed in the "thick" way). Thus the deprivation account can be defended.

It is not clear to us that it is impossible (in the relevant way—in some broadly metaphysical sense) for the same thick individual to have been born considerably earlier than he actually was born. But we grant that this sort of possibility is at best very far-fetched; it would appear to require wholesale changes in the past: various persons existing and events taking place considerably earlier than they actually do. About this Kaufman says:

> So even if it is not logically impossible for me, thickly conceived, to have existed slightly earlier, it is so extremely unlikely that an earlier existing person would turn out to be qualitatively identical (or even similar) to me as I currently am as to make it virtually impossible that I could have existed earlier.[5]

We will grant, then, for the sake of the argument, that human persons, thickly conceived, could not (in the relevant sense) have been born much earlier than they actually were.[6]

It will be helpful to lay out Kaufman's reasoning in some detail. Kaufman is concerned to distinguish between thick and thin conceptions of personhood. The thin conception involves nothing more than "metaphysical essences." Kaufman says:

> A person, on this view, is simply a particular essence, and that person exists in all possible worlds which contain that essence. The details of one's actual life are wholly contingent features of an individual. On this understanding of 'person,' since the features of one's actual life are not in any way constitutive of the person one is, it is possible for one to be shorn of all the attributes of one's actual life and remain the same person throughout the changes.[7]

Kaufman concedes that one's metaphysical essence could have been born earlier—could have been associated with a different thick self. But he considers this irrelevant to the issues about death and earlier birth. He says:

> [I]nsofar as concern about death is driven by concerns that one's conscious personal existence will be extinguished forever, the fact that one's metaphysical essence might occur in different times and places seems beside the point. This is why certain possible occurrences that leave my metaphysical essence intact but which nevertheless extinguish my subjective sense of myself as myself are things which, like death, I could not survive, such as brain zaps, philosophical amnesia, permanent coma, some versions of reincarnation, or 'merging with the infinite.'[8]

In defending his view, Kaufman presents the following intriguing example:

> My metaphysical essence—whatever it is—might have led a very different life. I could have lived as an Eskimo, for example, had my parents given 'me' to an Eskimo tribe upon my birth. I would speak Aleut, live in igloos and hunt seals. That person—metaphysically me—would be otherwise unrecognizable to the person I currently am, the one who grew up in middle-class America. The conscious

personal life of the Eskimo 'me' would consist of completely different memories, projects, beliefs and commitments. Whatever point of
view the Eskimo 'me' would have on his life and circumstance, it will
be vastly different from my current subjective awareness.... Were the
'thin' metaphysical me to be raised by an Eskimo tribe, the conscious
personal entity that I currently am would regard him as a complete
stranger. I wish him well, but I am no more concerned about his
death than I am about the death of any other stranger.[9]

Thus, on Kaufman's view, it is important to distinguish between the
thin person (the metaphysical essence) and the thick person (the person with a particular set of memories, histories, projects under way,
beliefs, and values). Kaufman holds that what we worry about, when
we consider our own deaths, is the elimination of the thick person.
But this sort of person cannot have been born earlier than he or she
actually was born, and thus the time of one's birth cannot deprive
the thick person of goods he or she otherwise would have had. Thus,
the deprivation account of death's badness is perfectly compatible
with our asymmetric attitudes toward prenatal and posthumous
nonexistence.

III. CRITIQUE OF KAUFMAN

We are willing to concede that the actual time of one's birth cannot
deprive the thick person of goods he or she otherwise would have had.
But why exactly should this be the *only* relevant issue? That is, why
should we agree with Kaufman's contention that it is irrelevant that the
thin person—the metaphysical essence—could indeed have been born
earlier (and thus could have been associated with a different thick person)? We will contend that persons often make judgments that presuppose that it is coherent to care—and perhaps care deeply—about which
thick person one's metaphysical essence is, as it were, attached to. (For
the purposes of this discussion, we will adopt Kaufman's terminology.)

Imagine that you read in the newspaper that a certain hospital has
had various problems with "baby-switching" cases: babies have been
mixed up in the maternity ward, and couples have been given babies
who are not biologically theirs to take home. Assuming that you had
a generally pleasant and favorable set of childhood experiences, you
might say to yourself, "I'm relieved that sort of thing did not happen
to me! I'm glad that my biological parents brought me home from the
hospital and raised me." This seems to be a perfectly natural and not
uncommon kind of thought, and it seems to presuppose that one can
coherently make judgments about which thick person one's thin self
is attached to. If one's family life was particularly pleasant, one might
explicitly contrast, in one's mind, one's early childhood experiences

with (as one would naturally assume) the experiences one would have had, had one gone home from the hospital with another couple.

Suppose, however, that one's early childhood experiences were particularly horrid, involving significant poverty and physical and psychological abuse. Under such circumstances, it would not at all be unreasonable, upon reading the newspaper article, to wish that one had in fact gone home from the hospital with another family. One might wistfully think about having gone home with a happy, loving, and financially secure family; it would be natural to say to oneself, "My life would have been very different...." Again, these sorts of judgments appear to presuppose precisely the coherence of stepping outside one's thick self in a certain way, contrary to Kaufman's supposition.

Return to Kaufman's Eskimo example. Recall that Kaufman concludes, "Were the 'thin' metaphysical me to be raised by an Eskimo tribe, the conscious personal entity that I currently am would regard him as a complete stranger. I wish him well, but I am no more concerned about his death than I am about the death of any other stranger."[10] But let us now fill in the details of the story a bit differently. Imagine that you were adopted when you were very young, so that you have never known who your biological parents are. It happens that you have been raised in a middle-class community in Anchorage, Alaska. One day —when you are (say) forty years old—you get a telephone call from an elderly couple who explain that they are your biological parents. They would like to see you, and you arrange to meet them at a restaurant in Anchorage. When they arrive at the restaurant, you are surprised to learn that they are from an Eskimo tribe who live some distance from the city. They apologize profusely for having had to give you up for adoption at birth, but they already had eight children, and they just could not manage another. They are a lovely, warm, generous couple who have learned to speak English in their later years, in anticipation of this meeting with you.

The meeting is very emotional, and your feelings and thoughts are chaotic for some time afterward. But as you think about your biological parents and the story they told, you develop a strong feeling of sadness that you were not in fact raised by them in the Eskimo tribal community. You do love your adoptive parents, and you are grateful for all the love they have given you. But you can't help wondering what your life would have been like had you been raised by your biological parents among your biological brothers and sisters in the Eskimo community. You wonder about it constantly, and although you know there is nothing now that can be done to change the fact that you were raised in a middle-class community in Anchorage, you nevertheless wish that it had been different.

Of course, the story need not be told in this manner; upon meeting your biological parents, you might have little or no regrets about not having been raised by them. But the point is that the story *can* be told in this way.

It seems perfectly natural for human beings to prefer to have been raised by their biological parents, even when they have had relatively favorable circumstances. It would seem even more reasonable to have such a preference, if the adoptive circumstances are unpleasant and difficult.

When Kaufman concludes that the "conscious personal entity that I currently am" would regard the individual raised by the Eskimos as a "complete stranger" and that he would be no more concerned about this individual's death than about that of any other stranger, this is a complex and puzzling claim. But it is interesting to ask why Kaufman focuses on whether the individual as raised in the middle-class community would be concerned about the *death* of the already-mature individual raised in the Eskimo community. This does not seem to be the relevant question. Rather, the question would appear to be whether the individual raised in the middle-class community could coherently form preferences about having been raised in the Eskimo community. If it is possible for the middle-class individual to prefer having been raised in the Eskimo community, then his not having been so raised could deprive him of significant goods. That is all that is required; the middle-class individual's alleged attitudes toward the death of the already-mature Eskimo individual seem beside the point.

If the judgments and preferences in the cases discussed above are coherent, then it is plausible that we can in general form judgments and preferences about which thick persons our metaphysical essences—or thin selves—are associated with. Put in simpler language, it seems plausible that we can make judgments and form preferences about which lives to lead, where the possibilities include lives with very different beginnings from those of our actual lives. It is not an uncommon thought experiment to wonder what it would be like actually to be someone else; one might wonder whether one would like to switch places with another person. Of course, some versions of the thought experiments are perfectly compatible with Kaufman's view. For example, it is compatible with Kaufman's view that a thick individual can imagine himself in some other person's job or life circumstances now. But what does appear to be incompatible with Kaufman's view is the possibility of imagining that one has led another individual's life from the beginning. And yet it does not seem incoherent to form the preference for having led another individual's life from the beginning or to be relieved that one has not.

Regrettably, we do not have a decisive argument that the judgments and preferences discussed above are possible. It is in fact hard to see how to argue for their possibility. We do, however, wish to point to a possible source of confusion in the considerations Kaufman adduces on behalf of the contention that such judgments and preferences are without any basis and thus irrelevant. Recall Kaufman's claim:

> This is why certain possible occurrences that leave my metaphysical essence intact but which nevertheless extinguish my subjective sense of myself as myself are things which, like death, I could not survive, such as brain zaps, philosophical amnesia, permanent coma, some versions of reincarnation, or 'merging with the infinite.' And, like death, I regard these possibilities as bad insofar as they deprive me of the goods of life. Knowing that my essence might continue on without me, as it were, is no comfort.[11]

Suppose a person is subject to a "brain zap" that significantly changes one's "quasi memories," preferences, values, and beliefs. As a result of this direct electronic stimulation of the brain, the individual has a very different personality from the one he had prior to the stimulation. We agree with Kaufman that this would be tantamount to death for the original individual. Once we have begun our lives and formed our personalities—our "thick selves," as it were—we have a strong interest in not having these personalities (the total configuration of memories, beliefs, preferences, values, and so forth) radically altered in certain ways. When such alterations take place, we consider this tantamount to death.

But there is a difference between an alteration of this sort and a hypothetical case in which one's life circumstances would have been different from the beginning (thus allowing for the development of a different personality or thick self). An alteration of the sort in question involves a radical *discontinuity* (to which one does not consent voluntarily). That is, one's metaphysical essence is associated with *one* thick self, and then this association is severed and *another* thick self becomes attached to the same metaphysical essence; we have strong negative reactions to these sorts of cases. We do not want our lives to be *discontinuous* in this sort of way, and thus we have a strong negative reaction when we contemplate such possibilities.

But Kaufman appears to infer from this sort of negative reaction to the "alteration" cases a conclusion about hypothetical cases in which one's circumstances are different *from the beginning* (thus allowing for the gradual and continuous development of a very different kind of personality or thick self). This kind of inference is problematic, because one's aversion to alteration and thus discontinuity (of certain sorts) is irrelevant to contexts that are different from the actual circumstances *from the beginning*. That an individual of course would object to being subject to an involuntary brain zap that would significantly alter his personality does *not* show that he could not reasonably prefer that he had been raised in very different circumstances from the actual ones.

Apart from the invocation of intuitions about cases of alteration and thus discontinuity, we do not see that there is any sort of *argument* in Kaufman's article that would establish that the judgments and preferences about leading entirely different lives discussed above are necessarily incoherent, mysterious, or without any basis. Although this kind of argument is not explicit in Kaufman's work, we suppose some-one might argue as follows. The thick individual has a point of view or perspective—a set of experiences, memories, desires, and values—by reference to which he can coherently form preferences about leading various kinds of lives. But a thin person by definition does not have such a point of view and thus cannot coherently be thought to form preferences about different lives. After all, where would such prefer-ences come from? What would they be based on?

But this argument rests on a mistake. It supposes that the prefer-ence for leading one total life (a life from the beginning) as opposed to another must be generated from the perspective of the thin self or meta-physical essence. This is admittedly impossible, but it is also unneces-sary. On the picture we are suggesting, it is possible for us, construed as thick persons (with the appropriately rich perspective of a thick per-son) to make judgments and form preferences about various scenarios in which our metaphysical essences are associated with different thick selves. So the preferences about such scenarios are generated from the perspective of our thick selves, even though they are about the possi-bility of our thin selves being associated with other thick selves. There is nothing incoherent in this picture, as far as we can see.

We have pointed to a number of contexts in which human beings naturally make judgments and form preferences about leading very different lives (from the beginning). We have not sought to dispute Kaufman's claim that thick persons could not have been born much earlier than they were actually born. We have instead raised ques-tions about Kaufman's claim that thick personhood is the *only* notion of personhood relevant to concerns about the dates of our death and birth. If it is coherent to prefer that one had been raised in very differ-ent circumstances from the beginning, then there is no bar to saying that it would be coherent to prefer that one had been born consider-ably earlier. In Kaufman's terms, one would be exhibiting a preference that one's metaphysical essence be associated with a different thick person.

It is of course possible to insist that the sorts of judgments and preferences we have claimed are coherent are at a deeper level sim-ply incoherent or without any basis. But it is important to see that one would thereby be calling into question some fairly common kinds of practices (of making certain judgments and forming certain prefer-ences).[12] Further, we do not see a strong *argument* in Kaufman's article (or elsewhere) to convince us that we *should* abandon these practices. When he seeks to argue for his conclusion, Kaufman appears to go from considerations pertaining to radical discontinuity and disruption to those pertaining to alternative circumstances that are different from the beginning (but involve no such alteration or disruption).

IV. BELSHAW'S "CONSERVATION CLAIM"

In his recent essay, "Death, Pain, and Time," Christopher Belshaw presents an approach that is very similar to that of Kaufman. As we understand Belshaw's argument, he wishes to start with the assumption that almost everyone does indeed have an asymmetric attitude toward prenatal and posthumous nonexistence. That is, the vast majority of people, if not everyone, will consider that the time of their death can deprive them of goods but will not think of the time of their birth as similarly depriving them of goods. He then wishes to offer an explanation for this asymmetry. Belshaw says:

> We want, most of us, for the past to be as it is, and so are neither indifferent to its shape, nor interested in amending it. Older people can, on occasion, express a wish to be younger. Historians sometimes, and unthinkingly, say they'd like to be older than they are. The rest of us generally do not. We recognise that our being born at a certain time is, in large part, responsible for who we are today. Someone born at a different time just wouldn't, in an everyday sense, be me. And so we want neither to reduce prenatal nonexistence, making ourselves older, nor, as a means of regaining youth, to increase it. Nor are we simply indifferent to past nonexistence, caring neither one way nor the other when we were born. Rather, our concern is with *conservation*, with keeping the facts of prenatal nonexistence just as they are. For many of us recognise, and many more can easily be brought to recognise, that a concern for the present to be as it is, and for us to be who we are, implies a concern that the past be as it was, and thus that we be born when in fact we were.... Indeed, the point can be put more dramatically: to want to be born at a different time is, in effect, to want not to exist, and for someone else to exist in your place. It's not surprising that this is something only a very few of us want.[13]

Belshaw's view is presumably similar to Kaufman's in that he is suggesting that to want to be born at a different time is to want to be a different thick person (in Kaufman's terminology) and that very few persons would want this. According to Belshaw, we do not want to have been born earlier because we recognize (or could easily be brought to recognize) that if we had been born earlier, our personalities would have been significantly different. The key assumption is that we would not want our personalities to be significantly different (from the beginning, as it were).

But this assumption has problems that are similar to those that plagued Kaufman. Belshaw is seeking to explain what he takes to be a very prevalent and almost universal attitude toward birth. His crucial supposition is that almost everyone would not prefer to have had a different personality from the beginning. But this does seem to be a *very* conservative principle, and it is not at all clear that it is true. Surely many individuals would not want to have had a different personality from the beginning. These individuals—perhaps they are a majority (even a large majority)—have led basically good lives under generally favorable circumstances. Even many people who have struggled considerably will no doubt prefer not to have had a different personality from the beginning (where they do not have control over the nature or features of this other personality).

But surely there are many deeply unhappy persons—persons who grew up under conditions of horrible poverty or terrible physical or emotional abuse. Many of these individuals suffer from the emotional scars of their troubled early childhoods, and quite a few of them lead very unhappy lives. Why wouldn't these people be willing to take the risks involved in having a different personality? And of course it is not only individuals from disadvantaged or troubled backgrounds who suffer from deep, persistent, and unpleasant emotional and mental problems; chronic depression and schizophrenia are not reserved for those who have grown up in poverty or suffered abuse. Why is it so obvious that *almost everyone* would want to keep the past as it is because they want desperately to keep the basic features of their personality as they are? This would seem to be conservative in the extreme and to be based on an unwarranted assumption that almost everyone is sufficiently satisfied with their personalities that they would be unwilling to take the risks associated with having a very different personality.

Now we want to emphasize that it does seem reasonable that *most* people would not prefer to have been "someone else" (in the sense of having a very different personality, and—importantly—not being able to select the nature and features of this personality). But this is not enough for Belshaw's stated purpose, because he believes that the desire to hold fixed the time of one's birth is almost universal. At the beginning of "Death, Pain, and Time," Belshaw states the point starkly: "We wish to die later. But we don't wish to have been born earlier. Our future nonexistence matters to us in a way that past nonexistence does not."[14] Later he criticizes approaches that seek to explain our asymmetrical attitudes toward prenatal and posthumous nonexistence in terms of our attitudes toward pain and pleasure, saying "our asymmetrical attitude regarding pleasures and pains is, I shall maintain, complex and untidy, while that concerning nonexistence is more straightforward, and relatively easy to understand."[15]

But the considerations discussed above indicate that it is not plausible to assume that there is an almost universal desire to maintain one's personality as it is (and not risk assuming another personality, over the features of which one has no control). The situation here is more "complex and untidy" than Belshaw supposes. If this is so, and if there is indeed an almost universal lack of a wish to have been born earlier, then this wish (and the attendant asymmetry in our attitudes toward prenatal and posthumous nonexistence) cannot be explained in terms of Belshaw's "conservation claim."[16]

NOTES

1. Thomas Nagel defends the deprivation account in "Death," reprinted in *Mortal Questions* (Cambridge: Cambridge University Press, 1979). For developments of this approach, see, for example, Brueckner and Fischer, chapter 2; and F. M. Kamm, "Why Is Death Bad and Worse than Pre-Natal Non-Existence?" *Pacific Philosophical Quarterly* 69 (1988), pp. 168–174; and *Morality, Mortality: Volume I* (New York and Oxford: Oxford University Press, 1993), esp. pp. 13–71.

2. Nagel, 1979, pp. 8–9.

3. For a discussion of these issues, see Brueckner and Fischer, chapter 2.

4. Frederik Kaufman, "Pre-Vital and Post-Mortem Non-Existence," *American Philosophical Quarterly* 36 (1999), pp. 1–19.

5. *Ibid.*, p. 14.

6. It is not clear that Kaufman needs so strong a conclusion as that it is *impossible* for an individual to have been born significantly earlier than he actually was born. It would seem to be sufficient, for Kaufman's purposes, that certain *counterfactuals* would be true (whether or not the impossibility claim is true). So it would seem to be sufficient that it is true that anyone born considerably earlier would not be identical to the individual in question. And this could be true compatibly with the (perhaps remote) possibility that the individual in question could have been born considerably earlier. The counterfactuals and the possibility claims correspond to different modalities, and strictly speaking, what appears to be relevant to Kaufman's argument are merely the counterfactuals. For a discussion of the logic of arguments involving these two importantly different kinds of modalities, see John Martin Fischer, *The Metaphysics of Free Will* (Oxford and Cambridge, Mass.: Blackwell Publishers, 1994), esp. pp. 87–110.

7. Kaufman, 1999, p. 11.

8. *Ibid.*, p. 11.

9. *Ibid.*, p. 12.

10. *Ibid.*, p. 12.

11. *Ibid.*, p. 12.

12. Consider the following parable, which we owe to Glenn Pettigrove. Odysseus, on his long journey home from Troy, is paid a visit by Zeus one Mediterranean afternoon. Zeus informs Odysseus that the gods have been contemplating human attitudes toward life and death. Not surprisingly, a heated dispute has arisen on Mount Olympus. In order to resolve the dispute, Zeus has proposed that they perform a little experiment. Because of his reputation for craft and cunning, Odysseus has been selected as the subject of the experiment. The experiment is simple, requiring nothing more from Odysseus than a single choice between two options: (1) complete, eternal annihilation, effective tomorrow, or (2) to be born fifty years earlier than he had been and live to the ripe age of one hundred (twice as long as his lifetime under option 1), at which time he would be completely and eternally annihilated.

After securing from Zeus the assurance that the life under option (2) would contain at least as much honor as his current life, it seems likely that the cunning Odysseus would choose an earlier birth over an immediate death. And it seems that many, if not, most of us would choose similarly. Of course, in Kaufman's terminology the choice would be for our metaphysical essence to have been associated with a different thick person. Perhaps Kaufman would contend that upon careful reflection most persons would not make the choice for earlier birth, but it is not at all clear that this is so. Our attitudes toward the time of our birth—and thus the possibility of having a different thick self—are more complex and ambivalent than Kaufman supposes.

13. Christopher Belshaw, "Death, Pain, and Time," in *Philosophical Studies* 97 (2000), pp. 317–341, esp. pp. 324–325.

14. *Ibid.*, p. 317.

15. *Ibid*, p. 317.

16. We are grateful to Dominick Sklenar for helpful conversations about the topics of this essay, and to Frederik Kaufman and Glenn Pettigrove for generous comments on a previous version.

5

Earlier Birth and Later Death: Symmetry Through Thick and Thin

John Martin Fischer

You see, he [Bob Marshall, the first Adirondack 46er and the founder of the Adirondack Society] had been so dreadfully afraid, so sure that he had missed it all, born too late ever to taste the freedom of the wilderness as, he imagined, Lewis and Clark had tasted it long ago in the wilder west. He tried to be rational about the deprivation. He allowed as how, had he been privileged to join that 'most thrilling of all American explorations,' he probably would have been 'bumped off' by Indians or typhoid fever before he was 25.

...Always, even after his most remote bushwhacks in the wilds of Idaho and Alaska, he would remember this lakeside country [the Adirondacks]: 'Real wilderness to me, as exciting in a different way as the unexplored continent which I had missed by my tardy birth'.[1]

I. THE ISSUES

Although we human beings typically think that death can be a bad thing or misfortune for the individual who dies, it is not easy to explain why or how death can be a bad thing, when (and if) it in fact is. (The commonsense view about the possibility of death's badness need not be interpreted so that it entails that death is *always* bad for the individual who dies, or that immortality would always and under all circumstances be good.) A natural way to seek to explain death's badness, when it is indeed bad, is to say that death deprives the individual of what would otherwise have been, on balance, good. Since death deprives the individual of life, it is bad insofar as it deprives the individual of what would have been (overall) good. In his classic paper, 'Death,' Thomas Nagel (1970) suggested this sort of explanation of death's badness, and various philosophers have followed him in defending the deprivation thesis about death's badness.[2]

The deprivation account of death's badness has various problems. It must explain how a mere deprivation—an experiential blank in this instance—can be bad for an individual. (Normally, we suppose that only unpleasant experiences can be genuinely bad for an individual, or at least that such badness includes or has as an accompaniment unpleasant experiences.) Also, if the dead individual no longer exists, how can he or she be harmed? That is, who is the subject of the harm (or bad or misfortune), and when exactly does this harm take place? These and other conundra have received considerable attention, and I will not address them in this essay.

Rather, I shall focus here on what Nagel (1986, p. 228) has called the most puzzling aspect of the family of puzzles pertaining to death: the intuitive asymmetry between prenatal and posthumous nonexistence. Lucretius, a Roman follower of Epicurus, agreed with the Epicurean idea that we should not fear our deaths, or regard them as something whose prospective occurrence should be deemed undesirable, precisely because death cannot be a bad thing for the individual who has died. One of the arguments presented by Lucretius is the Symmetry Argument. Because death (considered as an experiential blank—an indefinitely long period of nonexistence) is the mirror image of birth, and since we do not consider it bad or regrettable that we were born when we were born, rather than considerably earlier, we should not consider it an unfortunate or undesirable thing that we die when we actually die, rather than considerably later. After all, birth at the actual time of our births, rather than earlier, is a deprivation in a way similar to the way in which death at the actual time of our deaths, rather than later, is a deprivation. Holding fixed the time of my birth, if I were to die later than I actually die, I would have more life (good or bad, on balance); similarly, holding fixed the actual time of my death, if I were to have been born earlier than I actually was born, I would have more life (good or bad, on balance).

Of course, one could turn the Symmetry Argument on its head and conclude that we should begin to regret the actual time of our births. This is precisely what Fred Feldman does:

> There are, after all, two ways in which we can rectify the apparently irrational emotional asymmetry [between late birth and early death]. On the one hand, we can follow Lucretius and cease viewing early death as a bad thing for Claudette. On the other hand, we can at least try to start viewing late birth as a bad thing. My suggestion is that in the present case the latter course would be preferable. I think it must be granted that our emotional reactions toward pleasures lost by early death are quite different from our emotional reactions toward similar pleasures lost by late birth. If my proposal is right, this emotional asymmetry is irrational (1992, p. 222).

It is open to Feldman to point out that, just as it is not rational to be *excessively* concerned or *preoccupied* by our eventual deaths, it is also not appropriate to focus *excessively* on the fact of our late births. But it has seemed to many that our judgment that we are (and should be) indifferent to our prenatal nonexistence is on firmer ground than our prospective judgments about our future deaths. This, in conjunction with the mirror-image claim, yields the view that we ought to be indifferent about our prospective deaths (or, at least, that we should regard the fact that we will die at a particular time, rather than a later time, as a matter of indifference). The Symmetry Argument thus provides a compelling challenge for the proponent of the deprivation account of death's badness.

In his article, 'Death,' Nagel famously suggested a potential explanation of our asymmetry in attitudes in terms of a certain sort of asymmetry of possibility: whereas it is possible that an individual die later than he actually die, it is in some important sense *impossible* that an individual—that very same individual—be born considerably earlier than the actual time of his or her birth. In an important footnote, Nagel expressed doubts about this explanation:

> I confess to being troubled by the above argument, on the grounds that it is too sophisticated to explain the simple difference between our attitudes to prenatal and posthumous nonexistence. For this reason I suspect that something essential is omitted from the account of the badness of death by an analysis that treats it as a deprivation of possibilities. My suspicion is supported by the following suggestion of Robert Nozick. We could imagine discovering that people developed from individual spores that had existed indefinitely far in advance of their birth. In this fantasy, birth never occurs naturally more than a hundred years before the permanent end of the spore's existence. But then we discover a way to trigger the premature hatching of these spores, and people are born who have thousands of years of active life before them. Given such a situation, it would be possible to imagine *oneself* having come into existence thousands of years previously. If we put aside the question whether this would really be the same person, even given the identity of the spore, then the consequence appears to be that a person's birth at a given time *could* deprive him of many earlier years of possible life. Now while it would be cause for regret that one had been deprived of all those possible years of life by being born too late, the feeling would differ from that which many people have about death. I conclude that something about the future *prospect* of nothingness is not captured by the analysis in terms of denied possibilities. If so, then Lucretius's argument still awaits an answer (pp. 370–71).

The Nozickean spore example has its analogues in contemporary biomedical science. That is, it is (or may soon be) possible to freeze a fertilized sperm and egg, and thaw them out at some later time. Apart from considerations about technological feasibility, it certainly seems to be genuinely conceivable (not conceptually incoherent) and thus metaphysically possible that a particular sperm and egg have existed considerably earlier than they actually existed; thus, it is at least metaphysically possible (even if not feasible) that a particular individual have been born considerably earlier than he or she actually was born.[3]

II. THE BELSHAW/KAUFMAN SOLUTION: ASYMMETRY OF POSSIBILITY

Recently, Frederick Kaufman (1999, 2000, unpublished) and Christopher Belshaw (1993, 2000*a*, 2000*b*) have (in slightly different ways) defended Nagel's original suggestion of the asymmetry of possibility: although it is possible for us to die later, it is not possible for us to have been born much earlier. More specifically, these proponents of the 'asymmetry of possibility' view distinguish what might be called a 'thin' notion of selfhood or the individual from a 'thick' notion. The thin notion corresponds roughly to metaphysical personal identity (understood in a certain way); the thin self is perhaps individuated by reference to 'bodily identity' or, (slightly) more carefully, in terms of identity of the sperm and egg from which the body has developed. (Alternatively, I suppose the thin self could be understood in terms of a 'soul' or simple, nonphysical substance without particular mental contents.) The thin self can remain the same (metaphysically identical) through significant changes in 'mental' characteristics, including memories, preferences, beliefs, intentions, plans, values, and character traits. In contrast, the 'thick' self (to a rough first approximation that will be refined below) includes the mental characteristics. It corresponds to the idea of personality or basic character (as given by or generated from interaction with a particular set of experiences).

In this essay, I shall focus primarily on Kaufman's development of the asymmetry of possibility view (although I shall also allude briefly to aspects of Belshaw's position, as appropriate). Kaufman says:

> When we ask whether a currently existing person could exist at an earlier time and still be the same person who exists now, we need to be careful about how we construe 'person,' a multiply ambiguous concept. I shall argue that a version of Nagel's original response to the symmetry argument can be sustained if we are clear about the account of persons that is relevant to the issue of the badness of death.
>
> Consider an account of persons which focuses on metaphysical essences. A person, on this view, is simply a particular essence, and that person exists in all possible worlds which contain that essence. The details of one's actual life are wholly contingent features of an

individual. On this understanding of 'person,' since the features of one's actual life are not in any way constitutive of the person one is, it is possible for one to be shorn of all the attributes of one's actual life and remain the same person throughout the changes (1999, p. 11).

This is the 'thin' notion of personhood or 'selfhood.' In contrast stands the 'thick' notion:

> ... [I]nsofar as concern about death is driven by concerns that one's conscious personal existence will be extinguished forever, the fact that one's metaphysical essence might occur in different times and places seems beside the point. ... Hence, in discussions about the evil of death, a fuller account of 'person' is needed, one which incorporates the defining characteristics of our lives, characteristics which make up our conception of ourselves as particular persons with particular memories, beliefs, projects, and commitments. This, after all, is what death deprives us of.
>
> ... While large differences in the time or place of our thin selves will produce persons unrecognizable to the thick persons we currently are, less dramatic changes will result in persons with whom we will bear more or less affinity. ... when I reflect on my biography, it seems that being in the right (or sometimes the wrong) place at the right time makes all the difference. The opportunities seized (or lost), the accidents avoided (or encountered), the people met, the moral and physical challenges thrust upon me; these and many other life-defining events all depend on my existing at a particular time. Indeed, were my essence to have existed even slightly earlier, the effect on my present conscious personal life would be enormous. So even if it is not logically impossible for me, thickly conceived, to have existed slightly earlier, it is so extremely unlikely that an earlier existing person would turn out to be qualitatively identical (or even similar) to me as I currently am as to make it virtually impossible that I could have existed earlier (1999, p. 14).

Kaufman applies the distinction between thin and thick personhood to Lucretius's challenge as follows:

> ... So far all we know is that thick persons cannot exist earlier than they do. But if one's biography is, in some broad sense, constitutive of one's person, then it also seems that one cannot die later than one will, for longer life will change the conditions of one's life, and thus produce a different person. In other words, if thick persons cannot exist earlier, neither can they die later—the symmetry argument again.
>
> However, this objection can be met by noting that additions to one's biography do not necessarily produce a different person. Thick persons can, as it were, become 'thicker,' that is, acquire additional features without undoing what is already there. Thus, I, as I currently

am, could go live with the Eskimos; but I, as I currently am, could not have lived with the Eskimos all along.

... Irrespective of whether a future self would be me, the important point is that it is possible for some future self to be me, since additions to one's biography need not disrupt what has already been established. If the appropriate connections among my current psychological states and those of a future self hold, then, subjectively, I can reidentify myself as myself at a later time. What strains credulity, though, is how a prior existing self could be me, thickly conceived, since attempting to imagine myself existing at an earlier time does disrupt my biography thus far....A life might unfold in a variety of ways, but imagining it starting earlier destroys the current biographic self, and with it the subject who can be deprived by death (1999, p. 15).

In a recent paper, Kaufman encapsulates the view as follows:

I am suggesting, with Parfit, that metaphysical personal identity is not 'what matters' when we contemplate life and death; what matters is psychological continuity. Concern about one's own death has very little if anything to do with the extinction or continuation of one's metaphysical personal identity. Questions about death engage us at an intimate level and our concerns are understandably about the psychological continuum that we conceive ourselves to be. A god's eye perspective that identifies an earlier existing person as metaphysically identical to me seems beside the point.

A life conceived as a psychological continuum of overlapping memories, intentions, beliefs, commitments and structured by particular projects, events, loved ones and concerns, shows us how a person can be deprived of time after death but *not* similarly deprived of time before birth. Whereas a given psychological continuum can readily accommodate additional future experiences without disrupting its previous narrative structure, no existing narrative could accommodate earlier experiences and retain its previous narrative structure, given contingent facts of human life. What you do tomorrow does not disrupt what you have already done, but you cannot retain your current biography if 'you' were alive 100 years ago. For you would have to picture yourself remembering, say, your favorite TV show as a child and also amusing yourself before television was invented.

... Thus while a given person can conceivably die later than he or she in fact does, that same person (read: structured psychological continuum) cannot exist earlier and retain the biography of any currently existing person (unpublished, pp. 14–5).

It will be helpful (in coming to grips with the ideas suggested above) to consider the dilemmatic argument presented by Kaufman (2000). Either we are concerned about the thin notion of the self or the thick notion, when we are worried about our own death. In order for an individual to be deprived of something (in the relevant sense), he or she must at least be capable of desiring or preferring it; but a thin self has (and can have) no desires or preferences. And, whereas the thick self can have preferences, it is impossible that the thick self have existed earlier. What is impossible, in this sense, cannot be considered a meaningful deprivation.[4]

III. REPLY TO THE ASYMMETRY OF POSSIBILITY VIEW

Consideration of Kaufman's development of the Asymmetry of Possibility view will help us to gain a more nuanced understanding of the subject of the harm of death and also what we care about in caring about continuing to live. I begin by simply noting that we do in fact sometimes make judgments that appear to involve regret or disappointment at not having been born or raised in very different circumstances. I (and my coauthor) have discussed such judgments in chapter 4.[5]

Additionally, Glenn Pettigrove says:

The contestable nature of Kaufman's claim comes to the fore when one considers a variety of religious positions on the afterlife. Most doctrines of reincarnation hold that one has no conscious recollection of memories from one life to the next. If there is any remnant which one might loosely call a character which perdures over several incarnations, it is something well below the conscious, psychological threshold with which Kaufman is concerned. Nevertheless, untold numbers have found comfort in the face of death through a doctrine of reincarnation. Several Buddhist teachings provide an even more startling contrast to Kaufman's claim, insofar as the metaphysical substance which was connected with a particular biological and psychological profile merges indistinguishably with the vast sea of metaphysical substance which gives life to the cosmos. Here again hundreds of generations have found comfort in the thought that their lives would not end with death, even though their psychological continuum would be broken and their metaphysical substance would not even be readily isolable after death (2002, pp. 410–1).

I have some doubts about the coherence of the various doctrines of reincarnation alluded to by Pettigrove.[6] I find plausible Bernard Williams' contention that it is not rational now to care about the future states of an entity with a character not suitably related to one's character now (although, of course, it is tricky to specify the nature of the relationship in question).[7] It is even more difficult to understand how it can be comforting to envisage a future in which one has merged metaphysically with The Infinite.[8] But it seems to me natural to take seriously the idea that we could have been born and raised in very different circumstances; it is not *obvious* that this is based on a confusion. After all, it seems that one might regret not having been born to wealthier parents, or not having been born and raised in a more civilized century, and so forth.

But certainly, Kaufman might argue that our ordinary, commonsense ways of expressing these thoughts might not survive critical scrutiny. What about the first horn of Kaufman's dilemma, according to which one cannot be deprived of anything unless one has the capacity to desire or prefer it, and a thin self cannot have such mental states? Of course, there are well-known problems with the attempt to connect deprivation *too closely* with desires and preferences. For example, a newborn infant does not have the preference that his inheritance (which is in a trust fund on his behalf) not be embezzled; yet embezzling it would deprive him of something to which he is entitled and thus harm him. It is presumably necessary to refine the account of the connection between the relevant mental states and deprivation (and harm) to invoke the *potential* to develop such mental states; but this sort of revision threatens to lead to problems of its own (such as the apparent implication that abortion at even an early stage would be wrong).

I would suggest that when we speak of deprivation and harm, the subject is not the thin self (*qua* thin self), but some more complex entity, such as the thin self conjoined with a capacity to step back from any particular thick self and evaluate such selves. After all, we have points of view or perspectives on the world, and the 'I' that is a potential subject of deprivation and harm is a conscious entity with a point of view. This potential subject of deprivation and harm can be considered an aggregate or combination that includes at least a thin self ('metaphysical essence') and the capacity to step back from any particular associated thick self, evaluate it in light of various possible thick selves, and form desires and preferences about which thick selves should be associated with one's thin self (metaphysical essence). Perhaps the subject of the harm is an aggregate of *three components*: a thin self, a particular thick self, and the associated capacity to step back and reflect and form preferences of the sort sketched above. In any case, the 'I' who can be deprived by early death and also late birth can be interpreted to include the relevant capacity. Thus, there is no incoherence in supposing that an individual (the appropriate aggregate individual) can be harmed by an early death, even if it is granted that there is some plausible sort of connection between deprivation, harm, and preferences.

Now the question of whether I can be deprived and thus harmed by late birth becomes: is it possible for my thin self to have been born considerably earlier with the same sort of thick self as I currently have? And I do not see why not. Note, first, that it is coherently conceivable, and thus metaphysically possible, that one's thick self have come into being considerably earlier than it actually did (contrary to the second horn of Kaufman's dilemma). Here I am supposing that we need not hold *all* of the details of our lives fixed, in order to have the *same* thick self (in the relevant sense). It is just implausible that I care about *all of the details of my current thick self*, and Kaufman agrees, saying, 'Not every detail of our lives is absolutely necessary for us to be the psychological persons we currently are' (1999, p. 14).[9] So, for instance, it is implausible that I care about holding fixed the *exact times* of my various experiences, given that their fundamental contents are not altered. And it appears to be coherently conceivable, and thus metaphysically possible, that my thick self have come into existence, with all of its fundamental content, significantly prior to its actual birth.

Note that this claim is no less defensible than a claim Kaufman is willing to concede: that the thin self could have been born significantly prior to its actual time of birth. After all, if the Kripkean view of the essential features of the thin self is correct (and Kaufman does not reject it), then in order for my thin self to have been born significantly earlier, my parents would have had to have existed significantly earlier, and (among other things) the very same sperm and egg would have had to have been fertilized significantly earlier, and so forth. Of course, these scenarios are wildly and fantastically implausible, and yet Kaufman is willing to suppose that they are at least metaphysically possible.[10] I do not see how it would be relevantly different with respect to thick selves. Yes, it is wildly and fantastically implausible that the same thick self should have existed significantly earlier. But that is not the issue: just as with the thin self, it is at least *possible* that the thick self could have existed considerably earlier. So we do not as yet have an asymmetry of possibility (given the assumption, shared by everyone, that the thick self can die later than it actually dies).

The claim that it is possible, in the relevant sense, for my thick self to have come into being (along with my thin self) considerably earlier than it actually did points us to possible worlds that involve radical departures from the actual world. Since it is antecedently wildly and totally implausible and unlikely that such a thing should happen (that the same thick and thin selves came into being considerably earlier than they actually did), the possible worlds in which this does indeed happen are very 'distant' in logical or metaphysical space from the actual world. A proponent of the asymmetry of possibility view might seek to invoke this fact in some way, but I do not see how this is relevant to the argument. The argument posits a certain sort of asymmetry of metaphysical possibility, but there is no such asymmetry; the implausibility of the possibilities in question (and thus the distance in logical or metaphysical space of the relevant possible worlds) is quite beside the point.

It is significant to note that it is not uncommon, and arguably not clearly irrational, to regret the fact that a rather unlikely scenario did not become actual. Suppose one buys a lottery ticket, and it does not win. Still, one might regret that it did not win, knowing full well that the scenario in which this particular ticket wins is extraordinarily unlikely.

Unlikely scenarios, so long as they are metaphysically possible, can certainly be the object of hope (prospectively) and regret and disappointment (retrospectively). It is clearly not absurd to regret that one's ticket lost, and to regard it as unfortunate for one—even while admitting that it was an extreme long shot. Hope and disappointment can take as their objects possible scenarios that are unlikely (and thus correspond to distant possible worlds). One can find many examples of this sort of phenomenon, ranging from the stock market to the philosophical job market to one's loyal support for a particular sports team. I do not see any way to argue that it is not rational to regret, or consider it unfortunate for me, that my ticket did not win the lottery (or that I did not get a particular philosophy position for which I had the no-doubt-shocking temerity to apply, or even that the San Francisco Giants failed yet again to win the pennant...).[11]

Now it certainly is true that we ought not waste much mental energy thinking about remote possibilities. It would follow that I should not excessively focus on or obsess over my lack of success in the lottery (or, say, my failure, yet again, to secure that endowed chair in philosophy at Harvard). It is indisputably true that one should not focus *excessively* on these matters. But, of course, it is equally the case that one ought not focus too much on death—on the fact that I will die when I actually die and not later. I do not see any difference in this respect between our attitudes toward regrettable (although unlikely) scenarios and our attitudes toward matters concerning death.

Both Kaufman and Belshaw seek to brush aside wildly implausible scenarios as irrelevant. Kaufman says:

> So even if it is not logically impossible for me, thickly conceived, to have existed slightly earlier, it is so extremely unlikely that an earlier existing person would turn out to be qualitatively identical (or even similar) to me as I currently am as to make it virtually impossible that I could have existed earlier (1999, p. 14).

If this is correct, the same should be said about the thin self, as pointed out above. But Kaufman does *not* explicitly conclude that it is metaphysically impossible for the thin self to have been born earlier. In fact, as noted above, he concedes that this *is* metaphysically possible. The whole point of the distinction between thin and thick notions of the self, I would have thought, is that, whereas thin selves are conceded to have the possibility of considerably earlier births, thick selves are not; but I do not see how Kaufman, Belshaw, or anyone could defend this difference. Further, given that it is not obviously irrational or inappropriate to regret the nonoccurrence of even extremely unlikely (but metaphysically possible) scenarios, it has *not* been shown that our intuitive asymmetry in attitudes toward posthumous and prenatal nonexistence can be explained and justified.[12]

IV. MY ANSWER TO LUCRETIUS AND A DEFENSE

I and my coauthor, Anthony Brueckner, have suggested an alternative answer to Lucretius's challenge. We have argued that the intuitive, widespread asymmetry in our attitudes toward posthumous and prenatal nonexistence (or, if one prefers, experiential blanks) is a special case of a more general asymmetry in our attitudes toward our past and future experiences. More specifically, we care especially about future pleasures, and we are relatively indifferent to past pleasures. Since death deprives us of future pleasant experiences, whereas late birth merely deprives us of past pleasures, it is not surprising that we care about the time of our death, but are relatively indifferent to the time of our birth. The specific attitudinal asymmetry is an instantiation of a more general, apparently deep-seated asymmetry in our attitudes toward the future and past.[13]

Kaufman however offers the following criticism:

> Brueckner and Fischer purport to explain our asymmetric attitudes about the time before we exist and the time after our deaths by subsuming those attitudes under a more general Parfitian temporal bias. If we are interested only in explaining why our attitudes about these allegedly symmetrical times are so different, Brueckner and Fischer have indeed offered an explanation. But a general temporal bias is still a bias. If we ask instead whether we are justified or warranted or correct in holding such different attitudes about the time before our births and the time after our deaths, then Brueckner and Fischer's explanation for our having different attitudes misses the point. One does not justify a bias by putting it in the context of a larger bias; a racial bias is not justified by pointing out that people are xenophobic (perhaps because of evolution), even though a general xenophobia might explain the prevalence of racial bias.
>
> Brueckner and Fischer move from noting our preferences about prenatal and post mortem nonexistence to insisting on the rationality of those preferences. But our temporal preferences are not rational just because they are preferred (unpublished, p. 5).

Parfit struggles with the status of the general asymmetry in our attitudes. Although Parfit suspects that the general asymmetry is irrational, he does not argue for this view, and he only concludes that the asymmetry is, at best, not irrational (rather than rational). If the specific asymmetry in our attitudes about death and birth is not irrational, then this would indeed provide an answer of some degree of plausibility to the challenge posed by Lucretius. After all, Lucretius contends that since prenatal and posthumous nonexistence are mirror images of each other, our asymmetric attitudes are irrational.

I suppose however that one can pose a deeper challenge on behalf of Lucretius. One can ask how it can be rational to have the asymmetric attitudes, given the mirror-image fact. Granted, we have a natural tendency toward the asymmetry, and it is not obviously irrational. But why is it rational? Why continue to have the asymmetry? What is the point?

I do not know how to answer this difficult and probing question in a completely satisfactory way. I would like to end by trying, in a preliminary way, to sketch an approach to addressing the question. This approach, I fear, will leave more questions unanswered, but perhaps it will be fruitful as a way of beginning to think about the general asymmetry. At the macroscopic level in our universe, causation flows from past to present to future. That is, causation goes forward, and not backward, in time. Thus, insofar as we care about bringing about effects in the world, we care especially and distinctively about the present and future (rather than the fixed past). There is a clear survival benefit to creatures who care especially about the future, so from a purely evolutionary perspective, there seems to be a 'point' to some sort of general asymmetry in our concern about the past and future. Given this, and the difficulty of 'fine-tuning' such an asymmetry in attitudes, it would not be surprising (or inappropriate) that we have the general asymmetry in our attitudes toward our own future pleasures and our own past pleasures.

Again, presumably creatures with this specific sort of attitudinal asymmetry will have a greater chance of maximizing pleasure over time, and, arguably, being happier. Again, there is a clear survival advantage to having such an asymmetry. As above, given the difficulty of 'fine-tuning' such an asymmetry—of turning it off and on as the context requires—it would not be surprising or inappropriate that we would have asymmetrical attitudes toward our own future pleasures and our own past pleasures, even in particular instances in which it is clear that such an asymmetry will not affect one's long-term pleasure or happiness (or chances for survival). I hope it will emerge, at least in a preliminary way, that there can be a rationale or nonarbitrary point to the Parfitian general asymmetry of which our asymmetric attitudes toward early death and late birth are a specific instance. Insofar as it is rational to care about pleasure, happiness, and even survival, the general asymmetry is, arguably, rational. (Of course, one could call into question the rationality of caring about such things, but it is at least plausible that these are extremely widely regarded as rational to care about.[14])

I do not think it is plausible that being xenophobic can be justified in a similar way (by a *good* evolutionary argument). Certainly it is plausible that favoring one's own interests and those of one's family and friends (and perhaps nation) can have an evolutionary justification. But certain kinds of (excessive and inappropriate) fear of different people, and associated attitudes (say, of racism), are not similarly justifiable —indeed, one supposes that they could plausibly be shown to be *disadvantageous* across a wide variety of circumstances.[15]

REFERENCES

Belshaw, Christopher (1993), 'Asymmetry and Nonexistence,' *Philosophical Studies*, Vol. 70, pp. 103–16.

—— (2000a), 'Death, Pain, and Time,' *Philosophical Studies*, Vol. 97, pp. 317–41.

—— (2000b), 'Later Death/Earlier Birth,' in Peter A. French and Howard K. Wettstein, eds., *Midwest Studies in Philosophy*, Vol. 24 (2000), pp. 69–83.

Feldman, Fred (1992), *Confrontations with the Reaper: A Philosophical Study of the Nature and Value of Death*, Oxford University Press, New York.

Fischer, John Martin, ed. (1993), *The Metaphysics of Death*, Stanford University Press, Stanford.

Fischer, John Martin (1994), 'Why Immortality is Not So Bad,' *International Journal of Philosophical Studies*, Vol. 2, pp. 257–70 (chapter 6).

Fischer, John Martin and Brueckner, Anthony (1986), 'Why Is Death Bad?,' *Philosophical Studies*, Vol. 50, pp. 213–21 (chapter 2).

Fischer, John Martin and Brueckner, Anthony (1993a), 'The Asymmetry of Early Birth and Late Death,' *Philosophical Studies*, Vol. 71, pp. 327–31.

Fischer, John Martin and Brueckner, Anthony (1993b), 'Death's Badness,' *Pacific Philosophical Quarterly*, Vol. 74, pp. 37–45.

Fischer, John Martin and Curl, Ruth (1996), 'Philosophical Models of Immortality in Science Fiction,' in *Immortal Engines: Life Extension and Immortality in Science Fiction and Fantasy*, University of Georgia Press, Athens, GA, pp. 3–12 (appendix to chaper 6).

Fischer, John Martin and Speak, Daniel (2000), 'Death and the Psychological Conception of Personal Identity,' in Peter A. French and Howard K. Wettstein, eds., *Midwest Studies in Philosophy*, Vol. 24, pp. 84–93 (chapter 4).

Kaufman, Frederick (1999), 'Pre-Vital and Post-Mortem Non-Existence,' *American Philosophical Quarterly*, Vol. 36, pp. 1–19.

Kaufman, Frederick (2000), 'Thick and Thin Selves: Reply to Fischer and Speak,' in Peter A. French and Howard K. Wettstein, eds., *Midwest Studies in Philosophy*, Vol. 24 (2000), pp. 94–7.

Kaufman, Frederick (unpublished), 'Earlier Birth and Later Death: The Answer to Lucretius.'

Nagel, Thomas (1970), 'Death,' *Noûs*, Vol. 4, pp. 73–80. Reprinted in Fischer 1993, pp. 59–69 and pp. 370–1 (references to page numbers below are to the reprinted article).

Nagel, Thomas (1986), *The View From Nowhere*, Oxford University Press, New York.

Parfit, Derek (1984), *Reasons and Persons*, Clarendon Press, Oxford, pp. 165–85.

Perry, John (1978), *A Dialogue on Personal Identity and Immortality*, Hackett Publishing Co., Indianapolis.

Pettigrove, Glenn (2002), 'Death, Asymmetry and the Psychological Self,' *Pacific Philosophical Quarterly*, Vol. 83, pp. 407–23.

Williams, Bernard (1973), 'The Makropulos Case: Reflections on the Tedium of Immortality,' in *Problems of the Self*, Cambridge University Press, Cambridge, pp. 82–100. Reprinted in Fischer, 1993, pp. 73–92 and pp. 371–2.

NOTES

1. From *The Adirondack Explorer*, January 2001, p. 33 (this article first appeared in *Wilderness* magazine). I am grateful to Steve Schwartz for this

quotation. Steve also informs me that an Adirondack 46er is someone who has climbed all 46 peaks in the Adirondacks that are over 4000 feet. As he puts it, 'It is kind of like getting your Ph.D. in masochistic outdoors activity.'

2. Other defenses of the deprivation account include: Feldman, 1992; Fischer and Brueckner, 1986 (chapter 2), 1993a, and 1993b; Fischer and Speak, 2000 (chapter 4).

3. See Brueckner and Fischer, 1986.

4. Kaufman himself puts the dilemma as follows: 'I conclude that thick me cannot be deprived by there not being a different thick self in its stead, because thick me cannot be a different self, irrespective of how much I might wish it to be so; and since thin me has no preferences, it too cannot be deprived by not having had a different thick self attached to it.' But surely the issue is not whether thick me can be a different self, but whether thick me (holding fixed the fundamental content, but not necessarily all the details) could have existed at a much earlier time.

5. For similar examples, see Pettigrove, 2002.

6. Kaufman expresses his own doubts: 'This is why certain possible occurrences that leave my metaphysical essence intact but which nevertheless extinguish my subjective sense of myself as myself are things which, like death, I could not survive, such as brain zaps, philosophical amnesia, permanent coma; some versions of reincarnation, or "merging with the infinite"' (1999, p. 11).

7. See Williams, 1973, and Fischer, 1994.

8. There are interesting treatments of 'fusion' of selves in various works of science fiction. For a discussion, see Fischer and Curl, 1996 (appendix to chapter 6).

9. For a critical discussion of the extreme view that we care about holding fixed all of our thick selves, what Belshaw calls the 'Conservation Thesis,' see Fischer and Speak, 2000, pp. 91–2. It is very implausible that I want to hold fixed even the fact that I broke a blood vessel in my leg when I was young and had to stay in bed for weeks. After all, I can be confident that I would still have the same basic personality and character, and the same important configuration of memories, even sans this experience and associated memories....

10. Kaufman says, 'I am willing to concede, in other words, that on a thin account of "person," we could have existed earlier. But I deny that that conception of "person" is what is at issue when we ask about the badness of death' (1999, p. 12).

11. Gretchen Weirob, the philosophy professor (on her deathbed) in John Perry's (1978) delightful, *A Dialogue on Personal Identity and Immortality*, says: 'Even the possibility of something quite improbable can be comforting, in certain situations. When we used to play tennis, I beat you no more than one time in twenty. But this was enough to establish the possibility of beating you on any given occasion, and by focusing merely on the possibility I remained eager to play. Entombed in a secure prison, thinking our situation quite hopeless, we may find unutterable joy in the information that there is, after all, the slimmest possibility of escape. Hope provides comfort, and hope does not always require probability' (p. 2).

12. David Hershenov (in personal correspondence) makes an interesting point. He says: 'Leaving aside the possibility that the thick self exists earlier, aren't all accounts of a thick or biographical or narrative self committed to a first

moment or (vague period) of existence in which there is not much of a thick self or personality or narrative? (Doesn't there logically have to be a beginning of a narrative?) Since we existed at that time with very little in the way of a settled psychology and looked forward to a future, couldn't we at that state have been open to many possible experiences and thick selves developing? We could have been placed in countless different cultures and would have cared about ourselves and our futures. If that is so, then at least at a certain time in our existence we could have expressed prudential concern, but without a thick narrative or biographical self. We could have been happy at that moment raised a Moslem in Iran in another time period or Christian in modern America. So at least at one time in our existence, we should have been neutral between earlier (pre-birth) deprivation and future deprivation (so far as the narrative-self approach is concerned). And if we could care equally then about any number of thick selves we might acquire, why couldn't we recapture that concern?'

13. See chapter 2.

14. Note that I am not here contending that we can analyze or somehow 'reduce' value notions, such as 'good' and 'bad' (and so forth) to such notions as happiness, flourishing, or survival. For a discussion of related issues, see Parfit, 1984.

15. I have read an earlier version of this essay to the Department of Philosophy, University of Rochester; I am very grateful to various members of the audience for their helpful comments. Also, I have been helped by a discussion with David Hershenov's University of Buffalo graduate seminar, Fall 2004.

6

Why Immortality Is Not So Bad

John Martin Fischer

There's an old joke. Uh, two elderly women are at a Catskills mountain resort, and one of 'em says: 'Boy the food at this place is really terrible.' 'The other one says, 'Yeah, I know, and such...small portions.' Well, that's essentially how I feel about life. Full of loneliness and misery and suffering and unhappiness, and it's all over much too quickly.
Woody Allen, Annie Hall

I

I shall begin by laying out some of the key elements of Bernard Williams's fascinating and influential discussion of immortality, 'The Makropulos Case: Reflections on the Tedium of Immortality'.[1] Williams discusses a character in a play by Karel Čapek (which was made into an opera by Janáček.) This character had various names with the initials EM. When she was 42 years of age, her father gave her an elixir of life which rendered her capable of living forever (at the biological age of 42). At the time of action of the play, EM is aged 342. As Williams puts it, 'her unending life has come to a state of boredom, indifference and coldness. Everything is joyless...In the end, she refuses the elixir and dies, and the formula is destroyed by a young woman (despite the protests of some older men!).'

For my purposes here, it will be useful to begin by distilling from Williams's rich and intriguing discussion his general framework for analyzing models of immortality. This framework involves positing two criteria which must be met if a given model of immortality is to be appealing to an individual. First, the future person (posited by the model) must be genuinely identical to the individual. (This means not just being qualitatively similar or having several identical *properties*; it means being genuinely identical—the same particular person.) Second, the life of the future person must be attractive (in a certain way) to the individual—the life of the future person must be 'suitably related' to the goals and projects of the individual.

This framework is really very simple and natural. It says that, in order for a model of immortality to be attractive to an individual, the model must posit a future scenario in which the individual can recognize *himself*—someone genuinely identical to the individual. Further, the life of oneself in the future must be appealing; presumably, it cannot involve constant torture, onerous labor, tedium and so forth. The two conditions presented by Williams can be dubbed the 'identity condition' and the 'attractiveness condition'.

Now the problems with EM-type immortality are supposed by Williams to pertain primarily to the second condition, although he also adduces considerations pertinent to the first.[2] With regard to the second condition Williams constructs a dilemma. Either EM's character (her basic goals, projects, dispositions, and interests) remain the same over time, or they change. If they remain the same, then indefinitely many experiences will lead to detachment or boredom: 'a boredom connected with the fact that everything that could happen and make sense to one particular human being of 42 had already happened to her'.[3] But if the character changes, it is unclear whether the second condition is satisfied, because it is unclear how to assess the new projects and goals in light of the old ones.

Williams's point is that it is not merely a contingent fact that eternal life would be unattractive; this unattractiveness is alleged to be an *essential* feature of eternal life.[4] Williams says:

> ...perhaps, one day, it will be possible for some of us not to age. If that were so, would it not follow then that, more life being *per se* better than less life, we should have reason so far as that went...to live for ever? EM indeed bears strong, if fictional, witness against the desirability of that, but perhaps she still laboured under some contingent limitations, social or psychological....Against this, I am going to suggest that the supposed contingencies are not really contingencies; that an endless life would be a meaningless one; and that we could have no reason for living eternally a human life. There is no desirable or significant property which life would have more of, or have more unqualifiedly, if we lasted for ever. In some part, we can apply to life Aristotle's marvellous remark about Plato's Form of the Good: 'nor will it be any the more good for being eternal: that which lasts long is no whiter than that which perishes in a day' [*Ethica Nicomachea* 1096b4].[5]

II

I wish to examine Williams's thesis that immortality is essentially unappealing for creatures like us. First, I shall briefly consider Williams's suggestions about the identity condition. Then I shall turn to the attractiveness condition. Consider the following passage from Williams's essay:

> Some philosophers have pictured an eternal existence as occupied in something like intense intellectual enquiry....The activity is engrossing, self-justifying, affords, as it may appear, endless new perspectives, and by being engrossing enables one to lose oneself....But if

one is totally and perpetually absorbed in such an activity, and loses oneself in it, then as those words suggest, we come back to the problem of satisfying the condition that it should be me who lives for ever.[6]

Similarly, Williams argues against the appeal of the Spinozistic idea that intellectual activity is the most active and free state that a person could be in. Specifically, Williams argues against Stuart Hampshire's formulation of a doctrine he alleges is shared by both Spinoza and Freud, that

one's only means of achieving this distinctness as an individual, this freedom in relation to the common order of nature, is the power of the mind freely to follow in its thought an intellectual order.' The contrast to this free intellectual activity is 'the common condition of men that their conduct and their judgments of value, their desires and aversions, are in each individual determined by unconscious memories.[7]

But since Williams believes that such unconscious motivations are indeed part of the self, he accuses the Spinozistic conception of freedom of aspiring to be free from the self, which entails a loss of individuality itself. Thus, again, Williams claims that to lose oneself in intellectual activity is literally to *lose oneself*. If such activity were the dominant component of immortality, it could not be of interest to an individual in the sense in which the individual is especially interested in *his or her own future*; thus, Williams is here primarily concerned with his first criterion for the desirability of immortality—the *identity* criterion. Williams goes on to say:

As those who totally wish to lose themselves in the movement can consistently only hope that the movement will go on, so the consistent Spinozist—at least on this account of Spinozism—can only hope that the intellectual activity goes on, something which could be as well realised in the existence of Aristotle's prime mover, perhaps, as in anything to do with Spinoza or any other particular man.[8]

But it seems to me that an activity in which it is tempting to say that one 'loses oneself' is one in which the *content* of one's experiences is focused outward: one is thinking about something besides oneself. An engrossing and absorbing activity causes one to 'lose oneself' in the sense that one is not *self-absorbed*. But it is quite another matter to claim that the experiences involved in such activities are themselves not *one's own*. Even though one has 'lost oneself' in something in the sense that one is not narcissistically focused even in part on oneself, it does not follow that one cannot look at a future with such experiences as genuinely *one's own future*.

I would suggest, then, that Williams's remarks about 'losing oneself in the movement' do not call into question the possibility of an immortal life in which a certain particular individual continues to exist (and can envisage him or herself in the future). Even if one's life is heavily invested in activities in which one 'loses oneself', one can still understand these activities to be part of one's own future; the crucial distinction here is between the *content* of the relevant experiences and their *ownership*.

III

I now turn to Williams's second condition—the attractiveness condition. As pointed out above, Williams here constructs a dilemma: either one's character remains fixed, or it is allowed to change over time. I shall begin with the first horn of Williams's dilemma; that is, I shall be assuming that the individual in question has roughly speaking a fixed character over time.

The specific problem with the first sort of immortality (in which character is held fixed) is its putatively inevitable tendency to become boring and alienating. Williams puts the point as follows:

> In general we can ask, what it is about the imaged activities of an eternal life which would stave off the principle hazard to which EM succumbed, boredom. The Don Juan in Hell joke, that heaven's prospects are tedious and the devil has the best tunes, though a tired fancy in itself, at least serves to show up a real and (I suspect) a profound difficulty, of providing any model of an unending, supposedly satisfying, state or activity which would not rightly prove boring to anyone who remained conscious of himself and who had acquired a character, interests, tastes and impatiences in the course of living, already, a finite life.[9]

There are various philosophical defenses of the thesis that immortality (of the sort under consideration here) would be necessarily boring and thus would run afoul of the attractiveness condition. I certainly cannot here fully defend the idea that there are some pictures of such immortality which are *not* necessarily unattractive in this (or any other) way, but I wish to make a gesture in this direction by pointing to what appear to me to be some salient errors in Williams's defense of the thesis that such immortality is necessarily boring.

The first error can be seen to come from (or at least be encouraged by) a particular formulation employed by Williams. He says that the defenders of the desirability of immortality must provide a 'model of an unending, supposedly satisfying, state or activity which would not rightly prove boring to anyone who remained conscious of himself and who had acquired a character, interests, tastes and impatiences in the course of living, already, a finite life'.[10] The use of the phrase 'an unending, supposedly satisfying, state or activity', is infelicitous insofar as it suggests (but of course does not strictly speaking *entail*) that the endless life in question must consist in a *single* state or activity. Later, Williams says that the defender of the desirability of immortality must point to 'something that makes boredom *unthinkable*... something that could be guaranteed to be at every moment utterly absorbing. But if a man has and retains a character, there is no reason to suppose that there is anything that could be that'.[11] Again, this passage (especially the use of the singular pronouns 'something' and 'anything') at least suggests that the endless life must consist in some *single* utterly absorbing thing. Finally, Williams considers an eternal existence occupied in activities of intense intellectual inquiry. He says that 'it seems quite unreasonable to suppose that [these activities] would have the fulfilling or liberating character that they do have for [an individual who actually engages in such activities], if they were in fact all he could do or conceive of doing'.[12]

But why suppose that any one *single* supposedly absorbing activity must be pursued *at the expense of all others*? Why can't such activities be part of a *package* in an immortal life, just as we suppose that they should be in a mortal life? Certainly, an immortal life could consist in a certain *mix* of activities, possibly including friendship, love, family, intellectual, artistic and athletic activity, sensual delights, and so forth. We could imagine that any *one* of these would be boring and alienating, pursued relentlessly and without some combination of the others. In general, single-minded and unbalanced pursuit of any single kind of activity will be unattractive. But of course from the fact that one's life will be *unending* it does not follow that it must be *unitary* or *unbalanced*. That one's life is endless clearly does not have the implication that one must endlessly and single-mindedly pursue some particular sort of activity.

It might be useful again to consider Williams's demand for 'something that makes boredom *unthinkable*... something that could be guaranteed to be at every moment utterly absorbing'. His claim is that 'nothing less will do for eternity'.[13] But the justification for this demand is unclear. Why, in particular, should there be an asymmetry (of the sort implied by the demand) in the standards for the attractiveness of a finite life and an infinite life? Surely, we think of certain mortal lives which involve considerable stretches of boredom and even pain nevertheless worth living and even very appealing. Given this, why think that an immortal life with such features would not be on balance appealing? Why think that because a life is *unending*, it must be *uniformly* pleasing in order to be on balance attractive? The inference here is not more compelling than the inference noted above from the unending nature of immortal life to some single *unitary* activity which it putatively must contain.

Suppose one says that one finds some activity 'endlessly fascinating'. This could mean various different things. First, it could mean that whenever one turns to the activity (in the normal course of one's life), one finds it on balance fascinating. Second, it could mean that whenever one turns to the activity (in the normal course of one's life), one finds it *filled with* fascinating moments—perhaps even densely packed with fascinating moments. Finally, I suppose it *could* (just possibly) mean that one pursues the activity *forever* and finds it at every moment fascinating. Thus, with regard to the schema, 'endlessly—', one must distinguish at least three different notions: *reliability, density,* and *infinite extensibility.*

Now imagine that an unending life contains some activity which one finds 'endlessly fascinating'. It surely does not follow from the fact that an *unending* life contains an endlessly fascinating activity that the activity must be endlessly fascinating in the sense of infinite extensibility. An unending life can contain an endlessly fascinating activity in the sense of reliability or density. Further, I see no reason simply to *assume* (as Williams seems to) that in order for an endless life to be attractive, it must contain an activity (or even set of activities) that is endlessly fascinating (or endlessly appealing in any way) in the sense of infinite extensibility. I should think that it is even an open question whether in order for an endless life to be attractive, it must contain an activity that is endlessly fascinating (or endlessly appealing in any way) in *any* of the senses.

I wish now to develop a distinction which I believe is important to assessing the appeal of immortality. Having laid out the distinction, I will suggest that the tendency to think that immortality must be boring and alienating may come in part from attending solely to one of the categories involved in the distinction; this is another mistake of the proponents of the thesis that immortality is necessarily boring.

Some pleasurable experiences, it seems, are in some sense 'self-exhausting'. In the case of these pleasures, once (or perhaps a few times) is enough. That is to say, when one experiences such pleasures one tends not to want to repeat them—even at some point relatively far in the future. Some such pleasures are frankly *disappointing*; in the case of these, we find that some highly touted or much anticipated pleasure is just not what it was made out to be, and we simply conclude that it is not worth pursuing these in the future. But there are other such pleasures which are not necessarily disappointing; rather, they may be entirely fulfilling but in some way 'complete in themselves'. More specifically, they seem to be complete in the sense that, having experienced such a pleasure, one has no desire to experience it again at any point in the future.[14]

I take it that everyone has had his share of disappointments, so it is not necessary to dwell on these. But it will be useful to consider some examples of the 'non-disappointing' self-exhausting pleasures. Suppose, for instance, that you have the goal of doing something just (or at least primarily) to prove to yourself that you can do it. Imagine, for example, that you are somewhat afraid of heights, and you have been working hard to overcome this phobia. You form the goal of climbing Mt Whitney just to show yourself that you have overcome the fear—just to show yourself that you can control your life and overcome obstacles. Upon climbing the mountain, you may in fact be very pleased and proud. Indeed, you may be deeply satisfied. But also you may have absolutely no desire to climb Mt Whitney (or any other mountain) again. You have accomplished your goal, but there is no impetus toward repeating the relevant activity or the pleasure that issues from it.

I speculate that there are quite a few activities and resulting pleasures that are relevantly similar to those in the above case. Some of these are activities in which one sets out to prove something to oneself or other people. Others may be activities in which one sets a goal which is essentially 'comparative' in some way—one wants to win a race or some prize, one wants to be the brightest, most productive, most popular, fastest, and so forth (in some given context). Frequently (although certainly not invariably), upon reaching such essentially comparative goals, one finds them either disappointing or 'complete in themselves'; in any case, there is relatively little energy or impetus to repeat the accomplishments. (Of course, the energizing aspect of such accomplishments will vary with the nature of the accomplishment and the individual's personality; for some individuals, such achievements only whet the appetite for more, whereas this is not the case for others.)

I suspect, then, that the class of self-exhausting pleasures (both disappointing and not) is rather large. But these are *not* the *only* sort of pleasures. There are also 'repeatable pleasures'. Here an individual may well find the pleasure highly fulfilling and completely satisfying at the moment and yet wish to have more (i.e., to *repeat* the pleasure) at some point in the future (not necessarily immediately). Certain salient sensual pleasures leap immediately to mind: the pleasures of sex, of eating fine meals and drinking fine wines, of listening to beautiful music, of seeing great art, and so forth. These, or many of them, seem to be—at least for many people—repeatable pleasures. (Note that the distinction between self-exhausting and repeatable pleasures must be *relativized to particular individuals*; this having been said, there will presumably be some similarities across different individuals.)

It is not evident that the distinction between self-exhausting and repeatable pleasures can be understood or explained in terms of other notions. That is, it is not clear that the repeatable pleasures are 'higher', 'more noble', 'more intrinsically compelling', 'more complex', 'more intense', and so forth. It just seems to be a fact about us that we find that some pleasures are self-exhausting and some are repeatable, and it is not clear how even to begin to give an illuminating reductive account of this distinction.[15]

Of course, even repeatable pleasures may become boring or unappealing if distributed too closely (or in an otherwise inappropriate pattern). I suppose that even the most delectable lobster thermidor would quickly become revolting if consumed at every meal. But, as noted above, it is a mistake to suppose that the pleasures must be experienced in this way. Given the appropriate distribution of such pleasures, it seems that an endless life that included some (but perhaps not only) repeatable pleasures would *not* necessarily be boring or unattractive. Perhaps some of the proponents of the 'necessary boredom' thesis tend to attend solely or primarily to the self-exhausting pleasures (and associated activities). But once it is seen that there are also repeatable pleasures, the prospects of a certain sort of immortality are not nearly so grim.

I wish to say a bit more about the distinction between self-exhausting and repeatable pleasures. As the discussion proceeds, I hope it will become evident just how implausible it is to deny that there are repeatable pleasures (or that there can continue to be repeatable pleasures that form part of a mix of pleasurable experiences that extends indefinitely into the future). As a help in further discussing the nature and role of repeatable pleasures, I shall now relate the story of André and his beloved goose liver:[16]

> We had just been served the usual airline fare. The man sitting next to me, call him André, tasted his food deliberately, paused thoughtfully for a moment as if he were extracting what little pleasure could be found in the morsel, and then pronounced judgment: 'Surprising, yes this is really rather nice.' He had a cultured European accent and the appearance of a man dissipated not by wanton and reckless living, but by the civilized excess of too much of the good life. I said something to the effect that I thought all airplane food was awful and this seemed to be no exception. André looked at me with a type of patient parental disappointment. My comment had revealed how little I knew about life. 'Well, of course, this "food" is terrible— not really *food* at all. But this is an airplane, isn't it? And the point is that this turkey is much superior to what one normally finds in such environs. That is the pleasure in it.' It became clear that André's senses were far more refined than mine. He had trained himself to glean what little enjoyment could be found even in something so bland as a turkey sandwich on United.
>
> He began to relate the various meals he had eaten at different times. And this was how we at last came to the topic of the beloved goose liver. A goose liver, you see, properly nurtured and prepared, simply is better than the best of any other food. André became quiet for a time—lost in reveries like one remembering old and dear friends.

He began slowly, reverently to recall for me the rare times when he had found his beloved goose liver. There were the times growing up in Hungary—a country which, as everyone knows, really is the best country at producing goose liver. Later there were great moments when he would return to Hungary to visit his relatives; they would scrimp and save in order to have the week's wages necessary to procure the goose liver. Certainly this was extravagant, but so great was his joy eating the meal that everyone at the table felt it was a small price to pay.

There were other rare occasions in places like Vienna and New York where André would find and become reacquainted with his beloved goose liver in new surroundings. But such moments carried with them tremendous opportunities for disappointment. Not infrequently, the prized liver would be ruined by a clumsy chef who completely lacked the proper respect for the bounty he was preparing. Once, however, André was traveling through a little town in the Swiss Alps. He happened upon an average-looking restaurant around dinnertime. There on the menu was the daily special—goose liver. He inquired after the details of the dish— was it fresh, how was it prepared, and so forth. The answers encouraged him to order the meal. Upon its arrival at his table, André was surprised beyond his wildest dreams. He exclaimed to the waitress that he must meet the chef, for there were only two or three men in the world (he knew them all) who could prepare the beloved goose liver so expertly. How was it possible that the masterpiece could be produced so casually here? Much to André's surprise, when the chef was brought to the table, he turned out to be one of the famous chefs who had prepared André a meal years earlier. (The chef had some family business in the area and was cooking in the restaurant as a favor to the owner who was his friend.) The chef was, of course, delighted to find someone who truly appreciated the treasure which had been laid before him, and the two talked late into the night. André extended his stay in the town three days. He ordered goose liver every night.

Evidently, André's enthusiasm is food. Surely, the pleasures of the goose liver are *repeatable* pleasures for André. And it seems that André does not need such exotic culinary adventures to achieve significant repeatable pleasures; indeed, he gets such pleasures from a wide variety of gastronomic experiences, both elaborate and pedestrian. Further, I see no reason to think that André's pleasures would cease to be repeatable, if part of an immortal life (in which the pleasures are appropriately distributed. Goose liver for breakfast, lunch and dinner would no doubt rather rapidly turn even André's stomach).

To extend the point. Really, it seems that there are many repeatable pleasures; when one thinks about it—and specific accounts such as that of André help to bring home the point—Williams's necessary boredom thesis becomes very implausible. Think, for instance, of the pleasures of listening to great music. I get extraordinary pleasure from listening to Bach's Second Partita for the Unaccompanied Violin. (Whereas I am certainly not immune to gastronomical delights, Bach's Second Partita is my beloved goose liver.) And I see no reason why it would cease to be a repeatable pleasure, if part of an immortal life (in which there were an appropriate mix of activities and pleasures). Certainly, there are other such pleasures, such as the pleasures of visiting a great art museum, or a great and beautiful city, such as Paris, Venice or San Francisco. (I cannot imagine *ever* getting tired of the view of the city of San Francisco from the Golden Gate Bridge, or the feeling of the fog engulfing me in Golden Gate Park, or the beautiful plaintive sound of the foghorns in the distance. I have *no* tendency to think that these pleasures would become less compelling, unless pursued in a single-minded or compulsive fashion.)

In this section I have in a very sketchy way suggested a distinction between self-exhausting and repeatable pleasures. Although I have not analyzed or developed the distinction in detail, I have suggested that it is a mistake to suppose that all pleasures are relevantly similar to the self-exhausting sort. I wish briefly here to allude to a treatment of these issues which (like Williams's) is insufficiently attentive to the distinction in question. In Kierkegaard's pseudonymous essay 'The Rotation Method', the aestheticist 'A' properly rejects the idea that there must be *one* activity which is the sole source of pleasure and which is pursued relentlessly over the course of a lifetime. Rather, 'A' endorses a system of rotating pleasures just as an efficient farmer might rotate his crops to achieve a better result. But even with the rotation method 'A' finds life boring:

> Starting from a principle is affirmed by people of experience to be a very reasonable procedure; I am willing to humor them, and so begin with the principle that all men are bores. Surely no one will prove himself so great a bore as to contradict me in this.
> …All men are bores. The word itself suggests the possibility of a subdivision. It may just as well indicate a man who bores others as one who bores himself. Those who bore others are the mob, the crowd, the infinite multitude of men in general. Those who bore themselves are the elect, the aristocracy; and it is a curious fact that those who do not bore themselves usually bore others, while those who bore themselves entertain others.[17]

But whereas Kierkegaard's hedonist 'A' avoids some of the errors discussed above by adopting the rotation method, he evidently does *not* avoid the error of ignoring or underestimating the repeatable pleasures. Given the existence of such pleasures, a life with a suitable arrangement of them need not be boring. And I do not see why an immortal life with such a mix of repeatable pleasures would necessarily be boring.

Kierkegaard wished to convince us to turn away from hedonism and toward spiritual and religious experiences. I have suggested that he ignored the possibility of a range of pleasures which clearly are accessible even to persons who do not have spiritual or religious experiences. But for those who do indeed have such experiences, there would seem to be even more reason to embrace immortal life; surely, the deep and resonant rewards of spiritual and religious experience would not somehow become wooden or etiolated, if part of an endless life. What reason is there to suppose that such experiences would change their character in such circumstances?

Williams usefully distinguishes between 'conditional' and 'categorical' desires.[18] The conditional desires are desires for certain things, given that one will continue to live. Someone surely will want adequate clothing, food, shelter, and so forth, on the condition that he or she will continue to be alive. But such a person may not prefer to continue to live. Preferences which imply an answer to the question of whether one wishes to be alive are categorical desires. Presumably— although Williams does not explicitly say this—there can be both 'positive' and 'negative' categorical desires. A positive categorical desire implies the desire to continue to live, whereas a negative categorical desire implies the desire not to continue to live.

Perhaps the distinction between self-exhausting and repeatable pleasures can go some distance toward illuminating Williams's claim that one would lose one's positive categorical desires in an immortal life. Granted, this might be true if one focused exclusively on self-exhausting pleasures. After a while—perhaps a long while—these desires would lose their capacity to ground categorical desires and to propel one into the future. But I see no reason to think that the repeatable pleasures would lose their energizing and 'propulsive' character. Further, spiritual and religious experiences would seem to be relevantly similar to the repeatable pleasures in this respect; they seem capable of providing the basis for positive categorical desires, even in an immortal life.[19]

So far I have been concerned to discuss the first horn of Williams's dilemma pertinent to the attractiveness condition (presented above). That is, I have discussed the necessary boredom thesis in the context of a relatively fixed character. Let me now say just a few very brief words about the second horn, according to which the relevant individual's character changes over time. Williams suggests that it is now unclear that the individual will find such immortality attractive, given that it is unclear that there is the appropriate relationship between the individual's current character and future goals, values, and interests.

This sort of case notoriously raises fascinating but complex issues.[20] But the basic point is that it seems that an individual could value such an existence if he or she felt that the change in character would result from *certain sorts of sequences*. That is, if I felt that my future character will be different from my present one as a result of appropriate reflection at future times upon my experiences given my 'then-current' character, then I might well value such an existence. One's attitudes toward future changes of character depend on *how* and *why* the changes take place.

Surely in our ordinary, finite lives we envisage certain changes in our values and preferences over time. For example, one may currently value excitement and challenge; thus, one might wish to live in an urban area with many career and avocational opportunities (but with lousy weather and a high crime rate). Still, one might envisage a time in the future when one will be older and will prefer warm weather, serenity, and security. One can certainly envisage a time when one will prefer to live in a condominium in a warm, safe place, even if one currently thrives on life in Manhattan. And one need not look at the future stages of one's life (in which significant changes in values and preferences have taken place) as unattractive; certainly, they are not so unattractive as to render death preferable!

Thus, there are quite ordinary cases in our finite lives in which we envisage changes in our characters—our values and preferences—and which are not so unattractive as to render death preferable. Why, then, could not the same be true of immortal existence? As above, why set such radically different standards for immortal life and mortal life?

Granted, if one's character is changed by brainwashing, coercion, deception or various other methods, one might find the resultant existence thoroughly unattractive. But why assimilate all changes of character to these? And a devoted conservative republican may find it unthinkable that she become a liberal democrat, even by rather less exotic means of transformation. But it is not evident to me that such a person would actually prefer death. An even so, there is no reason to assimilate *all* changes of character to such a change; all that is required, in order to defend the thesis that immortality is not necessarily unattractive (on this horn of the dilemma), is that there be certain changes of character plausibly envisaged as part of an immortal life which would not be so unattractive as to render death preferable.

IV

In this essay I have explored some of the philosophical puzzles pertaining to immortality. More specifically, I have used Bernard Williams's important and influential discussion as a springboard for analyzing what I take to be certain problems with the claim that immortality is necessarily unattractive. I have argued that it is unfair to suppose that, in order for immortality to be attractive, it must consist of some *single* activity pursued at the expense of others. Further, it is unfair to demand that, in order for immortality to be attractive, it must consist of *entirely* pleasurable or agreeable experiences; why suppose the standards for immortal life are in this respect different from the standards for mortal life? Also, one may be entirely 'lost' in an engrossing activity in the sense of not *focusing* (primarily) upon oneself; it is quite another matter to say that the relevant experiences are not *one's own*. Finally, it is important to distinguish two different kinds of pleasures: self-exhausting pleasures and repeatable pleasures. A life without repeatable pleasures might well eventually become boring. But it is a mistake to suppose that an immortal life must contain only self-exhausting pleasures at the expense of repeatable pleasures. The repeatable pleasures—perhaps together with spiritual and religious experiences—could provide a reasonable basis for positive categorical desires even in an immortal life. It has been a recurrent theme of my discussion that it is quite unfair to set radically different standards for finite life and immortal life.

NOTES

I am very grateful to careful and insightful comments by Mark Ravizza. Also, I have benefited from the comments of anonymous readers for the *International Journal of Philosophical Studies*. Finally, some of the material in this essay is based on ideas that also appear (in telescoped form) in the introductory essay in *The Metaphysics of Death* and 'Models of Immortality' (see notes 1 and 2).

    1. Bernard Williams, 'The Makropulos Case: Reflections on the Tedium of Immortality', in Bernard Williams, *Problems of the Self* (Cambridge University Press, 1973), pp. 82–100; reprinted in John Martin Fischer (ed.) *The Metaphysics of Death* (Stanford, CA: Stanford University Press, 1993).

    2. For a general taxonomy of models of immortality and a discussion of the bearing of Williams's two criteria on several of these models, see the appendix to this chapter.

    3. Williams, op. cit. note 1, p. 90.

    4. Presumably, the essential boredom thesis is meant to apply to creatures of a certain sort—creatures relevantly similar to us. Otherwise, it would follow from the thesis that God's existence is boring and unattractive (insofar as God is essentially everlasting).

    5. Williams, op. cit. note 1, p. 89.

    6. *Ibid.*, p. 96.

    7. *Ibid.* p. 97.

    8. *Ibid.*, p. 98.

    9. *Ibid.*, pp. 94–5.

    10. *Ibid.*

    11. *Ibid.*

    12. *Ibid.*

    13. *Ibid.*

    14. This notion of 'completeness in itself' is different from Aristotle's notion according to which certain activities—*energeiai*—are complete in themselves.

Aristotle distinguishes *energeia* from *kinesis*, which are not complete in themselves. Roughly, Aristotle's distinction corresponds to activities which are movements toward a certain product and which are not complete until the production of the product, and activities which are not so understood.

At *Metaphysics* Theta Six, Aristotle introduces the 'tense test' to distinguish *energeia* and *kinesis*. According to the tense test, if the verb 'X-ing' is an *energeia* verb, then 'I am X-ing' entails 'I have X-ed'. For example, 'I am enjoying myself' entails 'I have enjoyed myself'. If the verb is a *kinesis* verb, 'I am X-ing' entails 'I have not X-ed'. For example, 'I am learning [something]' entails 'I have not learned [the thing]'. There is an analogue of the tense test which is a non-linguistic phenomenon. The proper parts of *energeia* X are also X's: the proper parts of enjoyings are enjoyings. The proper parts of *kinesis* Y are not also Y's: the proper parts of a walking from A to B are are not walkings from A to B. For some discussions of the tense test, see: J.L. Ackrill, 'Aristotle's Distinction Between *energeia* and *kinesis*', in R. Bambrough (ed.) *New Essays in Plato and Aristotle* (New York: Humanities Press, 1965); and Terry Penner, 'Verbs and the Identity of Actions—A Philosophical Exercise in the Interpretation of Aristotle', in O.P. Wood and G. Pitcher (eds) *Ryle: A Collection of Critical Essays* (Garden City, NY: Doubleday, 1970).

15. It is an interesting philosophical question: *Why* are some pleasures self-exhausting and others repeatable?

16. For the story of André I am indebted to Mark Ravizza. Since the original publication of this essay, I have become aware of the cruel practices involved in producing goose liver; I would not have used Mark Ravizza's otherwise nice (and true) story, if I had known of these practices.

17. Soren Kierkegaard, 'The Rotation Method', in *Either/Or*, in *A Kierkegaard Anthology*, ed. Robert Bretall (New York: The Modern Library, 1946), pp. 21, 23–4.

18. Williams, op. cit. note 1, pp. 85–6.

19. It has been brought to my attention that there may indeed be some experiences in life that we savor and value (to the extent we actually do) precisely because we know that we will not enjoy them forever. It is difficult for me to know whether this is really the case, and to what extent (if so). But let me grant that it is true. This admission would not in itself undermine my strategy of argumentation, for even if certain pleasures are expunged or diminished, the repeatable ones may still make immortal life worthwhile. And it is also worth noting that there certainly are painful and unpleasant experiences associated precisely with the fact that we *cannot* have certain relationships and experiences forever: loss and death notoriously impose great pain and suffering upon us. I see no reason to suppose that the diminution in pleasures issuing from immortality would be greater than the diminution in pain and suffering.

20. See, for example, Derek Parfit, *Reasons and Persons* (Oxford: Oxford University Press, 1984).

Appendix to Chapter 6: Philosophical Models of Immortality in Science Fiction

John Martin Fischer and Ruth Curl

Science fiction (SF) is often described as a literary genre well suited to philosophical speculation. SF and philosophy share a common interest in the question of immortality, and comparisons and contrasts can be made regarding their respective treatments of the theme. We propose here a sketchy taxonomy of different models or pictures of immortality offered by philosophers and SF writers. After noting important differences in these models, we shall suggest that some problems and concerns expressed by philosophers and SF writers alike are the result of conflating different models. It is our hope that these comparisons will provide a preliminary sense of the way SF can be said to function as philosophical discourse.

Our discussion will use as its base the analytical framework presented in Bernard Williams's influential discussion of immortality, *The Makropulos Case: Reflections on the Tedium of Immortality*.[1] This simple and natural framework involves two criteria to make immortality truly appealing: first, there must be a future in which an individual can recognize himself or herself—someone genuinely *identical* to the individual, not just qualitatively similar or with several identical properties. Second, the future life of the individual must be *appealing* (in some way) to that individual; it cannot involve constant torture, hard labor, tedium, or the like. These conditions can be dubbed the *identity condition* and the *attractiveness condition*. With these, we can construct a taxonomy of different models of immortality (see Table 6.1).

Although our focus will be the immortality of sentient creatures or constructs, another treatment of immortality in SF is also possible: universe immortality, in which there is an attempt to overcome laws of entropy to create an immortal world, forever self-perpetuating. The center of attention here is not the immortality of sentient creatures but rather the immortality of the physical universe.[2] Only SF seems to deal with universe immortality; and while it is not our focus, this vision of immortality merits attention because it has no corollary in other fields of literature or philosophy.

Table 6.1. A taxonomy of immortality

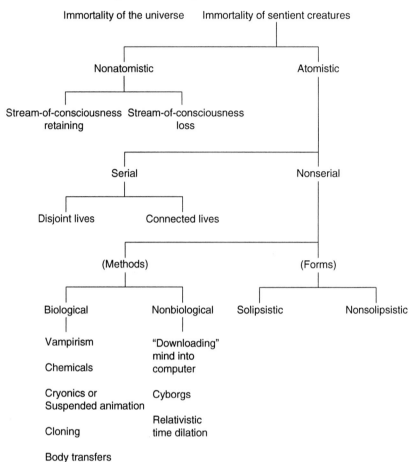

We turn now to depictions of immortality pertaining to sentient entities, beginning with a distinction between *nonatomistic* and *atomistic* concepts of immortality. The former involves a kind of *fusion* of different individuals into a type of immortal entity; the latter involves the immortality of individuals. The nonatomistic model usually involves the merging of various individuals into some sort of superorganism. The individual's stream of consciousness may either be retained, as in Greg Bear's *Blood Music*, or lost, as in Arthur C. Clarke's *Childhood's End* and one episode of Robert A. Heinlein's *Methuselah's Children*.[3]

In *Blood Music*, a brilliant researcher, after losing his job, injects himself with lymphocytes he has genetically manipulated so that he can smuggle them out of the lab and continue his research. The altered lymphocytes then invade the biosphere and trigger the mutation of humanity into a new organism composed of individually intelligent cells. Eventually the cells unite to form a superintelligent being. Each cell can either function separately or compartmentalize with other cells, which can then isolate themselves to work on various problems. Bear's vision of the mutation and transformation of humanity is best expressed in the novel's last lines: "Nothing is lost. Nothing is forgotten. It was in the blood, the flesh. And now it is forever" (*BM* 247).

In *Childhood's End*, children and adolescents transform beyond the comprehension of the rest of humanity. Clarke's vision clearly shows a complete but unintentional and uncontrollable break with human characteristics, memories, and emotions. In *Methuselah's Children*, members of the Howard Families (immortals in a mortal world) fleeing persecution on Earth and searching for a hospitable planet encounter the Little People, who "in an utterly basic sense…differed from humans in kind. They were not individuals. No single body of a native housed a discrete individual. Their individuals were multi-bodied, they had group 'souls.' The basic unit of their society was a telepathic rapport group of many parts. The number of bodies and brains housing one individual ran as high as ninety or more and was never less than thirty-odd" (*MC* 134–5).

Clearly, there can be different versions of the nonatomistic approach, including differences in the nature of the transition from individuals to composites, which can be a genetic mutation (as in *Blood Music*, ignoring for the moment the manipulation by Vergil) or a nonmutational evolutionary transformation (as in *Childhood's End*). And there can be differences in the nature of the composites: for example, there may be one or many composites, and the existence of the composites might be relatively desirable or undesirable.

But any sort of nonatomistic immortality—even one in which the nature of the composite's existence is relatively attractive—appears to run afoul of Williams's first criterion: the identity criterion. Arguably, the types of fusion envisaged in nonatomistic models (even ones that somehow preserve individual streams of consciousness) do not allow individuals to look forward to *their own* future existence. As such, these nonatomistic models are not very appealing models of immortality.

Is it then appropriate to eliminate nonatomistic models? When we look to the future we seem to care about the welfare of our communities and friends, the planet and its nations. We might care about the continued development of the arts, the preservation of natural beauty, and the attainment of human rights and distributive justice; but we care *especially* about how *we ourselves* will fare—we especially look forward to future pleasurable states of ourselves and particularly reject prospective unpleasant future states of ourselves. So, for example, if we are told that some future individuals will be tortured horribly for days, we can genuinely regret this; however, if we are then told that those people will be ourselves, we are horrified—we *especially* regret this. Thus, individuals might care to some extent about a future in which individuals have become group entities of certain sorts; indeed, it might even be desirable in some sense. But we do not and cannot look at such a prospect in the special and especially vivid way we look at future scenarios in which we exist as individuals. This special sense in which we care *particularly* about what happens to us is not engaged by nonatomistic models of immortality.

Since nonatomistic models seem to run afoul of the identity condition, let us instead turn to atomistic models of immortality. In this class there are *serial* and *nonserial* models. In serial models of immortality, the individual in question in some ways lives a series of lives; in nonserial models, the individual simply leads an indefinitely long single life.

The atomistic serial model of immortality comes in at least two versions: the *disjoint-lives serial model* and the *connected-lives serial model*. In the disjoint-lives model, one individual lives an indefinitely long series of lives without internal psychological connections: there are no significant continuities or connections of memory or other psychological states, such as values, beliefs, desires, and intentions, from one life to the next. In this view, the self is some sort of soul or bare particular without any essential mental contents. When the soul enters a new body, the person itself persists, even if there are no remaining memories, beliefs, preferences, values, or intentions. This model recalls the Hindu model of reincarnation. A possible metaphor is the tulip bulb—the different lives correspond to the different plants and flowers that spring from the bulb from one year to the next, whereas the persisting self corresponds to the essential bulb.

But, like the nonatomistic model, the disjoint-lives serial model runs afoul of the identity condition. It is unclear how an individual could recognize a future individual as genuinely identical to himself or herself if there is no psychological connection between the two (including connections of memory). We do not know if it is metaphysically coherent to suppose that persistence of personal identity means the persistence of a bare, psychologically empty soul; there are deep perplexities here into which we cannot go. Even if the model is metaphysically coherent, the identity condition does not seem to be satisfied in the relevant way, a way that makes it possible for us to *recognize* ourselves in the future scenario. That is, even if there is no insuperable ontological problem with the disjoint-lives serial picture, there is an epistemic problem: presented with a description of a future scenario, there is no way individuals can recognize or identify *themselves*. And, if the relevant future person has no psychological connection to the current individual, why should the individual care especially (in the way one cares especially about *oneself*) about this future person? Given this problem, the disjoint-lives model is unappealing—it cannot capture the sense in which we might value especially our own immortality.

Unfortunately, the connected-lives serial model fares no better. Imagine, if you can, what it would be like to lead one life—to go through childhood, adolescence, and all the stages of life—accumulate memories and associated values, and then begin again: go through a second childhood (but with memories of the previous life), a second adolescence (but with memories of the previous life plus the new childhood), and so forth. What would it be like to be a small child carrying memories of adolescence, marriage, raising a family, seeing one's children grow up, and so forth? The model of full or robust psychological connections within serial lives seems either entirely incoherent or entirely unattractive; in any case, it surely does not meet the two criteria. Nor does it seem possible to weaken the psychological connections in any natural or appealing way; in particular, it does not seem plausible that one could have only certain memories (just enough to be able to recognize oneself as a persisting entity) at certain stages of life. This would involve "blackouts" of parts of memory at some stages and not others—an almost stroboscopic and bizarre picture of memory. SF often puts a skeptical valence on this sort of connected-lives serial model. Consider Clarke's *The City and the Stars* (1956). In this novel people are reborn into new bodies without memories of previous lives; then, as they near adulthood, they gradually remember their previous lives. From the perspective of the "new" individual, it would surely be disconcerting to be suddenly flooded by a vast set of old memories of earlier lives; and—more relevant to the issue of immortality—from the perspective of the "old" individual, it would not be pleasant to stop being conscious one day, then reawaken with a new set of memories involving a new childhood and adolescence.

Thus, even though SF novels may claim that a character leads many lives, our ruminations above lead us to call this possibility into question. On closer scrutiny, these novels do not depict characters who themselves lead different lives in the senses required by the serial model. A particular character (say, Lazarus Long) does not lead many lives; rather, *he* leads *one* extended life in which many other people play roles. Many lives become part of his life when they intersect it—but Long himself does not genuinely lead a series of lives. (A life with a series of people need not be a series of lives.)

Our taxonomic trail leads finally to atomistic nonserial conceptions of immortality, of which there are various versions. Primarily, these involve different ways of *generating* or *maintaining* the indefinitely long life, and different ways of viewing the *nature* of the life (pattern and distribution of experiences, relationship to other lives, and so forth).

Let us first consider the different ways of generating or maintaining a nonserial atomistic form of immortality. There are a number of horror stories in which a vampire draws on the life force of another to continue existence. Literature and films have produced many variations on this theme; the vampire does not always follow the Count Dracula formula. Numerous films, for example, depict beautiful young women who seduce young men to feed off their energy; and Oscar Wilde's *The Picture of Dorian Gray* (1897) features a protagonist who remains young while his portrait ages. In E. E. "Doc" Smith's Lensman series the Overlords live off the life force of the Velantians. In one Balzac story, an old man lives off young girls. A recent Stephen King film, *Sleepwalkers* (1992), depicts a young man who gains vitality from the innocence or purity of young virgins, whom he kills in order to devour their life force, or souls. Obviously, the topic continues to generate discussion.

In Anne McCaffrey's series comprising *Crystal Singer* (1982), *Killashandra* (1985), and *Crystal Line* (1992), humans have developed a symbiosis with a spore, which makes them extremely long-lived. Unfortunately, they must periodically return to the planet of the spores to avoid a terrible death. (This somehow resembles the need to visit one's parents regularly—at least in our families!) In McCaffrey and Jody Lynn Nye's *The Death of Sleep* (1990), the protagonist, who engages in cryogenic sleep, ages only four or five years in seventy-two. Another type of life prolongation is envisioned in Hugo Gernsback's *Ralph 124C 41+: A Romance of the Year 2660* (1925), in which a man reacts to a scientist's revival of a dead dog by exclaiming, "I only regret for myself that you had not lived and conducted this experiment when I was a young man, that I might have, from time to time, lived in suspended animation from century to century, and from generation to generation as it will now be possible for human beings to do."[4] This would not be continued conscious existence with stroboscopic memory, but rather stroboscopic consciousness of a certain sort. In some novels, cloning gives characters a form of immortality. For example, in Heinlein's *Time Enough for Love* (1973), Lazarus Long is more or less cloned as his own daughters.

Another biological method of achieving immortality consists in so-called body transfers, which presupposes the falsity of the "bodily identity" criterion of personal identity. In *The World of Null-A* (1948) and *The Players of Null-A* (1956), by A. E. van Vogt, Gosseyn's consciousness transfers from one body (when it is destroyed) to another. As long as there are bodies, he can exist forever. Of course, conceptually one can distinguish between various sorts of body transfers. In some cases the brain is transferred to a different body. In others the brain itself is not transferred, but the mental state is, as in the film *Invasion of the Body Snatchers* (1956); in some of the latter sorts of cases, there can be teleportation as well as mental transfer.[5]

There are also rather less exotic (though by no means mundane) biological methods of generating and maintaining immortality, as portrayed in Mary Shelley's "The Mortal Immortal" (1910) and Larry Niven's *Ringworld* (1970), *Ringworld Engineers* (1979), and *Protector*

(1973), all of which feature immortal beings. In Shelley's story, a young apprentice drinks the creation of his master and becomes immortal. In Niven's books, individuals live for centuries by using a drug especially tailored for their chemistry; without the drug, they die. Any human who eats the Spice of Life becomes a Pak Protector. Human Protectors undergo a physical change that makes them almost unrecognizable as human and a mental change that makes them protect whatever society they are in at the moment. These beings seem to be biological analogues to Isaac Asimov's robots, and they follow laws (instincts, in this case) similar to his Laws of Robotics.

There are also nonbiological methods of generating and maintaining immortality. In *Neuromancer* (1984) William Gibson creates a kind of human immortality by allowing the transfer of human mental states to computers. In Gregory Benford's *Great Sky River* (1987) the transfer is accomplished through the insertion of computer chips into the human, resulting in a combination of biological and mechanical capabilities: though the body may die, the "mind" continues. These procedures involve mental transfer ("downloading" of the "mind") not accompanied by actual brain transfer.[6]

Other SF authors increase human longevity or create immortality by augmenting or supplanting normal human biological capacities through mechanical means. In McCaffrey's *The Ship Who Sang* (1969), a future society trains deformed but mentally functional babies to work in cyborg-type bodies if the parents so choose. This falls under the rubric of cyborg-type models of generating and maintaining atomistic nonserial immortality. In other works, robots are created and then allegedly made sentient. Their mechanical nature makes them more or less immortal. Thus, in Asimov's Robot and Foundation series, Daneel first acquires a feel for human phenomena and then leans more and more toward the human, becoming telepathic to get a better insight into human nature and reasoning. Finally, he makes plans to transfer his knowledge and memories (which in a robot are also his essence) to the brain of a Solarian child, thereby becoming mortal. But it is a prolonged mortality because Solarians, like all Spacers, live three or four hundred years. Further, if he can perform the operation once, he can do it again, particularly because this child is a hermaphrodite who will produce at least one offspring that is for all intents and purposes "itself." So, unlike Andrew Martin in "The Bicentennial Man," Daneel leaves his "option" of immortality open.

One other nonbiological way to produce immortality (one might call it "relativistic" immortality) involves time travel, as in Joe Haldeman's *The Forever War* (1974), in which time travel paradoxes are manipulated to achieve a sort of immortality.[7]

Having briefly surveyed the methods of generating and maintaining immortality (in particular, atomistic nonserial immortality), we now turn to the *nature* of immortal lives—their relationship to other lives and the pattern and distribution of their experiences.

First, consider a kind of solipsistic model. Heinlein's " '—All You Zombies—' " (1958) features an endless temporal loop in which the protagonist is a man who travels in time. But the pattern of his time travels indicates that he is in fact his own father, mother, and baby. There are other, nonsolipsistic, conceptions of the nature of atomistic nonserial immortality. One posits the "lone immortal" who lives among other individuals, all mortals. There are at least two versions of the lone immortal model—one in which the lone immortal is known by (certain) others to be immortal, and another in which the immortality is a secret. Such models appear, respectively, in Asimov's *The End of Eternity* (1955) and Shelley's "The Mortal Immortal." In another conception the immortal is not alone—perhaps others are immortal, as in *Methuselah's Children*, or perhaps everyone is immortal.

We have found problems with all models of immortality except for atomistic nonserial approaches. Nonatomistic models do not seem to meet the identity criterion, and some atomistic models—in particular the connected-lives serial models—run afoul of the attractiveness criterion (if not also the identity condition). But what about the atomistic nonserial models of immortality? Surely some methods of generating and maintaining immortality (such as feeding off the blood and vitality of others) make the resulting immortality less attractive. And some pictures of the nature of such immortality (such as the solipsistic model) make immortality unappealing. But not all methods of generating immortality are similarly problematic, and not all concepts of the nature of such immortality are straightforwardly problematic. Is there something about the nature of atomistic non-serial immortality that renders it, on reflection, *necessarily* undesirable?

Though some philosophers argue for this undesirability,[8] some SF models are not so pessimistic. A common trait in SF is its faith in the ability of technology to accelerate the moment in the process of history when desirable immortality can be experienced. And today, there is already the hope that the human life span can be extended (through cryonics, for example) long enough to allow us to outlive the immediate causes of death and in a sense live to see the dawn of immortality. Yet SF has negative models, too, and can be every bit as critical of positive aspirations as are many philosophers. One brief example: though some SF novels depict efforts to achieve immortality through transformation into robots or mechanical beings, perhaps an equal number offer the opposite maneuver: a reverse immortality, or "Pinocchio Syndrome," in which an immortal strives to become mortal (not to die, but to become "subject to mortality"). Somehow, even facing the prospect of immortal existence, human (mortal) qualities still retain such value that they are worth the reversal.

Despite a certain symbiosis between models in SF and philosophy, SF may be more open to the possibility of transformation of the human body and life span. But in the end, is SF any more *willing* to abandon human limits? That vast and intriguing question is, unfortunately, beyond the scope of this essay.[9]

NOTES

1. Bernard Williams, *The Makropulos Case: Reflections of the Tedium of Immortality* (Cambridge: Cambridge University Press, 1973), 82–100.

2. We see such concern expressed in Robert A. Heinlein's "Waldo" (1942) and Isaac Asimov's *The Gods Themselves* (1972), in which an alternate universe is discovered and energy is drawn from it, thus invalidating the law of the conservation of energy and avoiding entropy. In Poul Anderson's *Tau Zero* (1970) the universe contracts until there is too much energy contained in too small a volume and the contracting universe explodes to begin the process of expansion again. In Gregory Benford's *Timescape* (1980), tachyons—particles that travel faster than light—can make universal wave functions split into two or more universes if a causal paradox is created by the tachyonic interaction. These works all depict science fiction's underlying concern with the mortality of the universe.

3. Greg Bear, *Blood Music* (New York: Ace Books, 1986) [*BM*]; Arthur C. Clarke, *Childhood's End* (New York: Ballantine Books, 1980); Robert A. Heinlein, *Methuselah's Children* (New York: Signet Books, 1958) [*MC*]. Later page references are to these editions.

4. Hugo Gernsback, *Ralph 124C 41+: A Romance of the Year 2660* (New York: Frederick Fell, 1950), 65.

5. For various examples of this, along with an incisive and comprehensive philosophical discussion of the nature of personal identity, see Derek Parfit, *Reasons and Persons* (Oxford: Clarendon Press, 1984).

6. See Rudy Rucker, *Software* (New York: Ace Books, 1982).

7. For a philosophical discussion of time travel paradoxes, see Paul Horwich, *Asymmetries in Time* (Cambridge: MIT Press, 1987).

8. See Williams, *The Makropulos Case.*

9. For more complete citations and a bibliography of Science Fiction discussions of death and immortality, see John Martin Fischer, ed., *The Metaphysics of Death* (Stanford: Stanford University Press, 1993), pp. 411–413.

7

Epicureanism About Death and Immortality

John Martin Fischer

I want to live forever: but just what is it that I thereby want? Prior to 1874
(or thereabouts) my want would have seemed quite clear: I would have wanted to live for
an unending sequence of years, one year for each natural number—an omega-sequence
of years. But our horizon has since been expanded by the teachings of Georg Cantor.
The natural numbers all together amount only to the smallest order of infinity, aleph-null.
There are countess greater infinities that dwarf aleph-null as surely as aleph-null dwarfs
our customarily allotted three score and ten. Why settle for a piddling aleph-null years
if there are limit cardinals out there to vault over, inaccessible cardinals waiting
to be surpassed?
...trans-omega longevity is (conceptually) possible: there are possible worlds that endure
beyond a single omega-sequence of years, and a person can survive in these worlds from
one omega-sequence to another.
...I want trans-omega longevity, but not at any cost. Wanting to live beyond a single
omega-sequence of years is, for me, a conditional want, as is wanting to live to be 100.
Both wants are conditional, at the very least, upon my still having my wits about me,
and upon there still being a fair balance of pleasure over pain. In claiming that
trans-omega longevity is desirable, I claim only that there is some possible world,
even if quite remote from our own, in which I have trans-omega existence and the above
conditions are satisfied. Some, it is true, have argued that such conditions could never
be satisfied even for ordinary immortality because a life too long inevitably leads to
perpetual boredom. I suspect that those who argue in this way either lack imagination
or become too quickly jaded with the good things in life...

> Phillip Bricker, "On Living Forever" (*presented at The American Philosophical*
> *Association, March, 1985*)

I. INTRODUCTION

Epicureans take seriously Boethius' thought that philosophy has its consolations. In her important work on Hellenistic philosophy, Martha Nussbaum has offered an interpretation of Hellenistic philosophy according to the "medical model."[1] On this approach, philosophy is not a neutral, detached methodology, but a way of helping us to grapple with problems that otherwise would confuse and distress us. Philosophy, then, is a kind of therapy. Nussbaum both attributes this view to Epicurus and his followers (such as the Roman philosopher, Lucretius) and also endorses it. The Hellenistic philosophers sought to apply their philosophical therapy to such issues as the fear of death, the nature and mysteries of love, sexuality, and potentially unruly emotions, such as anger.

Here I shall focus on Nussbaum's reconstruction, interpretation, and defense of Lucretius's "main argument" that it is irrational to fear death.[2] I shall also offer some reflections on what she calls the "banquet argument" of Lucretius. According to this argument, we should realize that life is like a banquet: "it has a structure in time that reaches a natural and appropriate termination."[3] Here I wish briefly to add to my previous defense of the thesis that immortality would not necessarily be unattractive.[4]

In my view, philosophy is a perfectly neutral device. It can be employed by those who seek reassurance and freedom from anxiety. It can also increase confusion and perplexity. Even at its best, it may reveal puzzles and problems of which we were previously unaware. Of course, it is always up to us how exactly we use the deliverances of theoretical reasoning. It is not a good idea to ruminate excessively on insoluble dilemmas—a sensible view that would be endorsed, presumably, by practical philosophy—or to allow them to dampen our spirits. But it may be that philosophy shows us, what we feared inchoately, that, as Thomas Nagel puts it, "...a bad end is in store for us all."[5]

II. THE MAIN ARGUMENT AND PREVIOUS DISCUSSION

Nussbaum presents Lucretius's main argument as follows:

1. An event can be good or bad for someone only if, at the time when the event is present, that person exists as a subject of at least possible experience, so that it is at least possible that the person experiences the event.
2. The time after a person dies is a time at which that person does not exist as a subject of possible experience.
3. Hence, the condition of being dead is not bad for that person.
4. It is irrational to fear a future event unless that event, when it comes, will be bad for one.
5. It is irrational to fear death.[6]

Nussbaum points out that Nagel has rejected the first premise of the main argument because of its insistence on a connection between badness and experience. Nagel offers two examples. The first involves an individual who is betrayed behind his back; even though the individual never comes to know about this betrayal (or, let us say, experience any unpleasant consequences of it), Nagel contends that the betrayal can be a bad thing for the individual. In the second example, a person loses all higher mental functioning in an accident (or as a result of a stroke); this is alleged by Nagel to be a loss for the person, even if the individual is now (after the accident) contented. On Nagel's view, death is bad for the individual who dies not in virtue of involving unpleasant experiences, but insofar as it is a deprivation of the good things in life (the "deprivation thesis about death's badness").

Nussbaum disagrees:

> ...Nagel does not make it clear exactly how an event located completely outside a life's temporal span diminishes the life itself. The cases he actually analyzes are not by themselves sufficient to show this, since in each of them a subject persists, during the time of the bad event, who has at least a strong claim to be identical with the subject to whom the bad event is a misfortune. In the betrayal case, this subject is clearly the very same, and is a subject of possible, if not actual, experience in relation to that event. In the second case, it is hard not to feel that the continued existence of the damaged person, who is continuous with and very plausibly identical with the former adult, gives the argument that the adult has suffered a loss at least part of its force. Where death is concerned, however, there is no subject at all on the scene, and no continuant. So it remains unclear exactly how the life that has ended is diminished by the event.[7]

Why exactly is it thought to be so important to produce an example in which "the subject does not persist?" I shall return to this question below, but I would first suggest that a quite natural response would be that, in such a circumstance, it is *impossible* for the individual to have any unpleasant experience as a result of the event which purportedly is bad for him or her. That is, it is plausible to suppose that the reason why the subject's going out of existence is problematic is that (on the assumption that death is an experiential blank), the (nonexistent) agent *cannot* have any unpleasant experience. This thought makes it natural to seek to develop examples in which it is indisputably *impossible* for the (still existing) individual to have any unpleasant experience as a result of the purportedly harmful event, and yet the person *does* appear to be harmed.[8]

Consider the following two examples. The first is a modification of the case presented by Nagel; it employs the signature structure of preemptive overdetermination found in the "Frankfurt-type" counterexamples to the Principle of Alternative Possibilities.[9] Here is my presentation of the case:

> Imagine first that the example is as described by Nagel. You are betrayed behind your back by people who you thought were good friends, and you never actually find out about this or have any bad experiences as a result of the betrayal. But now suppose that these friends were (very) worried that you might find out about the betrayal. In order to guard against this possibility, they arrange for

White to watch over you. His task is to prevent you ever from finding out about the betrayal. So, for example, if one of the individuals who betrayed you should decide to tell you about it, White can
prevent him from succeeding: White can do whatever is required to
prevent the information from getting to you. Or if you should begin
to seek out one of the friends, White could prevent you from succeeding in making contact. I simply stipulate that White is in a position to thwart any attempt by you or your friends to inform you of
what happened.[10]

Since everything that actually happens among your friends and to
you and your family is exactly the same in my version and Nagel's
version, I claim that it is plausible that the betrayal harms you. That
is, it is plausible that the betrayal harms you in Nagel's version, and
if harm supervenes on what "actually happens to you" (in some
physico/causal sense) and your loved ones, then you are harmed in
my version of the case. But in my version, it is not just true that you do
not experience anything unpleasant as a result of the betrayal—you
cannot.

The second case owes much to an example by Jeff McMahon.[11] Here
is the example:

> ...your daughter is trekking in the Himalayas while you are at home
> in the United States. Tragically, she dies in an accident. I believe that
> you are harmed by your daughter's death—a bad thing has happened
> to *you*—even before you find out about it. Suppose, further, that you
> die without ever finding out about the accident in the Himalayas;
> imagine, for example, that you die of a heart attack just five minutes
> after your daughter dies. You never find out about her death, and,
> given plausible assumptions about the situations of you and your
> daughter, you *cannot* find out about it. Nevertheless, it seems to me
> that you have been harmed (at least, for the five minutes of your con-
> tinued life) by the death of your daughter. And here it is not merely
> the case that you do not have any unpleasant experiences as a result
> of your daughter's death; in addition, it is, at least on a very natural
> understanding of "possibility," *impossible* for you to have any such
> experiences as a result of her death.[12]

Nussbaum has responded to the latter case as follows (and, presumably, her comments would also apply to the former):

> I do not find Fischer's counterexamples altogether convincing:
> like the Nagel examples I criticize, they all involve a subject who
> continues to exist, however briefly, during the time when the bad
> event takes place. Even if the mother dies shortly after her daugh-
> ter's death, and without receiving news of it, the idea that a bad
> thing has happened *to her* surely rests, at least to some extent, on

the thought that the mother is there in the world when the daughter dies. There is a *her* for the bad thing to happen to. This, of course, is not true of one's own death; the bad event just is the cessation of the subject (Lucretius profoundly suggests that we believe death to be bad for us through a mental sleight of hand, in which we imagine ourselves persisting and watching our own loss of the goods of life). The right parallel, then, would be the case in which the mother and the daughter die at precisely the same instant. In this case I think we would not confidently assert that the mother has suffered a bereavement.[13]

III. SUITS AND HETHERINGTON

III.1. Suits

David Suits does not find my modification of Nagel's example entirely convincing.[14] Indeed, he says:

> This [the modified version of the Nagel example of betrayal behind one's back] seems to be a quite fanciful—no, a desperate—attempt to bolster the example. First of all, we are never in a position to know that any precaution against harm (for that is all White is) is guaranteed to be successful in a case such as betrayal, where the effects can be far-ranging and difficult to trace...
>
> Second, it seems to me that if White is really so clever as all that, then he could make his job immeasurably easier simply by preventing the secret betrayal in the first place. So now the question is this: What is the difference between, on the one hand, a secret betrayal which, on account of magic, can have no bad effects whatsoever on you, and, on the other hand, there never having been a secret betrayal after all?...Let's invent a counter-story: All your life is characterized, as far as you can tell, by the unwavering loyalty of your friends. Nothing whatsoever in your experience leads you to believe that any of your friends are not after all your friends; in fact, all your experience is to the contrary. All attempts to discover betrayal have come to naught. What shall you do with the hypothesis that there might nevertheless be some secret betrayal? What will your therapist say about your speculations that there is a very cunning Mr. White who is preventing all relevant effects of this secret betrayal from reaching you?
>
> In what sense then could it be said that something happened that was bad for you? Well, the only answer is that if there was a secret betrayal, then it was after all a *betrayal*. Now of course to call something a betrayal is to lead us to expect harmful consequences. That is the way we have come to know the world....The best that can be

said is that if, somehow, I *were* absolutely convinced that the "victim" would not and could not be harmed in any way, then I would have to say that what takes place is not a betrayal at all.[15]

In reply to Suits, I would begin by pointing out that the example is indeed fanciful, and admittedly so. It is a thought-experiment, with all of the attendant methodological risks (and, I believe, benefits). Granted: in ordinary life, we are never in a position to know that a given precaution against harm is guaranteed to be successful. I am not proposing this as empirically plausible or feasible, but as conceivable and thus metaphysically possible. Imagine, if you will, that White has Godlike foreknowledge of the future. I do not believe that the *philosophical* point is affected by Suits' contention that we (as we actually are) could never have the required sort of certainty.

Further, it is quite beside the point that White "could make his job immeasurably easier simply by preventing the secret betrayal in the first place." This may be true, but in the example as I presented it, White does not prevent the secret betrayal. One could certainly tell a different story, but, in the story I told, White is a merely "counterfactual intervener"; the example thus has the characteristic structure of a "Frankfurt-type case" (as pointed out above). If the story I told is coherent, then a theorist is intellectually required to take it into account—to show how its point fits with his own view, even if his own view fits nicely with *another* story.

In the "counterstory" told by Suits, there is no act of betrayal—at least as far as anyone can tell. This is fundamentally different from my story, in which an act of betrayal *does* in fact take place. Simply put, there is a basic, clear difference between a case in which a betrayal actually takes place and one in which a betrayal does not take place, but would have under certain hypothetical circumstances (would have, let us say, but for the intervention of White). In ordinary life, given no evidence of betrayal, it would be unhealthy obsessively to seek evidence of a betrayal (and one's therapist would legitimately be concerned!). But, again, that is quite beside the point. The example is one in which it is simply stipulated that there was a secret betrayal, and we are invited to consider whether this in fact harms an individual who never has any unpleasant experience as a result. Of course, it is *not* a suggestion of the story that in ordinary life one should obsessively seek evidence of the infidelity of friends and loved ones!

Suits continues to press his case:

The best that can be said [about the example as presented by Fischer] is that if, somehow, I *were* absolutely convinced that the "victim" would not and could not be harmed in any way, then I would have to say that what takes place is not a betrayal at all. I might not know what to call it . . .

A White-managed secret betrayal is no different from a merely hypothetical betrayal. Real betrayals, as we have come to know them, are like the incautious firings of guns: if they do not on some particular occasions have bad consequences, then they are at least very risky. And so we invoke precautions which, on the basis of past experience, we expect will minimize such risks. Suppose everyone agrees that all reasonable precautions are in place. We fire the gun, and no one is harmed. Is this bad for someone? We are having fun shooting at paper targets; we are in an enclosed firing range with thick concrete walls; no one else is around. Who dares to complain? Who comes forward and says that something bad has happened as a result of our target practice, *even though no one has been harmed, and even though no one can make out a case for possible harm, given our precautions*? Incautious firing of guns is risky, but once the precautions are in place, then firing the gun is not at all incautious. Similarly, betrayals are risky, but once White is in place, then there is no betrayal after all.[16]

For my purposes, it does not matter what we call the behavior in question—a "betrayal" or (say) "characterizing you negatively behind your back," or whatever. The question simply is whether such behavior harms you. It is stipulated that you experience nothing unpleasant as a result of the behavior in question; now the issue is whether, nevertheless, you have been harmed. It may be that a White-managed secret betrayal is no different from a merely hypothetical betrayal insofar as you do not experience anything unpleasant as a result of the behavior in either case; but it does *not* follow that there is no difference between the cases with respect to the issue of whether you are harmed. As I said above, an actual betrayal *is* different from a merely hypothetical betrayal: in the case of an actual betrayal, something *has happened* which (arguably) has harmed you. Suits does not discuss Nagel's other case (the case of the individual who is reduced to the state of a "contented infant" by (say) a stroke), but I would make the parallel claim about this case: an actual stroke is crucially different from a merely hypothetical stroke (even though, by hypothesis, the individual in question does not experience anything unpleasant in either case).

Yes, typically betrayals are risky; but the story does not purport to portray a typical case. A theory needs to be right even in atypical cases. A "real betrayal" (or a betrayal under normal circumstances) *is* like the incautious firing of a gun: there is a considerable risk of causing unpleasant experiences in both cases. When one has taken the sort of precautions described by Suits, then firing the gun is *not* incautious; as with the White-managed "betrayal" example, there is no risk of causing unpleasant experiences. But the cases are significantly different.

Whereas I am inclined to say that the negative characterizations of you by your so-called friends harm you, by the very nature of the behavior, I have no similar inclination to say that a mere firing of a gun, where there is no chance of hitting anyone, can harm anyone (except, perhaps, the gun-firer, but that raises different issues...). The contention is *not* that all riskless behavior (or that all riskless behavior which would be risky, but for the precautions) harms others; the contention is only that *some* does.

III.2. Hetherington

Stephen Hetherington offers a fascinating critique of Nagel's example of the (alleged) betrayal, even as modified a la the Frankfurt-type examples.[17] Hetherington says:

> By being betrayed, some of your beliefs are rendered *false*. More vitally, some of your personally *important* beliefs are rendered false. For a start, you believe that your friends are loyal to you in standard ways; moreover, you *care* that this belief of yours be true. The betrayal makes the belief false, though. And this harms you, even though you are wholly unaware of its doing so, indeed even if (as in Fischer's case) you *could never* experience any consequence of the betrayal. The harm occurs because the falsification of your belief diminishes you as someone who wishes to believe only what is true about whatever is important to you. You wish to have those true beliefs; your wish is not being fulfilled. So, although this harm is one of which you are unaware, it is a harm nonetheless. If you *were* to realize that your belief was false, you would be upset. And even if—perhaps because your circumstances are as described in Fischer's case—you could never come to realize that your belief is false, its being false still makes you that much less *cognitively* successful as a person than you would wish to be. You are—by now being *mistaken* about something that matters to you—that much "out of step" with the world, notably with some parts of the world that matter to you. Insofar as it matters to you to be right about what matters to you, therefore, your being mistaken about what matters to you harms you. That harm is of at least metaphysical significance, as your status as a true believer on what you care about is harmed.[18]

Hetherington goes on to elaborate the relevant sort of harm:

> Your *realizing* that you are being harmed in that way inflicts a further harm of its own; *a fortiori*, so does its being *impossible* for you ever to find out that you were harmed. What is that further harm? It is the harm of human *absurdity*. If the belief is important enough to you, and if the betrayal is sufficiently fundamental, then your life might well have become somewhat absurd as a result.

...I am talking about an *objective* sort of absurdity. It is objective, in that it is not an *awareness*, either actual or even possible, of a discrepancy; instead, it is the *existence* of a basic discrepancy, one that can exist between a person and the world as a whole, and one that can exist without the person being aware of it, perhaps even with her being unable to be aware of it. This sort of absurdity is also *cognitive*, in that it is a matter of a person's failing to be aware of how poorly at least some of her cognitive efforts are informing her about the world in which she has to live. It is essentially her being *mistaken* about that world.

...To the extent that your belief in your friends' loyalty is also *important* to you, that absurdity is even tragic, no matter whether or not you are aware of this tragic dimension to your life. You trust the friends; you show them your feelings; presumably, you interact with them in what you assume is a context of respect and honesty. All the while, however, they know that you do not know how untrustworthy they are in relation to you. They are aware of how *misplaced* is your trust in them.... Even if your friends are not laughing at you behind your back, they could be; and in that sense, the *world* is doing so, at any rate.[19]

On Hetherington's view, the badness of the betrayal is understood in terms of creating a certain sort of *dissonance* or *discordance*; one has a certain set of beliefs about important features of our lives, one structures one's life around these beliefs, and yet they are false. As Hetherington puts it, "A person can be harmed by something insofar as it renders false some belief of hers whose truth matters to her."[20] In contrast, of course, death cannot be a bad thing by creating a dissonance or discordance between one's cognitions and the external reality, since death destroys the cognizer. If what disturbs us about the Nagel-type betrayal case (in its various versions) is that it creates a kind of absurd discordance, then, since death cannot be bad in this way, the example cannot be legitimately employed in order to defend the deprivation thesis about death's badness.

Although I find Hetherington's analysis helpful, I am not sure that it captures the entire truth about the badness of the betrayal (or death). In any case, it is interesting to note that Hetherington (like Suits) only focuses on Nagel's betrayal example, and not on the example of an individual who is reduced to the mental status of a contented infant (as a result of a stroke or accident). It seems to me that the stroke (or accident) has indeed been a bad thing for the individual, even though (by hypothesis) he or she has not experienced anything unpleasant (and cannot do so) as a result. Further, it seems to me that the badness here cannot be analyzed in the way suggested by Hetherington in regard to the betrayal case.

As opposed to the betrayal case, in the case of the stroke victim there need not be a discordance of the sort pointed to by Hetherington. The stroke victim presumably has no memories of his previous activities, and need not be radically mistaken about his current situation and abilities. He does not believe that he has capabilities that are in fact wildly "out of sync" with reality; he need not be fundamentally *mistaken* about the world or his relationship to it. I do not believe that the stroke victim is *absurd*; his situation is sad and maybe even tragic (in a certain way), but not absurd. He has not *misplaced* loyalty or trust, and there is no tendency to suppose that the world is, as it were, laughing at him.

The two examples, then, are different. If one agrees that the stroke or accident has indeed harmed or been a bad thing for the individual, then one cannot explain the badness in terms of the sort of discrepancy and absurdity discussed by Hetherington. It seems to me that the badness is not so much a matter of the discordance or discrepancy between internal cognitive states and the external world, but more "direct"—the taking away of capacities to function and experience that were possessed prior to the unfortunate event. It is the lack of these more complex capacities and experiences in itself, rather than some sort of discrepancy between the individual's awareness and reality, that is bad. Or so it seems to me.

Nussbaum states, in a passage quoted above, "In the second case [the stroke case], it is hard not to feel that the continued existence of the damaged person, who is continuous with and very plausibly identical with the former adult, gives the argument that the adult has suffered a loss at least part of its force." One might then argue that there is even in this case a kind of discordance or discrepancy—between the former and current capacities of the individual. But the same can be said of death; it creates a disparity between prior and subsequent capacities—the latter having been reduced to zero. What cannot be said, in the case of death, is that there remains an existing individual who has been diminished (and thus that the remaining capacities are greater than zero, as it were)—but it is essentially controversial, within this dialectical context, whether the removal of the subject is consistent with badness: it cannot simply be assumed here that the removal of the subject is not consistent with badness, and thus that there must be a nonzero capacity remainder. I turn now to a more careful discussion of precisely this sort of dialectical subtlety.

IV. DEATH AND DIALECTICAL STALEMATES

Elsewhere I have sought to describe an argumentative structure I have called a "Dialectical Stalemate." I have suggested that this sort of structure is found in many of the most intractable philosophical puzzles:

Frequently in philosophy we are engaged in considering a certain argument (or family of arguments) for some claim C. The argument employs a principle P. Allegedly, P supports C. Now the proponent of the argument may be called upon to support the principle, and he may do so by invoking a set of examples (or other considerations). Based on these examples (or other considerations), he argues that the principle and thus also the philosophical claim are to be accepted.

But the opponent of the argument may respond as follows. The examples are not sufficient to establish the principle P. One could embrace all the examples and not adduce P to explain them: rather, it is alleged that a weaker principle, P*, is all that is decisively established by the examples (or other considerations). Further, P*, in contrast to P, does not support C. Finally, it is very hard to see how one could decisively establish P. One reason it is so difficult is that it at least appears that one cannot invoke a particular example which would *decisively* establish P without begging the question in a straightforward fashion against either the opponent of P or the opponent of C. Further, it *also* seems that one cannot invoke a particular example which would *decisively* refute P without begging the question against the proponent of P or the proponent of C. These conditions mark out a distinctive—and particularly precarious—spot in dialectical space.

I shall call contexts with roughly the above form, "Dialectical Stalemates."[21]

Take, for example, the Basic Argument for the Incompatibility of Causal Determinism and the sort of free will that involves alternative possibilities.[22] The argument, dubbed the "Consequence Argument" by Peter Van Inwagen, proceeds from the point that causal determinism implies that all our behavior is the *consequence* of the past and the laws of nature to the conclusion that we lack the sort of free will that involves genuine access to alternative possibilities (if causal determinism obtains).[23] The argument can be given in different forms, but typically it employs principles that putatively encode our commonsense views about the fixity of the past and natural laws. Sometimes the argument employs a modal principle that allegedly captures intuitive ideas about the transfer of powerlessness: if one is powerless over one thing, and powerless over that thing's leading to another, one is powerless over the other thing.

A number of examples can be adduced that seem to support a Principle of the Fixity of the Natural Laws. The problem is that there are different ways of seeking to capture the intuitive, commonsense notion of the fixity of the laws of nature. None of the examples appear to support the incompatibilist way of capturing the kernel of truth in those examples *over the compatibilist way*. That is, consider the following two Fixity of the Laws Principles:

(IFL) For any action Y, and agent S, if it is true that if S were to do Y, some natural law which actually obtains would not obtain, then S cannot do Y.

(CFL) For any action Y, event b, agent S and times $t1$, $t2$, and $t3$, ($t1$ prior to $t2$ prior to or simultaneous with $t3$), if (1) Y's occurring at $t2$ is inconsistent with the laws of nature, or (2) Y's occurring at $t2$ would cause some event b's occurring at $t3$ and b's occurring at $t3$ is inconsistent with the laws of nature, then S cannot at $t1$ do Y at $t2$.[24]

The problem is that none of the examples adduced by incompatibilists such as Carl Ginet and Van Inwagen, or by anyone else (as far as I know), can show decisively that IFL is to be preferred to CFL. That is, the relevant data do not support one principle *over* the other.

Consider, for example, Van Inwagen's examples of someone producing a machine that would cause things to go faster than the speed of light, or someone engaging in selective breeding to produce a human being who could get along without vitamin C. He points out that no one has it in his power to do such things, insofar as the laws of nature entail that nothing travels faster than the speed of light, and that human beings cannot get along without vitamin C. It is obvious, however that such examples do *not* support IFL *over* CFL.[25] If one states that causal determinism might turn out to be true, and, after all, it is "just obvious" that we are free in the sense that involves alternative possibilities, this would clearly be question-begging in the relevant dialectical context. Exactly similar considerations apply to the notion of the fixity of the past, as well as to the modal principle (or related principles) sometimes employed in the argument for incompatibilism.[26]

As I said above, a modal principle is sometimes employed as part of the Consequence Argument (for the incompatibility of causal determinism and freedom). The modal principle, the "Principle of the Transfer of Powerlessness," is structurally parallel to the "Principle of Closure of Knowledge Under Known Implication." Indeed, the principles are the same, except for the different interpretations of the relevant modality.[27] On this principle, if someone knows that p, and knows that p implies q, then he knows that q. Just as the Principle of the Transfer of Powerlessness is employed to generate a sort of free will skepticism (i.e., incompatibilism about causal determinism and the sort of freedom that involves genuine access to alternative possibilities), so the Principle of Closure of Knowledge Under Known Implication is sometimes employed to generate epistemological skepticism.

The argument would go as follows.[28] Evidently, I know that there is a laptop in front of me. But there being a laptop computer in front of me entails that I am not a brain-in-a-vat being stimulated to falsely believe there is a laptop in front of me, and I know this. Thus, given the Principle of the Transfer of Knowledge Under Known Implication, it follows that I know that I am not a brain-in-a-vat being stimulated to falsely believe (for instance) that there is a laptop in front of me. I do not, however, know this; in the lingo, I cannot "rule out this skeptical counterpossibility." Thus, *modus tollens* gives us the conclusion that I do not know that there is a laptop computer in front of me (or, for that matter, any contingent proposition about the external world).

Now one could simply state that it is "just obvious" that I know that there is a laptop in front of me, even though I cannot rule out the skeptical counterpossiblity and thus I do not know that I am not a brain-in-a-vat. Thus, someone could insist that the Principle of the Transfer of Knowledge Under Known Implication is invalid. The problem here is painfully clear: the data invoked are essentially contested, and thus it is question-begging, in the relevant dialectical niche (in which epistemological skepticism is being considered seriously), simply to assert it.

Consider, also, the "Principle of the Transfer of Nonresponsibility." This is the same modal principle as above, except for the interpretation of the modality. It states that if you are not responsible for one thing, and you are not responsible for that thing's leading to another, you are not responsible for the other.[29] An incompatibilist about causal determinism and moral responsibility might use this modal principle in an argument for this sort of incompatibilism. Assuming causal determinism, some fact about the distant past, together with the laws of nature, entail the present and future facts. I am not morally responsible for the past fact. Further, I am not morally responsible for the laws of nature, and thus, I am not morally responsible for the past fact's leading to the present and future situations of the universe.[30] Now, given the Principle of the Transfer of Nonresponsibility, it follows that I am not morally responsible for the present (and thus for my behavior).

There are various ways of responding to this sort of argument. I believe there are promising ways of seeking to show the modal principle—the Principle of the Transfer of Nonresponsibility—to be invalid.[31] But I do not think the following strategy is promising. A compatibilist might simply point out that it is "just obvious"that I am morally responsible for my behavior, even if causal determinism is true. (Perhaps this is because it is "just obvious" that I am free to do otherwise, even if causal determinism obtains.) Further, such a compatibilist might concede that I am not morally responsible for the distant past, nor am I morally responsible for the connection between the past and the present (given that this connection instantiates a natural law). So this sort of compatibilist simply insists that it is "just obvious" that the Principle of the Transfer of Nonresponsibility is invalid. It should however be (painfully) clear that this move is dialectically "traif" (unkosher). It simply begs the question against the incompatibilist. A compatibilist about causal determinism and moral responsibility might be entirely justified in rejecting the modal transfer principle, but *not* on this basis.

In my previous work on these subjects, I suggested that it is one of the salient characteristics of a perennial or classic philosophical problem that it involves the signature structure of a Dialectical Stalemate.[32] I added that the Free Will Problem (which is really a family of related problems and puzzles) is a "true philosophical classic" in part because it is an environment rich with Dialectical Stalemates.

It should be evident that the debate discussed above about death is a Dialectical Stalemate. Nussbaum points out that the examples invoked by Nagel, even as modified by me, cannot decisively show that death is a bad thing for the individual who dies. Even if it is plausible to say that the examples of betrayal and stroke involve badness for the relevant individuals, the examples are different from death in that they involve the persistence of the subject. Thus they cannot *in themselves* decisively show that death can be a bad thing for the individual who dies. In framing and considering general principles relating to harm, it is evident that there will be different principles, and that the examples in question will not in themselves decisively support a principle strong enough to entail that death can be bad for the individual who dies *over* a slightly weaker principle—*a principle that does not have this conclusion.* As Nussbaum points out, all of the examples "involve a subject who continues to exist, however briefly, during the time the event takes place."[33] But it is hard to see how one can get rid of this feature and have an example that would not beg the question at issue about death's badness. It would seem that, given the definition of death, any case in which the event in question removes the subject would be essentially contested. Thus we have a classic Dialectical Stalemate.

It is important, however, to keep in mind that a Dialectical Stalemate need not result in our inability to make any philosophical progress or to come to any useful philosophical conclusions. In a Dialectical Stalemate, no example *can in itself decisively establish* the relevant conclusion (without begging the question). Nussbaum is completely correct to point out that none of the examples above can in themselves decisively establish that death can be a bad thing for the individual who dies. But I want to highlight what I have written about how to proceed in this sort of argumentative neighborhood:

> I do not however think that Dialectical Stalemates should issue in philosophical despair. An opponent of the principle under consideration may demand that its proponent provide examples which absolutely *require* one to accept the principle. But I would claim that this is *unreasonable.* It may even be true that it is *necessarily* the case that if a philosopher argues for a certain general principle by giving examples, a weaker principle can be found that is the strongest principle the examples support (strictly speaking). The crucial issue becomes whether it

is plausible to accept the stronger principle, if one accepts the weaker principle. Considerable philosophical ingenuity can be displayed in generating examples, which invite one to accept the *stronger* principle as well as the weaker principle, or in explaining in a non-ad hoc fashion exactly why one should *only* accept the weaker principle. Alternatively, philosophical creativity can issue in a restructuring of the problem; that is, one might find some other principle *P** that can be employed to establish *C*, or perhaps one can show in some way that *C* wasn't that interesting after all.[34]

In my work on Free Will, I have suggested a certain kind of *restructuring* of the traditional debates. I have contended that there are importantly different kinds of freedom (or control), and that seeing this can help us to sidestep some of the Dialectical Stalemates embedded in traditional debates about Free Will. In our discussion of death here, I would opt for the other course of action alluded to above. That is, I would insist that it is unreasonable to demand an example that would in itself decisively show (in a nonquestion-begging way) that death can be a bad thing for an individual. (I actually believe that Nussbaum may well be in agreement with me about this; her explicit contention is merely that the examples in themselves do not show that death can be a bad thing for the individual who dies, and this leaves it open that other considerations may be invoked.)

I stated above that the crucial question in a Dialectical Stalemate may be whether it is plausible to accept the stronger principle, if one accepts the weaker principle. So the key issue is whether the difference between the stronger and weaker principles *makes a difference* to the issue at hand. I would argue that, whereas the Nagel-type cases discussed above all involve the persistence of a subject, it does not seem plausible that *this feature* is crucial—that it is *this feature* (perhaps together with others that are present in the examples) that inclines us to say that the relevant individual is harmed, and in the absence of which we would *not* be so inclined. So, my view is that if it is plausible to hold that the individual is harmed in the betrayal, stroke, and trekking cases, it would *also* be plausible to maintain that he is (or can be) harmed by death.

Recall that Nussbaum stated (about the trekking case), "The right parallel, then, would be the case in which the mother and the daughter die at precisely the same instant. In this case I think we would not confidently assert that the mother has suffered a bereavement."[35] It is correct that it would not be dialectically kosher to invoke the original version of the example as *decisive* evidence on the basis of which to conclude that death can be a bad thing for an individual. And I would agree with Nussbaum that one cannot conclude with confidence that the mother has suffered a bereavement, simply in virtue of consideration of her version of the example. But it would not be inappropriate to employ the original version of the example, together with suitable versions of the other examples, to generate the preliminary conclusion that a persisting subject can be harmed even in contexts in which he is unaware of the harm and does not suffer as a result. Then, if it is plausible that the difference between death and these contexts *does not make a difference to badness*, one could conclude that, even in Nussbaum's version of the trekking example, the mother has been harmed.

Nussbaum holds that the Nagel-type examples do not in themselves decisively establish that death can be a bad thing for the individual who dies. She does however have reservations about the main argument.[36] Her worries stem not so much from the examples, but from considerations about our ongoing projects in life. Although I am in agreement with Nussbaum that the examples do not in themselves decisively establish that death can be a bad thing for the individual who dies, they are helpful insofar as they point us to that conclusion; they help to provide a strong plausibility argument for it. They challenge the Epicurean to state why one should think that the examples are importantly different from death. More specifically, why exactly should the pertinent feature—that death deprives us of the subject—make the difference in question? It is perhaps natural to suppose that the problem with there being no subject is that this issues in an *impossibility of experience*; but we have seen that the mere impossibility of experience is *not* what makes it the case that death cannot be bad, if it were indeed the case that death cannot be bad for the individual who dies. So why exactly does it matter that the subject is removed?

V. LUCRETIUS'S "PROFOUND INSIGHT"

Nussbaum states, "Lucretius profoundly suggests that we believe death to be bad for us through a mental sleight of hand, in which we imagine ourselves persisting and watching our own loss of the goods of life."[37] Stephen Rosenbaum also highlights this view of Lucretius, according to which at least part of our view that death is bad can be explained in terms of a natural, pervasive mistake—a tendency mentally to project ourselves into the future as somehow "there" and "watching" and perhaps even "suffering," even after our death. The mistake consists in covertly assuming that one will continue to exist and have a point of view, even after death.

In his more recent work on death, Nagel also emphasizes this subjective tendency to project oneself into the future:

> It hardly needs saying that we are accustomed to our own existence. Each of us has been around for as long as he can remember; it seems the only natural condition of things, and to look forward to its end feels like the denial of something which is more than a

mere possibility. It is true that various of my possibilities—things I might do or experience—will remain unrealized as a result of my death. But more fundamental is the fact that they will then cease even to be possibilities—when I as a subject of possibilities as well as of actualities cease to exist. That is why the expectation of complete unconsciousness is so different from the expectation of death. Unconsciousness includes the continued possibility of experience, and therefore doesn't obliterate the here and now as death does.

The internal awareness of my own existence carries with it a particularly strong sense of its own future, and of its possible continuation beyond any future that may actually be reached. It is stronger than the sense of future possibility attaching to the existence of any particular thing in the world objectively conceived—perhaps of a strength surpassed only by the sense of possible continuation we have about the world itself.[38]

I believe that we do indeed have the sort of tendency noted by Lucretius (and Nagel), but that it is unclear whether its removal would, on balance, be helpful. This is because I think that sometimes, at least, our subtle projection of our perspective into the future, even after death, is comforting; we picture ourselves at our own funeral (listening to the no-doubt glowing eulogies of family, loved-ones, or friends), or, perhaps less nobly, we picture ourselves enjoying other emotions upon observing reactions by others to our own deaths. Now perhaps, strictly speaking, we are simply picturing the eulogies and the reactions, and not our own enjoyment of them. But it is Lucretius's suggestion that we tend to assume, perhaps subtly, that we are (somehow) still able to experience or be aware of the world, even after our deaths.

Consider these passages from an amusing piece by the comedian, Richard Lewis:

[Eulogizing myself at my own funeral] would be sort of a dream come true…My feeling is that since everyone in my life (except God) puts some kind of spin on me as to what and why and who and where I am, I at least deserve to get my licks in when it's me in that…casket.

I really don't want to scare people who show up to pay their last respects for me, but I feel that I owe it to my soul (before it gets too set in its ways) to put in my own two cents. At the risk of sounding cocky, I expect and want a lot of people at the *last good-bye* and the more crying the better, because I suffered a lot of emotional shit and it would do my corpse good to hear a little sobbing, albeit too little too late.

I don't want a small, private funeral. Not just because I will probably be forever narcissistic but also because I so rarely left my house when I was living. I think it would be nice to see people for a change, even if I am *dead*. So come on down!!!39

David Sedaris's short story, "The Last You'll Hear from Me," also contains some deliciously malevolent projections into the future:

Dear Friends and Family,

By the time you receive this letter I will be dead. Those of you attending this service are sitting quietly, holding a beautiful paperweight, a gift from the collection, which, in life, had been my pride and joy. You turn the paperweight over in your hands, look deep inside, at the object imbedded in the glass, be it a rose of a scorpion, whatever, and through your tears you ask, "What is death like?" By this time I certainly know the answer to that question but am unable to give details...

If my instructions were followed the way I wanted them to be (see attached instruction envelope #1), this letter is being read to you from the pulpit of The Simple Shepherd Church of Christ by my best friend, Eileen Mickey (Hi, Eileen), who is wearing the long-sleeved Lisa Montino designer dress I left behind that always looked so good on me. (Eileen, I hope you either lost some weight or took it out some on the sides or you're not going to be able to breathe. Also, remember it needs to be dry-cleaned. I know how you and your family love to skimp, but please, don't listen to what anyone says about Woolite. Dry-clean!)

Most of you are probably wondering why I did it. You're asking yourselves over and over again, "What could have driven Trish Moody to do such a thing?"

You're whispering, "Why, Lord? Why take Trish Moody? Trish was a ray of bright sunshine, always doing things for other people, always so up and perky and full of love. Pretty too. Just as smart and sweet and pretty as they come."

You're probably shaking your heads and thinking there's plenty of people a lot worse than Trish Moody. There's her former excuse for a boyfriend, Randy Sykes, for example. The boyfriend who, after Trish accidentally backed her car over his dog, practically beat her senseless. He beat her with words but still, it might as well have been with his fists.... The Dog's death was a tragic accident but perhaps also a blessing in disguise as Randy tended to spend entirely too much time with it....

What did Trish's mother say when her daughter, heartbroken over her breakup with Randy, came to her in search of love and understanding?

"If you're looking for sympathy you can find it between shit and syphilis in the dictionary."

Perhaps my mother can live with slogans such as this. I know I can't.

Neither can I live surrounded by "friends" such as Annette Kelper, who desperately tries to pretend that nobody notices the fact that she's balding on top of her head. That's right. Look closely—balding just like a man. Perhaps Randy feels sorry for chrome-dome Annette. Maybe that's why he was seen twice in her company in a single five-day period...

Is everyone on earth as two-faced as Annette Kelper? Is everyone as cruel as Randy Sykes? I think not. Most of you, the loved ones I left behind, are simple, devoted people. I urge you now to take a look around the room. Are Randy Sykes and Annette sitting in the audience? Are they shifting uncomfortably in the pew, shielding their faces with the 8-by-11 photograph of me I had reproduced to serve as a memento of this occasion?

Fancy little shitheads! Look at them, take a good hard look at them. It's their fault I'm dead. They are to blame. I urge you now to take those paperweights and stone them. Release your anger! The Bible says that it's all right to cast the first stone if someone dead is telling you to do it and I'm telling you now, pretend the paperweights are stones and cast them upon the guilty. I've put aside my savings to pay for damages to the walls and windows. It's money I was saving for my wedding and there's plenty of it so *throw*! Hurt them the way they hurt me! Kill them! No one will hold you responsible. Kill them![40]

Much of the "fun" described above comes from illicitly assuming that one would still be around to witness the events in question, even after death. Much humor surrounding death, as well as many funerary practices, involve treating the dead as like the living in certain ways (ways obviously seen to be inappropriate, in the case of the humor).[41] I simply wish to point out here that our (perhaps clandestine) assumption of our continued presence and capacity to be aware of the world, even after death, can be a source of comfort and consolation. If death is like life in this respect, even if it is unpleasant, it is not entirely mysterious and frightening—it has the ring of familiarity (note that chronic pain sufferers sometimes think of their pain as "an old friend"). In any case, removing this tendency to project ourselves into the future (as having a persisting point of view) may lead to *enhanced* anxiety about death; the tendency tames death, and without it, the stark nothingness and total annihilation can seem more frightening. When death is completely different from life and lacking even in awareness, it can arouse less tractable, more unruly fears.

VI. THE BANQUET ARGUMENT

Let us turn to Lucretius's "Banquet Argument." As in the case of a banquet, there is a definite pattern or temporal structure to a human life (in the typical case). The conclusion of the Banquet Argument is something like this: that our mortality is a necessary condition of our various activities having meaning and value of the sort we can comprehend and find attractive. Nussbaum writes, "...the removal of all finitude in general, mortality in particular, would not so much enable these values [the values we find in friendship, love, justice, and the various forms of morally virtuous action, for example] to survive eternally as bring about the death of value as we know it."[42] She contends that we would not have the virtues without death. For example, Nussbaum says that courage involves "a certain way of acting and reacting in the face of death," and moderation "is a management of appetite in a being for whom excesses of certain sorts can bring illness and eventually death...."[43]

I have pointed out, in contrast, that death is not the only condition that could provide a point or content to the virtues. Even in an immortal life, there could be long stretches of physical and/or emotional disability, depression, anxiety, boredom, loneliness, and so forth. These sorts of potential conditions could certainly give a shape to our lives and content to the virtues. We do not need death in order to have danger, and to provide considerable impetus to ourselves to strive to avoid terrible disability, dysfunctionality, and suffering. Nussbaum has subsequently expressed her agreement with this point, saying, "So I agree with Fischer: we need to take apart the different limitations of a human life much more precisely, asking exactly how each of them works in connection with the shaping of value."[44]

In this section I wish to make a few tentative gestures toward understanding these issues better. First, note that the proponent of the view that immortality is necessarily bad (such as Bernard Williams[45]) insists that there are no conceivable circumstances in which immortal life would be recognizably human and attractive. If in our immortal lives we became decrepit or permanently disabled, this would certainly give the relevant sort of "shape" to our lives, but there would emerge the concomitant danger that our lives would be unattractive. Thus, the sort of circumstances I am envisaging would involve the potential for long-term and significant disabilities and suffering, but with subsequent regeneration and recovery. This certainly seems both conceivable and potentially attractive.

It is often stated that an immortal life would have no shape. How could we care about something essentially amorphous? Consider, for example, an ordinary physical object, such as a carpet. You might think that you could simply expand the size of the carpet in your imagination indefinitely and that you would thereby imagine a very large carpet—indeed, an infinitely large carpet. But the problem is that a carpet is what it is—a particular carpet—in virtue of its borders. As one expands the carpet in one's mind, it inevitably explodes into shapelessness as the distinction between the carpet and the noncarpet surroundings becomes blurred. Similarly, a statue is the particular statue it is, in part, because of the contours of its borders; expand them indefinitely and one is in danger of having no sculpture at all, but a huge, formless blob of marble.

But I believe the analogies are misleading here. First, it is not entirely evident that the thought-experiments issue in their putative conclusions. Perhaps one can think of an indefinitely large carpet! But, more important, why not think of infinitely long life as similar to an indefinitely long electrocardiogram? (What could be more appropriate in this context than the representation of one's heartbeat—the physical engine of life?) I do not see why one could not have an indefinitely long electrocardiogram, with a given pattern displayed at any given temporal period. After all, one need not expand to infinity *all of the spatial dimensions* of the relevant object; one can have an indefinitely long electrocardiogram with specific structure and content along the way, since the vertical dimension need not be extended along with the horizontal one. It is surely a mistake to think that "shape" need be conflated with features of one dimension—the boundless horizontal dimension.

Yes, a banquet has a definite and bounded temporal structure: appetizers, soup, salad, main course, dessert and so forth. Also, our lives typically have a certain narrative structure with a beginning, middle, and end (carved up very roughly). It is of course normally thought to be a virtue—a sign of great wisdom—to accept the finitude of our lives and not engage in what the Greeks called "plenoexia" or a certain sort of inappropriate "overreaching." But the question at issue here is not about our ordinary, normal lives, but about life's possibilities, considered from a distinctively philosophical point of view. Why can a banquet not be a kind of "temporal all-you-can-eat buffet?" Better, why can we not imagine an indefinitely extended banquet, with suitable intervals for recovery (and enjoyment of other activities)? This is, after all, the way "foodies" tend to look at life already!

And our lives have a narrative structure, but why suppose that essential to this sort of structure is finitude? After all, many people watch soap operas, which are stories that are seemingly endless. Perhaps, more carefully put, it seems to me that our lives could have certain of the distinctive features of narrative structure *without* finitude. Specifically, our lives can be thought to have value based on narrative structure, even apart from whether the lives are bounded temporally. So, for example, we value succeeding as a result of striving or learning from past mistakes, rather than merely as a result of a windfall (such as winning the lottery). The values encoded in human narratives could still exist, even if the stories were infinitely long; these are a function of *relationships*, not *finitude*. We mean different things when we advert to the notion that our lives are (or correspond to) "stories," and that they have narrative structure. I believe that the chief element is narrative value, rather than finitude.[46]

Consider, finally, what I would dub the "Super-Powers Problem." In an immortal life, presumably one would know that one has immortality. By the way, this raises interesting questions about the concept of immortality, as it plays a role in philosophical discussions. I am assuming that the relevant individuals *know* that they are immortal, and *not* simply contingently so; they know that they are invulnerable to death, not just that in fact they will not die. But if one knows one is invulnerable to death, one knows one could do lots of things without having to worry about death—skydiving (without a parachute), rock climbing in the most exotic and precarious places, and so forth. Further, one knows that, no matter what happens to one, one will not die: so, someone could riddle you with bullets and you would nevertheless continue to live. Given these realizations, one might conclude that one could do just about anything, and, although such a life might seem at first attractive, it would be so fundamentally different from our own, finite, limited human lives as to be incomprehensible to us.

The reply is again that, although the envisaged circumstances would be very different from our current status, they would not be *sufficiently* different to justify the purported conclusion. As with the virtues, we must remember that there are dangers other than death. So, even if I realize that I am invulnerable to death and thus that I would continue to live, even if I were to fall from a high mountain cliff or were riddled with bullets, I would still realize that I would no doubt be significantly damaged by such things. Consequent pain, suffering, and disability would be a constraint against trying such antics, and would also temper any inclination to suppose that one had "infinite" or super-powers. Life would be different, but, arguably, *analogous* to our finite human lives.[47]

NOTES

1. Martha Nussbaum, *The Therapy of Desire* (Princeton: Princeton University Press, 1994); Martha Nussbaum, "Reply to Papers in Symposium on Nussbaum, *The Therapy of Desire*," *Philosophy and Phenomenological Research* 59 (1999), pp. 811–819.

2. The main argument is laid out in Nussbaum, *The Therapy of Desire*, pp. 201–202. I make a preliminary stab at discussing these matters in John Martin Fischer, "Contribution to Symposium on Nussbaum's *The Therapy of Desire*," *Philosophy and Phenomenological Research* 59 (1999), pp. 787–792.

3. Nussbaum, *The Therapy of Desire*, p. 203.

4. Fischer, chapter 6; and Fischer, "Contribution to Symposium on Nussbaum's *The Therapy of Desire*."

5. Thomas Nagel, *Mortal Questions* (Cambridge, Cambridge University Press, 1979), pp. 1–10; reprinted in John Martin Fischer (ed.), *The Metaphysics of Death* (Stanford: Stanford University Press, 1993), pp. 61–69. The quotation is on p. 69 of the reprinted version.

6. Nussbaum, *The Therapy of Desire*, pp. 201–202.

7. *Ibid.*, pp. 205–206.

8. Various philosophers have faulted Nagel precisely for providing examples in which (allegedly) the individual merely does not, rather than *cannot*, experience anything unpleasant as a result of the event in question: Harry S. Silverstein, "The Evil of Death," *The Journal of Philosophy* 77 (1980), pp. 401–424; reprinted in John Fischer (ed.), *The Metaphysics of Death*, pp. 95–110; Stuart Rosenbaum, "How to Be Dead and Not Care: A Defense of Epicurus," *American Philosopohical Quarterly* 23 (1986), pp. 217–225; reprinted in Fischer (ed.), *The Metaphysics of Death*, pp. 119–134; and Walter Glannon, "Temporal Asymmetry, Life, and Death," *American Philosophical Quarterly* 31 (1994), pp. 235–244. I attempt to reply in chapter 3.

9. Fischer, chapter 3. The Principle of Alternative Possibilities states that an individual is morally responsible for an action only if he could have done otherwise. Harry Frankfurt first presented a purported counterexample to this principle (or a template for such a counterexample) in Harry G. Frankfurt, "Alternate Possibilities and Moral Responsibility," *The Journal of Philosophy* 66 (1969), pp. 828–839. I have discussed such examples in (among other places) John Martin Fisher, *The Metaphysics of Free Will* (London: Blackwell Publishers, 1994); John Martin Fischer "Recent Work on Moral Responsibility," *Ethics* 110 (1999), pp. 93–139; and John Martin Fischer, "Frankfurt-Type Compatibilism," in S. Buss and L. Overton (eds.), *Contours of Agency: Essays on Themes from Harry Frankfurt* (Cambridge: The MIT Press, 2002), pp. 1–26.

10. Fischer, chapter 3, p. 39.

11. Jeff McMahan, "Death and the Value of Life," *Ethics* 99 (1988), pp. 32–61; reprinted in Fischer (ed.), *The Metaphysics of Death*, pp. 233–266.

12. Fischer, "Contribution to Symposium on Nussbaum's *The Therapy of Desire*," p. 789.

13. Nussbaum, "Reply to Papers in Symposium on Nussbaum, *The Therapy of Desire*," pp. 811–812.

14. David Suits, "Why Death Is Not Bad for the One Who Died," *American Philosophical Quarterly* 38 (2001), pp. 69–84.

15. Suits, "Why Death Is Not Bad for the One Who Died," pp. 76–77.

16. Suits, "Why Death Is Not Bad for the One Who Died," p. 77.

17. Stephen Hetherington, "Deathly Harm," *American Philosophical Quarterly* 38 (2001), pp. 349–362.

18. *Ibid.*, pp. 351–352.

19. *Ibid.*, pp. 355–356.

20. *Ibid.*, p. 352.

21. Fischer, The Metaphysics of Free Will, p. 83.

22. For a more complete discussion, see Fischer, *The Metaphysics of Free Will.* I discuss the application of the structure of Dialectical Stalemates on p. 84.

23. Peter Van Inwagen, *An Essay on Free Will* (Oxford: Clarendon Press, 1983). Also see Carl Ginet, *On Action* (Cambridge: Cambridge University Press, 1990); Fischer, *The Metaphysics of Free Will.*

24. Fischer, *The Metaphysics of Free Will*, pp. 67 and 70.

25. *Ibid.*, pp. 67–76.

26. For a discussion of the issues related to the Fixity of the Past, see Fischer, *The Metaphysics of Free Will*, pp. 78–86. I discuss the Dialectical Stalemates relevant to the modal principle, where the relevant modality is "nonresponsibility,"

in John Martin Fischer, "The Transfer of Nonresponsibility," in J. Campbell, M. O'Rourke and D. Shier (eds.), *Freedom and Determinism* (Cambridge: The MIT Press, 2004), pp. 189–209.

27. Fischer, *The Metaphysics of Free Will*.

28. For a helpful discussion of such arguments, see Anthony Brueckner, "Skepticism and Epistemic Closure," *Philosophical Topics* 13 (1985), pp. 89–118. Also, see Fischer, *The Metaphysics of Free Will*, pp. 23–45.

29. This principle was first formulated and discussed by Peter Van Inwagen (see Peter Van Inwagen, *An Essay on Free Will*, pp. 182–188).

30. For an interesting discussion, see David Widerker, "Farewell to the Direct Argument," *The Journal of Philosophy* 99 (2002), pp. 316–324.

31. Mark Ravizza, "Semicompatibilism and the Transfer of Nonresponsibility," *Philosophical Studies* 75 (1994), pp. 61–93; and John Martin Fischer and Mark Ravizza, *Responsibility and Control* (Cambridge: Cambridge University Press, 1994), pp. 151–169.

32. Fischer, *The Metaphysics of Free Will*, p. 84.

33. Nussbaum, "Reply to Papers in Symposium on Nussbaum, *The Therapy of Desire*," p. 811.

34. Fischer, *The Metaphysics of Free Will*, p. 85.

35. Nussbaum, "Reply to Papers in Symposium on Nussbaum, *The Therapy of Desire*," pp. 811–812.

36. *Ibid.*, p. 812.

37. *Ibid.*, p. 811.

38. Thomas Nagel, *The View from Nowhere* (Oxford: Oxford University Press, 1986), p. 226.

39. Richard Lewis, *The Other Great Depression* (New York: Plume Books [Penguin], 2002), pp. 244–245. Lewis goes on to write:

I have this gut feeling that if I made a "live" appearance it would be a friendly and cool visitation and everyone would have a sense of calm about it. Everyone except former "dates from hell" who are still actresses and see my demise as a great opportunity to showcase. As I've mentioned before, if I don't settle down in a good relationship but instead drop dead while still adolescently dating much younger women, I'm certain that my memorial service will mean nothing more to these vixens than a golden opportunity to display some histrionics (after catching a glimpse of some industry heavies in the synagogue) with the hopes of turning some heads (not mine anymore) and getting considered for a future role. After first feigning screams to plan a seed for future auditions for a potential horror-flick part, they would then, apparently out of the blue, go into powerful, well-rehearsed monologues from some Mamet play while paying lip service to my death by frivolously changing a few words here and there to refer to things that clearly come from my life–like too much masturbation and self-pity, my limitless quantity of neediness, or my sickening, debilitating habit of believing that I never did enough for the jerky people who knew how to make me feel guilty and worthless if I didn't go to bat for them (p. 245).

40. David Sedaris, *Barrel Fever* (Boston: Little Brown and Company, 1994), pp. 18–21.

41. Fischer (ed.), *The Metaphysics of Death*, pp. 29–30.

42. Nussbaum, *The Therapy of Desire*, p. 226.

43. *Ibid.*, pp. 227 and 228.

44. Nussbaum, "Reply to Papers in Symposium on Nussbaum, *The Therapy of Desire*," p. 813.

45. Bernard Williams, *Problems of the Self* (Cambridge, Cambridge University Press, 1973), pp. 82–100.

46. I explore these issues in greater depth in chapter 9.

47. I benefited from reading a truncated version of this essay at the University of Buffalo "Conference on Metaphysics and Medicine," November 2004, organized by Barry Smith. I also discussed the essay with members of David Hershenov's University of Buffalo philosophy department graduate seminar; I am grateful for their thoughtful comments. I have also read versions of this essay at the philosophy departments at Duke University, The John Hopkins University, and Washington University in St. Louis. I am very grateful to thoughtful comments on these occasions.

8

Stories

John Martin Fischer

Stories are those parts of our memories
we can afford to reveal.
    Garrison Keillor, "A Prairie Home Companion"

I. VIRTUE AND COMMUNITY IN LE NIÈVE

Recently, at a conference in California, Professor Jules Levain (University of Paris) gave an interesting talk on the relationship between virtue and community.[1] More specifically, he wished to distinguish various claims about the relationship between virtue and community and to evaluate some of them. Two particularly salient claims discussed by Levain were that community *sustains* virtue and that community gives *content* to virtue. That is to say, Levain wished (among other things) to evaluate the claims that certain sorts of communities perform crucial and indispensable sustaining and content-providing functions for various virtues.

Whereas it is relatively clear what it means to suggest that a community has the function of sustaining certain virtues, it might be useful to say a few words about the alleged content-providing function of communities. The point here is that forms of communal life "fill in the detailed prescriptions that make abstract principles into a lived morality." As Levain put it,

> communities tell us how to gear our general moral principles into a
> complex world; without them we would not know what our prin-
> ciples bid of us in the particular contexts of social life.... For exam-
> ple, we might hold to the general principle of respect for others; but
> it is only a particular form of communal life which tells us what it

is to respect others, how one does this in different contexts, what the different forms of respect are, and the like. It is only by living within a complex form of communal life that we can learn these particularities.

One of the most interesting features of Levain's presentation was his extensive use of facts about a town in France during the Second World War to substantiate the two claims about the relationship between virtue and community. He pointed out that the village of Le Chambon, a French Huguenot enclave which during the Nazi occupation of France sheltered about five thousand refugees (mostly Jewish), is often cited and discussed.[2] But Levain claimed that there was another village in the vicinity of Le Chambon—Le Nièvre—in which the citizens were also actively involved in sheltering refugees from the Nazis. Recent work by a French historian has brought to light some of this activity, and Levain employed this evidence to good effect.

Levain pointed out that the rescue enterprise in Le Nièvre had a *collective* nature; the community as a whole had an impact on the decisions of its members to engage in rescue. This influence of the community was felt despite the fact that the efforts were not explicitly organized, and many of the decisions to rescue were made by individuals and families acting outside any organized structure. As Professor Levain put it,

> A refugee would show up at someone's door, or someone would be asked if she would put one up, and she would have to decide there and then whether to help out. Sometimes the refugee would be brought by another villager, who either had no room or no more room for refugees, or whom the Nazi or Vichy officials had come too close to discovering. The person asked, or presented with a refugee, would not always have to put the refugee up at her own house. She could search for other shelter for the refugee. Other tasks were also essential—getting false papers, sometimes smuggling persons out of the village into Switzerland. Simply helping to keep up the facade that nothing worthy of the Nazis' attention was going on was a task shared by all. Yet engaging in any of these activities was very risky. It was a punishable offense to shelter Jews or to help to do so and in fact three of the town's leaders were jailed for a time for engaging in these activities.

Levain argued that the virtuous way in which individual citizens of Le Nièvre made their choices was deeply affected by the community in which they lived. He adduced the recent research of the historian, who did extensive interviews of surviving citizens of Le Nièvre. These citizens did not see their actions and practices as having been supererogatory. When pressed to say why they tried to help the refugees they said, "It was simply what one had to do," "She was standing at my door;

how could I fail to help?" and so forth. Levain analyzed the evidence as follows:

> the role of community in sustaining the virtuous activities becomes clearer. For the fact that others were engaging in, helping, and supporting the rescue activities—even though this was seldom directly discussed—is part of what helped everyone to define them as "everyday" and unremarkable. In a context in which one is doing what one regards as the right thing, yet no others are joining one in this effort, it is much more difficult to sustain a sense that one is doing precisely what can simply be expected from anyone and is nothing remarkable or noteworthy.

Thus, Levain pointed out that the evidence about the people of Le Niève supported both the claims about the sustaining and also the content-providing role of community.

In the discussion that followed the talk, many of the participants praised Levain's use of a "real-life" example. Indeed, just about everyone appeared to think it extremely important that the evidence came from an actual historical example rather than a mere hypothetical case. Too often, it was noted, philosophers simply make up stories—evidently, "out of thin air"—and precipitously generate conclusions from them. But why have any confidence that these made-up scenarios can reveal anything useful about the real world? Further, there was general consensus that the evidence adduced by Levain did indeed provide considerable support for the pertinent claims about the relationship between virtue and community.

At the end of the discussion period, Levain said, "I thank all of you for this illuminating conversation. I have learned much that will be of benefit to me in my thinking about these issues in the future. I should however mention one final point: as far as I know, there is no village of Le Niève, and no French historian who has unearthed evidence about it. I simply made up the story."

At the reception following the talk, there was much distress and animated conversation. Even the brie and chardonnay could not diminish the anger and mortification of many of those who had attended the talk; they felt duped and cheated. And no doubt they were justified in these feelings. But some at the reception began to wonder: Did it matter at all to the evaluation of the claims about virtue and community that Levain had simply made up the example rather than employing an actual example? (Would it have made any difference to the evaluation of the relevant claims about the relationship between virtue and community if Levain had used true evidence from Le Chambon rather than Le Niève? Would it have made any difference if Levain had used evidence which he falsely—although with justification—believed to be true of Le Chambon?) Doesn't the moral force of an example depend on its "intrinsic" features—its content—rather than on features of its "genesis"? (Would it have made any difference if Levain had begun by stating that the town of Le Niève and its inhabitants are the focus of a recently unearthed novel by a great French novelist?)

Indeed, one of the members of the audience found the professor's duplicity highly enlightening (although no doubt regrettable in certain respects). So enlightening, in fact, that he said to himself that it would be useful to present the story of the professor's talk as if it had actually occurred, even if it had not.[3]

II. HYPOTHETICAL AND STREAMLINED EXAMPLES

II.1. The Criticism

The story of Professor Levain might prompt one to reflect on certain aspects of the role of hypothetical examples in philosophy. In this essay, I shall be particularly interested in the role of hypothetical and schematized or abstract examples in ethics. There are of course many ways of thinking about ethical problems and many different approaches to doing ethics. One traditionally powerful (but by no means uncontroversial) approach to ethics rather liberally employs what might be called "streamlined" hypothetical examples. These are schematized hypothetical scenarios in which only a few details are filled in, and all the other details are left out.[4]

Although this methodology has many proponents, it also has its vigorous critics. In various contexts (although not perhaps as explicitly and frequently in print) one encounters criticisms of the use of hypothetical examples in ethics.[5] Sometimes the criticism takes the form of mere disdain, but on other occasions it is articulated with a bit more precision. I wish to attempt to understand this kind of criticism and to do some preliminary work toward defending the use of streamlined hypothetical examples in ethics.

It is striking that although many philosophers object—viscerally if not intellectually—to the use of streamlined hypothetical examples in ethics, they rarely offer explicit reasons for their view. The reasons they offer (when they offer reasons at all) are multifarious. Notoriously, Elizabeth Anscombe objects to the use of such examples in her classic essay, "Modern Moral Philosophy."[6] She criticizes philosophers who employ these examples on the grounds that they help to "corrupt our youth" and make them less likely to accept the absolute moral strictures of religious dogma. According to Anscombe, these hypothetical examples—in which graphic moral conflicts and dilemmas are represented—help to foster the false impression that God would allow such situations to occur frequently and one might have to depart from the clear rules given by the church. In her essay, "Does Oxford Moral Philosophy Corrupt the Youth?" Anscombe says:

A point of method I would recommend to the corrupter of the youth would be this: concentrate on examples which are either banal: you have promised to return a book, but…and so on, or fantastic: what you ought to do if you had to move forward, and stepping with your right foot meant killing twenty-five young men, while stepping with your left foot would kill fifty drooling old ones. (Obviously the right thing to do would be to jump and polish off the lot.)[7]

Similarly, Peter Geach says:

Spiritual writers warn us that the devil often suggests to us the question of what we ought to do in circumstances that have not arisen and may never arise, and tries to hurry us into a wrong hypothetical decision: he thus may have all the satisfaction of leading us to a morally sinful intention, without any of the trouble of contriving circumstances in which an actual decision would be unavoidable; and we ought to foil his malice and cunning by giving no other answer to the question he presses upon us than "I will do as the Lord wills," and by trusting in God that in an actual case we shall be given the grace to decide rightly.[8]

Now it would be convenient for my purposes to suppose that all the critiques of streamlined hypothetical examples were as implausible as these, or equally dependent on very special and not widely shared assumptions. But this is clearly not the case, and it is important to attempt to crystallize some more plausible versions of the critical view. It should be evident from Levain's story about Le Niève that the criticism of such examples cannot be merely that they are *hypothetical*. The story of Professor Levain helps to show that the force and relevance of hypothetical examples depends on their "intrinsic content" and not on their veracity or their etiology (for instance, whether they are concocted by a philosopher or borrowed, say, from a novel).[9] While holding fixed the intrinsic content of these stories but varying their veracity or etiology one gets *no* changes in the relevance of the stories to the ethical problems under consideration.

But the primary thrust of the skepticism about the use of the typical hypothetical examples in ethics is not based on the fact that these stories are not true. These examples are *both* hypothetical and *streamlined*. It seems to me that the most important basis of criticism is that the examples are streamlined. And I think the brunt of the criticism is based on the idea that schematized and abstract examples—that is, streamlined examples—are not *realistic*.

But while it is clear to me that this is the kernel of the critique of streamlined hypothetical examples, it is not yet clear exactly what the critique consists in and amounts to. Of course, insofar as a streamlined example lacks robust details, it is to that extent unrealistic. But why exactly does this matter? Why precisely is it important for an example to be in this way realistic? In a number of insightful essays, Martha Nussbaum has developed interesting criticisms of the use of hypothetical examples (of a certain kind) in ethics.[10] Further, she has argued in favor of turning to novels (by certain authors) for ethical insight. In seeking to understand the criticism of streamlined examples, it will be helpful here to lay out some of Nussbaum's main points.[11]

Nussbaum argues in favor of reading not just novels but other works of literature, saying that

> many serious dramas will be pertinent as well, and some biographies and histories—so long as these are written in a style that gives sufficient attention to particularity and emotion, and so long as they involve their readers in relevant activities of searching and feeling.... [12]

She goes on to say:

> But the philosopher is likely to be less troubled by these questions of literary genre than by a prior question: namely, why a literary work at all? Why can't we investigate everything we want to investigate by using complex examples of the sort that moral philosophers are very good at inventing? In reply, we must insist that the philosopher who asks this question cannot have been convinced by the argument so far about the intimate connection between literary form and ethical content. Schematic philosophers' examples almost always lack the particularity, the emotive appeal, the absorbing plottedness, the variety and indeterminacy, of good fiction; they lack, too, good fiction's way of making the reader a participant and a friend....
>
> We can add that examples, setting things up schematically, signal to the readers what they should notice and find relevant. They hand them the ethically salient descriptions. This means that much of the ethical work is already done, the result is "cooked." The novels are more open-ended, showing the reader what it is to search for the appropriate description and why that search matters.... [B]y showing the mystery and indeterminacy of "our actual adventure," they characterize life more richly and truly—indeed, more precisely—than an example lacking those features ever could; and they engender in the reader a type of ethical work more appropriate for life.[13]

II.2. Preliminary Points

Before going on to analyze Nussbaum's main point, I wish to pause to note a few things. First, being realistic implies a certain sort of richness of detail, but of course mere richness of detail does not imply that a scenario is realistic. Thus, there are various different ways of failing to be realistic. An example may not be realistic simply in virtue of not being very detailed; such an example might not be "far-fetched" or "fantastic" (to use Anscombe's term), and thus may be "realistic as far as it goes." Nevertheless, this sort of example would still be unrealistic in the sense of lacking the richness of detail present in reality. Of course, another way of failing to be realistic is to be far-fetched or "fantastic"; and this is quite compatible with richness of detail. Note that Nussbaum does not recommend careful perusal of the works of Robert Heinlein, for example; she prefers Henry James and Marcel Proust!

Second, one might wonder why we should turn to literature for illumination at all; that is, why not simply use real life? Montesquieu and Voltaire held that history is philosophy teaching with examples. Why not simply employ life itself (or full depictions of it) rather than literary works? To this Nussbaum responds:

> One obvious answer was suggested already by Aristotle: we have never lived enough. Our experience is, without fiction, too confined and too parochial. Literature extends it.... We can clarify and extend this point by emphasizing that novels do not function, inside this account, as pieces of "raw" life: they are a close and careful interpretative description.... The point is that in the activity of literary imagining we are led to imagine and describe with greater precision, focusing our attention on each word, feeling each event more keenly—whereas much of actual life goes by without that heightened awareness, and is thus, in a certain sense, not fully or thoroughly lived.[14]

A rather extreme version of this view about the importance of literature—a view not endorsed by Nussbaum—is held by the Hindu sage in the following very brief story. A great Hindu sage lived in a remote cave and offered advice to people who flocked to him for his wise counsel. When asked how he could give such good advice even though he never leaves his cave, he responded, "Every evening I read the Ramayana, and that is all I need to know." But one need not hold such an extreme position to maintain the basic plausibility of Nussbaum's response.

II.3. Reply to the Criticism

These preliminary points having been made, let us return to the criticism of streamlined examples based on their purportedly unrealistic character. Clearly, ethical reflection and practical reasoning—thinking about morality in general, thinking about particular moral problems, teaching morality, and so forth—is extremely complex and has many different aspects. I cannot here attempt to construct a general account of such reflection and deliberation, but consideration of Nussbaum's remarks can help one to distinguish some of the aspects in a fashion that illuminates the criticism of streamlined examples. I now wish to try to distinguish at least three different facets of ethical reflection.

Undeniably, part of ethical reflection involves enhancing our capacities to see what is morally salient and to respond sensitively and appropriately to it. These aspects of ethical reflection involve seeking to refine and deepen our capacity for moral perception and moral response.

The moral perception aspect of ethical reflection is itself complex and multifarious.[15] But I can say a few words to indicate part of what moral perception involves. We often face highly nuanced, complicated, and ambiguous situations in which we must first identify the ethically relevant features. Before we can properly decide how to respond or what to do, we must—either explicitly or implicitly—see what is morally relevant and important. As we confront the situation, we "frame the moral issues": we give a structure to a moral situation, identifying and making salient (admittedly sometimes in an inchoate fashion) the features that are relevant to a moral assessment and to an appropriate response.[16]

Having identified what is morally relevant, we are in a position to begin to make a suitable response, perhaps (but not exclusively) by applying or relating general principles to the particular elements we have identified as relevant. The second aspect of ethical reflection—the moral response aspect—involves seeking to improve our abilities to make acceptable moral judgments (given our background ethical theories or moral orientations), our propensities to have emotional responses which fit with these judgments, and our capacities to act in accordance with these emotional responses and judgments. Clearly, in this aspect of moral reflection, we seek to educate ourselves and develop our characters and emotions in light of our general ethical theories or orientations.

Another aspect of ethical reflection (not emphasized by Nussbaum, but of course compatible with her discussion) is moral analysis. The moral analysis aspect involves seeking to generate, test, and refine our general principles and theories—or, if one wishes to eschew the "theory approach," one's general moral orientation. The picture here is that there are times when we step back from our moral lives and engage in critical reflection on it; this reflection attempts to systematize and order the situations as given by our capacity for moral perception. Here the features identified and described by moral perception are evaluated and may be combined into more general principles and theories that give expression to our general moral outlook.

Let me emphasize that these are brief and very incomplete characterizations of the aspects of our moral lives. Further, I again state that these are only *some* of the many components of our ethical reflection and practical reasoning. Further, in practice these aspects do not exist in airtight compartments; there are considerable overlaps and interlacings of the various aspects. But, nevertheless, the preliminary distinctions I have made can help us to see what is correct in the criticism of streamlined examples, and what is incorrect.

I suggest that reading novels and other works of fiction fits nicely and naturally with the purposes of the first and second aspects of ethical reflection: enhancing the capacities of moral perception and response.[17] Nussbaum is correct to point to the importance of these aspects of morality and to the relevance of fiction (of certain sorts) to them. Further, it seems to me that philosophers' streamlined examples fit most naturally with the purposes of the third aspect: analysis. Here, one primary task is to test the generality and plausibility of principles which "latch onto" or embody features deemed morally relevant. By distinguishing the various aspects of ethical reflection, one can give an appealing account of the role of *different* sources of illumination; one can see how *both* fiction (i.e., rich stories) and philosophers' examples (streamlined stories) can play important roles (although at different points in ethical reflection).

Further, perhaps one can see why *certain* critiques of the use of schematized examples in ethics are unfair (or at least misguided). Of course, if one wishes to enhance and improve one's capacities of moral perception and response, the abstract and schematized examples will by and large be inappropriate.[18] If one is seeking to improve the capacity to pick out and describe the morally relevant features of highly complex situations, a schematized example in which one is "handed the ethically salient description" probably will not be useful. Further, such an example may not be particularly helpful in enhancing one's emotional responsiveness and sensitivity. But to infer from these facts that such examples can play *no* useful role in practical reflection is unfair; it illicitly presupposes that the first two aspects exhaust the domain.[19] My suggestion, then, is that the *complete dismissal* of schematized, hypothetical examples in ethics is too abrupt; it may issue from an exclusive focus on the first two aspects of practical reasoning at the expense of the third.

II.4. Further Challenges

I have suggested that the view that streamlined examples are completely inappropriate in ethics is incorrect because it wrongly leaves out an aspect of our moral lives: the aspect of analysis. But I now wish briefly to consider some further challenges to the legitimacy of streamlined examples. Someone might press the point that precisely because streamlined examples are unrealistic, they are even inappropriate to the aspect of analysis.

First Version of the Worry. The following version of this worry is indeed suggested by Nussbaum. Unless our emotions are engaged in a certain way by an example, our moral judgments about it are not to be trusted, and streamlined examples simply do not adequately engage our emotions. If this is true, then even if we set aside the aspects of moral perception and response, there will still be a problem with employing schematized examples for the more narrow task of evaluating a proposed moral principle or analysis.[20]

This view raises deep and difficult questions which are intractable to quick resolution. It is not absolutely clear to me that Nussbaum's thesis about the necessity of emotional engagement for trustworthy judgment is actually true. While it has some plausibility, we sometimes trust our moral judgments only when they are made from a cooler, more detached, less emotionally engaged, perspective. So Nussbaum's thesis here may not be true in its general form. Further, even if it is true, it can be accommodated compatibly with holding that streamlined examples have a legitimate place in moral reflection.

To explain: Nussbaum's critique of the use of hypothetical and streamlined examples in ethics rests not only on the thesis of the necessity of emotional engagement for trustworthy moral judgment, but also on what might be called an "atomistic" picture of emotional engagement. And I believe it is highly implausible to think that, one's emotions having been engaged, they suddenly *disengage* when one's attention is focused on a streamlined example. Imagine that one is in the process of ethical reflection on a given topic. Suppose one fully immerses oneself in relevant fiction (Henry James, Proust, and so forth) which appropriately engages one's emotions. Having identified salient ethical features and generated appropriate principles, one turns to the assessment and testing of those principles—and here one uses certain streamlined examples (as well as other ingredients). Why suppose that in this process somehow the emotions suddenly "turn off" or disengage when considering the streamlined examples; is emotional engagement this atomistic and episodic?

It seems to me that a more holistic and less atomistic conception of emotional engagement is closer to the truth about us. Surely, our emotional investment in and engagement with other persons does not work in a way analogous to the episodic view apparently presupposed by Nussbaum's criticism; it is a sometimes painful feature of our lives that we do not and cannot simply disengage from other persons when they are absent. And it is also perhaps a comforting feature of us that our emotional attachments are not so adventitious. If a less episodic conception of emotional engagement is accurate, one can hold the thesis of the necessity of emotional engagement compatibly with giving a place to streamlined examples in the analysis component of moral reflection.

Second Version of the Worry. There is another version of the worry that precisely because streamlined examples are unrealistic, they are inappropriate to the aspect of analysis. The idea is this. A streamlined example presents us with a very special, artificial, and rarified context. If a conclusion is drawn about this sort of context, it does not necessarily transfer straightforwardly to the real world. As a crude example, suppose you strike a match in a room with no gas in it, and you note that

striking a match there does not cause an explosion. You then proceed to
strike a match in a different room—one with lots of gas in it. Needless
to say, you would have made a rather unfortunate mistake—the mistake of failing to see that striking a match has different consequences
depending on the *other factors* that are present in the given context. A
given event may have one meaning in one context (and against a given
set of background conditions), and quite another meaning in another
context (and against another set of background conditions).[21] And so a
given moral event or factor may have one moral meaning in a streamlined example, and quite another meaning in reality.

I wish to grant the basic insight behind this criticism, but still maintain
that streamlined examples have a place in analysis. The objection shows
that one must be very careful to consider the various possibilities of
"meaning shift" in doing one's analysis, but it does not show that streamlined examples are worthless or inappropriate. Streamlined examples,
even when they cannot be employed to achieve closure, can be highly
suggestive; they can establish strong presumptions and can suggest further
examples in which the factor in question is tested against various backgrounds, or in which *clusters* of potentially synergistic factors are tested.

I believe that the meaning shift problem is the most significant reason
why one might be tempted to say that streamlined examples ought to be
avoided precisely because they are unrealistic. But I have suggested—in
an admittedly brief and tentative way—that even this possibility leaves
room for legitimate use of streamlined examples. And it is very important to keep in mind the potential benefits of employing streamlined
examples; these need to be weighed against the risks. A primary goal of
abstraction and schematization in moral reflection is to create the analogue of "controlled experiments" in science: one wants to hold all other
factors fixed, and test one particular factor for ethical relevance.[22]

The fruits of controlled experimentation in ethics, as in the sciences,
can be quite significant. And it must be kept in mind that this procedure
does *not* in itself imply that individual morally relevant factors combine
"additively" and "non-synergistically" to determine an overall moral
assessment of a situation, just as the procedure in the sciences does
not imply that striking a match will not have different consequences,
depending on the background conditions. The procedure of abstraction
and schematization—of "streamlining," if you will—can assist in deter-
mining whether a factor is morally relevant; but *how* this factor combines
with others is left open, and it is useful to keep in mind the possibility of
significant interactions, synergisms, and "meaning shifts."

III. CONCLUSION

My purpose has been to seek to find a place for philosophers' streamlined examples—hypothetical and schematized—in moral reasoning.

I have attempted to accommodate the insights of such philosophers as Nussbaum about the role of reading fiction and using less schematized (and in this respect more "realistic") examples. I have most definitely *not* argued that one should *exclusively* employ such examples in ethics; rather, I have emphasized that practical reasoning and ethical reflection has many aspects in which various sorts of examples are appropriate. I have attempted to explain why I believe that there are legitimate and appropriate uses of streamlined examples in ethical reflection.[23] Whereas this may seem to be a fairly weak thesis, it will provide some comfort to those who have been rebuffed by the proponents of the thesis that such examples are *never* appropriate and are to be shunned completely.[24]

NOTES

1. Professor Levain is one of the most distinguished ethicists in France. Although he is well known in France, he is not widely known in the United States. It is ironic that Jacques Derrida has received so much attention here whereas Levain remains obscure, given Levain's stature in French academic circles.

2. P. Hallie, *Lest Innocent Blood Be Shed*. Also, P. Sauvage's film, "Weapons of the Spirit."

3. As far as I know, there is no Professor Jules Levain—I simply made him up. The idea for this section was suggested to me by a talk delivered by Lawrence Blum to the Riverside Philosophy Conference, May 1991. The sort of duplicity portrayed in the text did *not* actually occur. The idea for this section was in part suggested by interesting remarks by David Solomon in response to Blum, and I have borrowed from Blum's nice essay. Blum's essay, "Virtue and Community," has subsequently been published in his collection of essays, *Moral Perception and Particularity* (New York, 1994), 144–69.

4. The "Trolley Problem" cases, and related cases, are frequently discussed examples of this sort, but of course there are many others. For a selection of essays that present and discuss many such hypothetical and streamlined cases, see *Ethics: Problems and Principles*, edited by John Martin Fischer and Mark Ravizza (Fort Worth, Tex., 1992).

5. Recently Jonathan Dancy has argued for "particularism" about moral reasons: *Moral Reasons* (Oxford, 1992). According to particularism, considerations count as moral reasons only given their entire context (pp. 55–7, 89). For a sustained critique of the use of thought experiments primarily in metaphysics, see Kathleen V. Wilkes, *Real People: Personal Identity Without Thought Experiments* (Oxford, 1988).

6. *Philosophy* 33 (1958): 1–19.

7. G. E. M. Anscombe, "Does Oxford Moral Philosophy Corrupt the Youth?" *The Listener*, February 14, 1957, p. 267. (Subsequent issues of *The Listener* contain what can only be described as vituperative correspondence about the issues raised by this piece.) Taking a similar tack to that of Anscombe, Tom Weller asks, "If A and B were drowning, and you could only save one of them, would you…have lunch or go to a movie?" (*The Book of Stupid Questions* [New York,

1988]; as quoted in F. M. Kamm, *Morality, Mortality Volume I: Death and Whom to Save from It* [New York, 1993], 75).

8. Peter Geach, in *Nuclear Weapons and Christian Conscience*, edited by Walter Stern (London, 1981), 91. I am indebted to Gerald Dworkin for bringing this passage to my attention.

9. Note that Levain's story of Le Nièvre pertains to moral matters, but more properly to *descriptive* features of practical reflection (rather than normative features, strictly speaking). That is, the story is about how communities function to sustain and give content to virtues, and these are primarily descriptive features of moral matters. I would contend that the point developed in the text about the irrelevance of etiology or veracity also applies to normative features of moral matters.

Given that Levain's story of Le Nièvre pertains to descriptive aspects of morality, shouldn't the falsity of the story be relevant? I do not believe it is. Stories are told, and examples adduced, for various purposes; if the story is told to bring some general phenomenon to the attention of the relevant audience—some phenomenon which otherwise might escape notice and for which there is considerable independent evidence—it can be perfectly useful and appropriate even if false.

10. Martha C. Nussbaum, *Love's Knowledge: Essays on Philosophy and Literature* (New York and Oxford, 1990).

11. It is helpful to turn to Nussbaum's work to understand the criticism of certain uses of hypothetical examples in ethics. But I wish to emphasize that Nussbaum herself does *not* argue that such examples are *never* appropriately employed in ethics. Thus, Nussbaum might well agree with the overall thesis for which I am arguing in this essay.

12. Nussbaum, *Love's Knowledge*, 46.

13. *Ibid.*, 46–7.

14. *Ibid.*, 47.

15. For a very useful discussion, see Lawrence Blum, "Moral Perception and Particularity," *Ethics* 101 (1991): 701–25; and various essays in Blum, *Moral Perception and Particularity*.

16. Barbara Herman discusses these issues within a Kantian framework in "The Practice of Moral Judgment," *Journal of Philosophy* 82 (1985): 414–36.

17. For a similar point, see Michael DePaul, "Argument and Perception: The Role of Literature in Moral Inquiry," *Journal of Philosophy* 85 (1988): 552–65.

18. One might usefully distinguish two sorts of capacities which are relevant here. First, there is the capacity to generate factors which are relevant to moral assessment; to *this* capacity the streamlined stories may indeed be relevant. I owe this point to Michael Otsuka. But given a set of factors which an agent believes may be relevant, there is the capacity to look at a complex and ambiguous situation and apply the possibly relevant factors in order to identify the particular factors relevant to the situation. To *this* capacity the abstract and schematized examples will be largely irrelevant, and this is the sort of capacity on which I focus in the text.

19. I should emphasize that this inference is *not* made by Nussbaum.

20. I am indebted to correspondence with Michael DePaul for this point.

21. For a very illuminating presentation of this sort of problem, see Shelly Kagan, "The Additive Fallacy," *Ethics* 97 (1988): 5–31.

22. In our introductory essay to *Ethics: Problems and Principles*, Mark Ravizza and I pose the question of why it should be thought that ethics is relevantly

different from social sciences such as economics or linguistics with regard to the appropriateness of the use of abstraction. We said:

> An economist constructs a model which is really a hypothetical "world." This hypothetical world is characterized by the assumptions of the model and is presumably considerably simpler than our world (or even the part of our world pertinent to the model). Having constructed this simpler world, the economist considers its properties and (ideally) generates conclusions. These conclusions may to some extent illuminate features of our world.
>
> Similarly, when we construct thought-experiments in ethics, we are constructing hypothetical worlds (albeit very small ones). These worlds are characterized by the assumptions of the examples, and they are in many ways simpler than real-world situations. We then scrutinize the hypothetical worlds and (ideally) generate conclusions. Again, these conclusions may to some extent illuminate features of our world. In ethics, hypothetical examples are very much like the models of economics.
>
> If the techniques of model-building and abstraction are useful and worthwhile in economics, then why should these techniques not yield similar benefits in ethics? (p. 47)

Although, admittedly, the issues are put rather starkly here, I do think the question deserves serious consideration. For further reflections on these issues, see *Thought Experiments in Science and Philosophy*, edited by Tamara Horowitz and Gerald J. Massey (Lanham, Md., 1991); and Roy Sorenson, *Thought Experiments* (Oxford, 1992).

23. Of course, the standard "philosophers' examples" are *not* the only schematized cases that are widely used in thinking about moral matters. Consider, for example, the extensive use of parables and stories in *moral education* and practical reflection quite generally, and, in particular, in the teachings and educational practices of various religions. Immediately, one thinks of the parables and stories of the Old and New Testaments, Hasidic Tales such as the Tales of Rabbi Nachman, and the stories of Chuang Tsu. Consider, just for fun, the following example:

> Two monks, having taken a strict vow of chastity, approach a stream in which a woman is drowning. The older monk immediately jumps in, rescues the woman, and carries her to the shore. Then they continue their walk. Some time later, the younger monk questions his elder, wondering whether the action of the older monk violated his sacred vow. The older monk replies, "See, I carried the woman for a few minutes and left her there by the side of the stream, but you have carried her with you all this way...."

Surely, no one would deny the prevalence of such stories in moral education and practical reflection. Nor would anyone insist that their relevance depends in any way upon their veracity or richness of detail. If such stories have a place in practical reflection, why couldn't philosophers' streamlined examples also have a place (although a different place)?

I suppose there could be many purposes of telling the story of the monks. One point is that one should not take certain rules or principles narrowly or "literally," but one should interpret them in light of their purpose. Often such stories are useful insofar as they remind us of some point we are apt to lose track of in ordinary life. They put things in unusual and striking ways and can help us either to see issues in new ways or to remind us of important points. Although these purposes are slightly different from the purposes of introducing stream-lined philosophers' examples, they share certain similarities: they in some sense involve "meta-reflections" on the first-order considerations of morality, and to this extent are similar to the purposes of the streamlined examples.

For the above story of the monks, I am very grateful to Mark Ravizza. Perhaps it has special significance for him, as he told it to me a few days before he entered a Jesuit novitiate!

24. Richard Rorty argues against the use of schematized philosophers' examples: *Essays on Heidegger and Others: Philosophical Papers*, vol. 2 (Cambridge, 1991). In his essay, "Heidegger, Kundera, and Dickens" (66–82), Rorty argues that such examples are misleading insofar as they (unlike certain examples from literature) foster the impression that there is an "essence" of morality—a true answer or set of answers to moral questions that can be codified and pre-sented in some sort of theory. Rorty's "postmodernist" anti-theory position leads to a denial of even the role I have found for schematized abstract phi-losophers' examples in ethics; Rorty's position is considerably stronger than Nussbaum's in this respect. Also, it should be noted that Rorty's objection to the use of examples is *driven* by his substantive view about ethics; in this way it is not a "neutral" objection to a particular methodology.

I believe that certain other objections to the use of streamlined hypothetical examples are also driven by particular substantive positions in ethics. For exam-ple, a proponent of virtue ethics might object to such examples on the grounds that they inappropriately tend to point us toward thinking of *general rules* as central in ethics. Similarly, a Kantian might object to such examples to the extent that they are not rich enough to help us to crystallize the agent's motive and thus his or her "maxim." It is important to see that these sorts of objections are "theory-driven" (or perhaps in Rorty's case "anti-theory-driven"); they issue from a particular sub-stantive view and are to this extent *not* neutral objections to a methodology. How such objections are properly viewed is a dialectically delicate and difficult matter. It must be conceded that it is fair to require that a particular methodology not be significantly "tilted" toward (or against) a particular approach. But as regards this latter point, recall that the methodology I have been defending here does not hold that hypothetical examples should be the only or even the primary considerations in ethical reflection. It would be difficult to argue that a methodology which sim-ply finds *some room* for such examples is significantly biased against particular approaches (which themselves have some minimal claim to plausibility).

Various friends have read pieces that have become parts of this essay and have offered encouragement. I am *very* grateful to them: Howard Wettstein, Alex Rosenberg, David Glidden, Dwight Furrow, Kerrin McMahan, Larry Wright, Anthony Brueckner, Gerald Dworkin, Stephen Munzer, John Heil, Andy Coats, Antonio Rauti, Michael DePaul, and Geoffrey Sayre-McCord. Also, I am indebted to David Solomon and Lawrence Blum for their interesting discus-sion at the Riverside Philosophy Conference, 1991, and to the UCLA Law and Philosophy Discussion Group, especially David Copp, David Dolinko, Michael Otsuka, and Seana Shiffrin. Finally, I owe many thanks to Mark Ravizza for the example of the monks, for encouragement, and for numerous helpful and enjoyable conversations

9

Free Will, Death, and Immortality:
The Role of Narrative

John Martin Fischer

Although the future is uncertain, we can at least be confident
of one thing: the past is always changing.

Slavic Folk Saying[1]

I. INTRODUCTION

The notion of 'narrative' is rich and suggestive, but, at the same time, vexed. The notion is invoked by philosophers and literary theorists (and others) in very different ways. Despite the confusions engendered by its multiple meanings and uses, I believe that the notion of narrative can be illuminating with respect to issues about freedom, death, immortality, and the meaning of life. Care must be taken, however, to distinguish different ideas, and to apply them appropriately.

In previous work, I have made some tentative and sketchy suggestions.[2] I have claimed that the value of acting freely, or acting in such a way as to be morally responsible, is the value of self-expression. When I act freely, I 'make a statement,' and the value of my free action is the value of writing a sentence in the book of my life (my narrative), rather than the value of 'making a difference' (of a certain sort) to the world. I have not suggested that artistic self-expression is the only value, or a hegemonic one; rather, the suggestion was that the value of free action is the value, whatever that is, of artistic self-expression. Further, I have suggested that our lives' having the signature features of narrative does not in itself imply that immortality would necessarily be undesirable (or even unrecognizably similar to our current lives).[3]

Here I wish to develop and tie together these ideas a bit further (although, perhaps inevitably, not as fully as I would like). I shall begin by laying out and discussing relevant aspects of the work of David Velleman on these topics.[4] I shall then argue that the value of our lives as free creatures is indeed a species of the value of artistic self-expression. More specifically, I shall contend that acting freely is what makes us the sort of creatures that live lives that have the characteristic features of narratives. Acting freely is what changes the depictions of our lives from mere characterizations to stories (or narratives). Further, I shall distinguish the claim that our lives can be explained in the distinctive manner of narrative explanation from the claim that our lives can be evaluated in the characteristic narrative fashion. Finally, I suggest that understanding our lives as narratives (in either sense) is compatible with the possibility that unending life would be attractive to human beings. Narrativity need not entail the necessity of endings.

II. VELLEMAN ON NARRATIVE VALUE AND NARRATIVE EXPLANATION

II.1 Velleman on Narrative Value

Velleman argues that the overall value of our life, considered as a whole, is not determined by a function that merely adds together all of the levels of momentary well-being in our lives. Additionally, he contends that our levels of momentary well-being are not simply the marginal increment in our level of overall welfare or value. The two dimensions of value—momentary and overall—are not analyzed in terms of each other or reducible to each other.[5]

According to Velleman, we care not just about the total amount of momentary well-being in our lives, or even its temporal ordering; we care about the story of our lives, the narrative structure of our lives.[6] More carefully, the function that specifies the overall value of our lives takes into account in an important way certain characteristics that are signature features of what we take to be 'good'" (in some sense) narratives.

As Velleman concedes, his point is not that we value narratives that are 'better stories' in a sense that would be of interest to potential readers of novels or (say) literary critics or reviewers. A life that makes a rather boring story might well be preferable, in terms of overall value, to a life filled with unexpected twists and turns, excitement, titillation, and tragedy. So exactly what does Velleman mean when he says that the overall value of our lives is importantly sensitive to narrative content? What are the signature features of narratives that help to shape the functions that determine the overall value of our lives?

I suggest that we begin by considering the examples Velleman employs. Velleman starts with an example of Michael Slote's:

A given man may achieve political power and, once in power, do things of great value, after having been in the political wilderness throughout his earlier career. He may later die while still 'in harness' and fully possessed of his powers, at a decent old age. By contrast, another man may have a meteoric success in youth, attaining the same office as the first man and also achieving much good; but then lose power, while still young, never to regain it. Without hearing anything more, I think our natural, immediate reaction to these examples would be that the first man was the more fortunate...[7]

Whereas Slote concludes from this sort of example that we have a 'time preference for goods that come late in life,' Velleman concludes that we care about the narrative content of our lives (and not just the total levels of momentary well-being, added up or even added up and weighted according to temporal position). It is a distinctive feature of narratives that later events can alter the 'meaning' or 'significance' of earlier events. In this sense narratives can have 'loops,' as Derrida (notoriously, in some quarters) contended. It is not that we can change the physico-causal past; but we can sometimes change its meaning and thus its contribution to the value of our lives overall.

Velleman says:

Why would a person care about the placement of momentary goods on the curve that maps his changing welfare? The answer, I believe, is that an event's place in the story of one's life lends it a meaning that isn't entirely determined by its impact on one's well-being at the time. A particular electoral victory, providing a particular boost to one's current welfare, can mean either that one's early frustrations were finally over or that one's subsequent failures were not yet foreshadowed, that one enjoyed either fleeting good luck or lasting success—all depending on its placement in the trend of one's well-being. And the event's meaning is what determines its contribution to the value of one's life.

...The meaning of a benefit depends not only on whether it follows or precedes hardships but also on the specific narrative relation between the goods and evils involved. Slote's politician would have experienced an improvement in his well-being whether his years of toil were capped by electoral victory or merely cut short by his winning the lottery and retiring young. But the contribution of these alternative benefits to the overall value of his life wouldn't be determined entirely by how well-off each would make him from one moment to the next. Their contribution to his life's value would also be determined by the fact that the former would be a well-earned

reward, and would prove his struggles to have been a good investment, whereas the latter would be a windfall in relation to which his
struggles were superfluous. Thus benefits that would effect equal
improvements in his momentary well-being might contribute differently to the value of his life, by virtue of lending and borrowing different meanings in exchange with preceding events.[8]

Velleman contends that it is better to thrive as a result of learning from
one's misfortunes than simply as a result of (say) winning the lottery or
some other windfall. As Velleman puts it:

> A life in which one suffers a misfortune and then learns from it may
> find one equally well-off, at each moment, as a life in which one suf-
> fers a misfortune and then reads the encyclopedia. But the costs of
> the misfortune are merely offset when the value of the latter life is
> computed; whereas they are somehow cancelled entirely from the
> accounts of the former. Or rather, neither misfortune affects the
> value of one's life just by adding costs and benefits to a cumulative
> account. The effect of either misfortune on one's life is proportionate,
> not to its impact on one's continuing welfare, but to its import for
> the story. An edifying misfortune is not just offset but redeemed, by
> being given a meaningful place in one's progress through life.[9]

Velleman believes that the following pair of stories illustrates the same
point. In both lives your first ten years of marriage are unhappy and
are followed by equal amounts of contentment. But in the first life you
get divorced and consider your first marriage a 'dead loss'; you just
happen to meet someone else with whom you live happily (ever after!).
In the second life, you learn from the troubles of your first ten years,
and you save the marriage (and live happily ever after). Indeed, in the
second story you think of the initial segment of the marriage as the
'foundation of your [later] happiness.' Velleman says that we would
prefer the second life. He says, 'You can simply think that a dead-end
relationship blots the story of one's life in a way that marital problems
don't if they lead to eventual happiness.'[10]

So it seems that the primary examples suggested by Velleman of
salient features of desirable narratives (in the sense relevant to the function that determines overall value of a human life) are of hard work
being rewarded and learning from mistakes, rather than simply profit-
ing (comparably) from windfalls. My suggestion is that we interpret
Velleman's claim that we take narrative content into account in evaluating overall welfare as involving the idea that 'narrative content' is a
shorthand for a kind (or perhaps kinds) of relationship among events
of which his cases are instances. 'Narrative content' is not explained
generally, but it involves the sort of relationships that are present in his
cases and other, similar cases. When this sort of temporally extended

pattern of events occurs, the kind of 'exchange of meaning' that is characteristic of narratives can take place.[11]

Velleman applies his claim (that human beings are distinctive insofar as the overall value of our lives is partly a function of narrative content) to issues pertaining to the badness of death. A decision about physician-assisted suicide depends at least in part on whether the individual's life would on balance be worth continuing (on some appropriate metric). Velleman says:

> The choice between heroic medical treatment and passive euthanasia is therefore frequently said to require so-called quality-of-life considerations. Whether days should be added or subtracted from a patient's life is to be judged, according to the prevalent view, by whether the days in question would be spent in a state of well-being or hardship.
>
> In my view, however, deciding when to die is not (despite the familiar saying) like deciding when to cash in one's chips—not, that is, a decision to be based on the incremental gains and losses that one stands to accumulate by staying in the game. It is rather like deciding when and how to end a story, a decision that cannot be dictated by considerations of momentary well-being. Hence a person may rationally be willing to die though he can look forward to a few more good weeks or months; and a person may rationally be unwilling to die even though he can look forward only to continued adversity. The rationality of the patient's attitude depends on whether an earlier or later death would make a better ending to his life story.[12]

II.1a Some Reflections

The idea of employing the notion of narrative as a guide in potential cases of physician-assisted suicide is fascinating and suggestive. I think it has limitations, though. We saw above that the pertinent notion of 'better ending to his life story' cannot be the notion of 'better' important to a reader of a work of fiction or a literary critic. But we do not have a general account of the relevant notion of narrative content and thus of 'better story' or 'better ending of the life-story.' We *do* have a set of examples, and we can intuitively recognize similar sequences of events that have the requisite 'narrative' characteristics. But I think that this will only provide guidance in some cases—by no means all.

Certainly we can say that the death of someone in the prime of her life, with many ongoing professional and personal projects underway, and no significant health problems, would be a bad ending to her story, in the relevant sense. Similarly, we can presumably say of an elderly woman who has had a full, rich life and has completed all her important life-projects, has said goodbye to her loved ones and friends and made arrangements for the disposition of her estate, and is in significant pain, that it would not be a bad thing for her to die; death now rather than later would be a better ending to her life story. Velleman's notion of narrative content arguably does help to sort through such examples.

But there will be many other cases in which it simply does not give sufficiently definite guidance. What about a person who has completed all his life-projects, but still to some extent enjoys simply watching certain television programs or reading the newspaper? He is physically confined to a bed, but is not in intolerable or significant pain. He knows however that he has a condition that will slowly incapacitate him further, and he has decided that now is the time to die. Would death now rather than in six months or a year or two years be a better ending to his story? Are his interests in television and the newspaper sufficient to say that death now would rob him of a 'better' ending to his story? What if he did not have such interests, or any interests? That is, what if he were largely indifferent to everything, including television and the newspaper and even news of his family, and so forth? Would this make a difference, and, if so, would the narrative account suggested by Velleman entail (or help to explain) the difference in question?

The ideas that people should thrive because of their efforts, or in virtue of learning from their mistakes, do not provide sufficient guidance about the sorts of cases just sketched. Further, it is not clear how to extrapolate or extend the ideas to provide definite guidance in these and a whole range of cases. I would think that many (although certainly not all) cases of potential physician-assisted euthanasia pertain to elderly individuals who have completed the major projects of their lives, at least so far as 'projects' are understood in a fairly standard way. It is already the case that either they have learned from their mistakes or not, either they have flourished because of their efforts or not, and so forth. These considerations don't seem to help with the decision about when exactly the decision to terminate life should be made, if at all. Of course, we could try to interpret 'narrative content' in such a way as to apply to anyone with ongoing interests of any kind, but this seems a stretch; here considerations of quality of life appear to be driving our judgments, rather than considerations of narrative content or structure. Thus, whereas Velleman's idea is highly suggestive, it can give only a partial guide to the difficult decisions concerning physician-assisted suicide.[13]

Velleman also applies his insights about the significance of narrative content to the question of the distinctive badness of the death of a person. A human being can see his life as an extended sequence over time; also, he can see it as a story. A human being can thus care about the narrative structure of his life. According to Velleman, a nonhuman animal, such as a cow, cannot conceive of itself as a continuing entity—cannot even take an extended temporal perspective at all. What the animal cannot conceive it cannot care about. As Velleman puts it, '...a person can care about what his life story is like, and a premature death can spoil the story of his life. Hence death can harm a person but it cannot harm a cow.'[14]

Velleman believes that, because a nonhuman animal cannot take a temporally extended perspective, it is incoherent to say that one sequence of moments can be better for a cow than another sequence of moments. He says, 'For a lower animal, then, momentary well-being fails not only of additivity but of cumulability by any algorithm at all. Consequently, the totality of this subject's life simply has no value for him, because he cannot care about it as such...'[15]

It is not clear to me that value (and harm) should be tied so closely to a subject's ability to conceive of the relevant thing. I do not know how to adjudicate this sort of issue. But I would simply point out that even if we granted that a cow's death deprives the cow of a sequence of future experiences (which on balance are positive), this is not the distinctive sort of value of which death can deprive a human being. That is, death can be bad for a person in a special way: it can rob a person of a good ending to his life-story, whereas it cannot so rob a cow. The lives of human beings (or, more carefully, persons) have a dimension of value over and above the accumulation of momentary well-being, whereas at best this sort of accumulation exhausts the value of a cow's life. Thus death can be bad for a person in a distinctive way, even if we grant that there is a cumulative dimension to the value of a nonhuman animal's life.

Note that Velleman contends that the capacity to adopt a temporal perspective from which one can see an extended period of time is necessary for the capacity to care about the story of one's life. Thus, on Velleman's view, such a capacity is a necessary condition for the overall value of humans' lives being affected by narrative considerations.[16] I do not however believe that the capacity to take this sort of perspective is *sufficient*. Consider a human being who is being thoroughly controlled by remote-control direct stimulation of the brain, so that his choices and actions are intuitively not his own free choices and actions. This individual may well have the normal capacity to take a more expansive temporal perspective, but the fact that he never acts freely inclines me to say that his overall level of well-being is to be determined by simply adding his momentary welfare values. For an individual who does not act freely, there is no separate dimension of value—the narrative dimension—irreducible to the intertemporal aggregation of momentary welfare. Such an individual would be 'in between' mere animals (on Velleman's account) and ordinary human beings (and other persons). That is, he would have the capacity to take the relevant temporal perspective, and yet not act freely. Thus, unlike mere animals (on Velleman's account), his momentary welfare values could be added together; but unlike ordinary human beings, he would not have a separate narrative dimension of value.

If I am correct about this supposition, then acting freely is the ingredient that gives us the distinctively narrative dimension of value. Acting freely is the feature which, when added to the others (including the capacity to take the appropriate temporal point of view and thus to care about one's story), transforms us into creatures whose lives can be evaluated by reference to salient sorts of narrative relationships.[17]

It is typically held that only a free creature—only a creature capable of acting freely—can have a meaningful life. It emerges now that acting freely is the specific ingredient that endows our lives with the distinctively narrative dimension of value. Only a creature who can act freely can affect the 'meanings' of past events by virtue of affecting the narrative relationships among various events in his life. Death robs a person of something especially important—the capacity to continue to lead a meaningful life. That is, it can now be seen that it robs a person of the capacity to continue to lead a life with a narrative dimension of value, and thus with a specific sort of meaning. It is sometimes said that death is bad because it deprives us of possible future goods. On the view I have sketched, it is also bad because it can deprive us of the possibility of changing the narrative meaning of the past.

On this sort of view (to which I am attracted), one can disagree with Velleman's claim that death cannot be bad for a cow, but still maintain that the death of a person is bad in a special way. Death arguably can be bad for the cow insofar as it deprives the cow of future pleasures (pleasures that would be part of an extended sequence that overall has considerably more pleasure than pain). But death can be bad for a person insofar as it deprives him of past goods as well as future goods: it cuts off the accumulation of momentary well-being, and it can prevent us from writing a better ending to our story (and thus vindicating our pasts).[18]

I follow Carl Ginet in holding that our freedom is the freedom to add to the given past, holding the laws of nature fixed.[19] This sort of 'fixity-of-the past' view pertains to the physico-causal events and features of the past, and not to their 'meanings.' This constraint applies to both the notion of 'freedom to do otherwise,' and the notion of 'acting freely.' Whereas we cannot go backward in physico-causal space-time and 'change the past,' we can readily go backward in narrative space-time. Whereas it is a constraint on our freedom that the physico-causal past be fixed, and that our actions be extensions of the given (physico-causal) past, it is precisely our capacity to act freely that provides the ingredient that allows for backward travel in narrative space-time.[20]

II.2. Velleman on Narrative Explanation

In a fascinating recent article, David Velleman has sought to give an account of narrative explanation (which, of course, is distinct from narrative value).[21] As Velleman puts it, 'A story does more than recount events; it recounts events in a way that renders them intelligible, thus conveying not just information but also understanding.'[22] Velleman seeks to describe the distinctive explanatory force of narrative, and to distinguish narrative explanation from explanation in the social and natural sciences.

Velleman says:

> This question arises for various disciplines in which narrative comes into play. For historians, it is the question whether narrating historical events conveys understanding over and above that conveyed by subsuming the same events under the generalizations of economics, political science, or sociology. For clinical psychologists, it is the question whether fitting symptomatic behaviours into a life-story adds to the understanding gained by fitting them into diagnostic categories. Even the police or the jury must ask themselves what sort of explanatory value there is in a suspect's giving his alibi in the form of a story.[23]

In providing his account of the distinctive potency of narrative explanation, Velleman builds on the work of Louis Mink and W.B. Gallie.[24] Both of these theorists emphasize the importance of characterizing events in terms of their relations to outcomes or 'endings'. Velleman says:

> A narrative must move forward not only in the sense of telling one event after another but also in the sense of approaching or at least seeming to approach some conclusion to those events, some terminus, finish, or closure.
>
> Here I should elaborate on a point...about the difference between narrative and the artistic genres that employ it. A novel or a theater piece need not reach a conclusion or even seem to approach one. But a novel or a theatre piece need not be a work of narrative, either; it may be a work of narrative only in parts, or it may be 'of' narrative only in the sense of commenting on the requirements of narrative only by pointedly defying them. A bad story can make for a great novel (though perhaps not the sort of great novel that one likes to read). The necessity of an ending is not inherent in the aesthetics of the novel or play but in the nature of storytelling, a form of discourse that a novel or play need not employ.[25]

On Velleman's view, a narrative explains by allowing the audience to assimilate the events in the story to a familiar emotional pattern or 'cadence.' He says:

> A story therefore enables its audience to assimilate events, not to familiar patterns of *how things happen*, but rather to familiar patterns of *how things feel*. These patterns are not themselves stored

in discursive form, as scenarios or stories; they are stored rather in experiential, proprioceptive, and kinesthetic memory—as we might say in the muscle-memory of the heart. Although the audience may have no discursive memory of events such as those of the story, it nevertheless has an experience of *deja senti*, because its emotional sensibility naturally follows the ups and downs of the story, just as a muscle naturally follows the cycle of tension and release.

What's more, the emotion that resolves a narrative cadence tends to subsume the emotions that preceded it; the triumph felt at a happy ending is the triumph of ambitions realized and anxieties allayed; the grief felt at a tragic ending is the grief of hopes dashed or loves denied. Hence the conclusory emotion in a narrative cadence embodies not just how the audience feels about the ending; it embodies how the audience feels, at the ending, about the whole story.[26]

So, on Velleman's account, narrative explains by getting the audience to understand the relevant events because it '*knows how they feel*,' in the sense that it experiences them as leading it through a natural emotional sequence, and also because '*it knows how it feels about them*,' in the sense that it arrives at a stable attitude toward them overall.[27]

II.2a Some Reflections

Above I distinguished two notions of 'better story' and, derivatively, 'better ending of the life-story.' One notion is, as I put it, especially relevant to potential readers of the story or critics, such as reviewers. Employing this notion, one might say that a certain story is better insofar as the ending is unpredictable, or there are unexpected and exciting twists and turns of plot, and so forth. It is clear that it cannot be this notion that is pertinent (say) to questions about physician-assisted suicide. Rather, a second notion is pertinent, and we can get a grasp on it by considering salient examples from what are considered 'good' (in the relevant sense) life-stories: persons thriving because of their efforts (and not merely because of unexpected windfalls), persons learning from their mistakes and thus flourishing (rather than deeming their mistakes 'dead-weight losses' or flourishing by lucky accidents), and so forth. It is this second notion that is relevant to questions about physician-assisted suicide.

In his essay on narrative explanation, Velleman says:

> ...the question how storytelling conveys understanding is inseparable from the question what makes for a good story. Of course, a good story can be good in many accidental respects, ranging from the elegance of its diction to the personal attractions of its characters. But what makes a story good specifically as a story—what makes it a good example of storytelling, or narrative—is its excellence at a particular way of organizing events into an intelligible whole.[28]

I am not sure whether Velleman intends to be making the following sort of suggestion, or whether he would agree entirely, but I would recommend that we interpret Velleman's remarks as suggesting a way of giving more concrete content to the first notion of 'better story.' That is, I suggest that 'good story,' in the sense relevant to potential readers and reviewers, is goodness in presenting a sequence of events in such a way as to have emotional resonance (i.e., to map onto the natural cadence of our emotions in a natural way). The various devices of plot and literary style can be seen as ways of seeking to achieve a resonance with our natural emotional cadences—to achieve *'deja senti'* in various ways. Some such devices work considerably better than others (for individual readers and also groups of readers). The classic literary (as well as musical) forms can be considered 'tried and true' ways of evoking emotional resonances. (It then becomes the challenge of the author—or composer—to work creatively and in original ways within the structure of these forms, or perhaps to transgress the boundaries set by these forms, so as to achieve emotional resonance.) Now I certainly doubt whether the notion of 'good story' of interest to readers and reviewers of literature can be reduced to a single idea, but this suggestion can perhaps illuminate at least a central aspect of the notion.[29]

Velleman says:

> Any sequence of events, no matter how improbable, can provide material for storytelling if it completes an emotional cadence. Twins separated at birth are ideal protagonists for a story even if their eventual reunion is a fluke. A discovery due to serendipity, a tragedy narrowly averted by dumb luck, a mundane act that unforeseeably becomes the last in a life accidentally cut short—these are the stuff not only of literary storytelling but of legend, gossip, and other forms of everyday narrative. Whether a winning lottery ticket or a fatal housefire makes enough of a story to be featured on the local news depends, not on whether its causes can be told, but rather on whether the surrounding circumstances will call up feelings that can be brought to some resolution by this inexplicable stroke of good or bad fortune. So long as we feel an anxiety relieved or a hope dashed, we have the sense of hearing a story, even if we have no idea why events took the relevant turn.[30]

How exactly do these remarks fit with the point made above that the narrative value of a life in which efforts are rewarded is greater than that of a life in which one thrives by serendipity or lucky windfall? We have to distinguish between narrative understanding and narrative value. We can achieve narrative understanding, and we could even say that the story is a good story, when we are told of someone flourishing by winning the lottery. Depending on the details of the presentation, the sequence of events can resonate with an emotional cadence—the story can depict the sequence of events in such a way that it feels familiar—it feels like a recognizable human drama. Upon hearing the presentation, we are inclined to say, in our hearts, 'Ah yes...' But it does not follow that such a story depicts a life with great *narrative value*. So, for example, such a story does not depict a life with more narrative value than the story of a life of flourishing as a result of lessons learned or simply hard work. A better story in the telling need not make for a story of a life with more value. An ending that is 'better' in the sense of narrative understanding need not be 'better' in the sense of narrative value.

Return to Velleman's claim, '...the question how storytelling conveys understanding is inseparable from the question what makes for a good story.' The question of how storytelling conveys understanding is inseparable from what makes for a good story, in the sense that is relevant to readers and reviewers of literature. Further, it seems that only a life that can be explained in the distinctively narrative way is capable of having the characteristic narrative value—is capable of being evaluated through a function that is sensitive to the sorts of structural relationships sketched above. So the possibility of narrative explanation is inseparable from the possibility of narrative evaluation; being a narrative is a necessary condition for having narrative value. Of course, it does not follow from anything said thus far that the better a story is in the telling—the greater its virtues along the dimension pertinent to narrative understanding—the higher the value of the function that determines overall value of the life will be (other things equal).

As I said in the introductory section of this essay, I have suggested in previous work that the value of acting freely is the value (whatever that is) of writing a sentence in the narrative of one's life. On some approaches, acting out of character is inconsistent with the idea of one's life's having narrative structure (and admitting of narrative explanation). But I do not employ the idea of narrative in a way that would rule out free action that is 'out of character.' The situation here is a bit like the possibility of narrative explanation of flourishing as a result of a windfall, such as winning the lottery. If the storyteller is adept, the story will resonate; that is, the structure of the story will map onto the emotional memory of the 'listener' or 'reader.' As above (in the case of succeeding as a result of a lucky accident), the story of action out of character can be told in such a way that it feels familiar—it feels like a recognizable human drama. It all depends on the way the story is told, and it is a delicate matter to tell the story in such a way as to elicit an emotional response of the proper sort. Certain ways of telling the story will result in puzzlement, whereas more skillful storytelling will evoke that heartfelt, 'Ah yes...,' indicating an isomorphism with a human emotional cadence. One can freely act out of character, even on an approach that invokes the importance of narrative explanation, and identifies the value of acting freely with the value of a certain sort of aesthetic activity (defined in terms of narrative).

On certain views of moral responsibility, one is morally responsible insofar as one expresses an enduring 'character trait.' This approach follows David Hume. But the basic problem with the Humean approach is that one can act freely, and be morally responsible, even when one acts out of character. The Humean may try to find some more 'complicated' character trait that is expressed in the behavior, but I believe that this trail leads inevitably to an unacceptable etiolation of the ordinary notion of 'character trait.' On this approach, it will turn out in the end that 'character traits' do not play any substantive, independent explanatory role. Despite the considerable attractions of a Humean approach to such matters, I believe that the possibility of acting out of character—and doing so freely—constitutes a significant and, indeed, insuperable problem.

On my view of acting freely and moral responsibility, one need not be expressing any sort of enduring character trait, or expressing any sort of 'commitment' or 'positive evaluation' of the relevant behavior. Rather, one is expressing oneself in the sense of writing a sentence in the narrative of one's life. If the story of one's past, and one's behavior, resonates appropriately, then one is acting freely and is morally responsible for the behavior in question. Again, it all depends on whether the storytelling is adept. In some cases the story can be told in such a way that the behavior under consideration is 'prefigured,' even if it is out of character. When the behavior is in this way prefigured, the story resonates with the listener (or 'audience') in the indicated way, and the agent is morally responsible.[31]

III. NARRATIVE, ENDINGS, AND IMMORTALITY

On the view of narrative explanation under consideration here, a narrative must have an ending. If our lives are narratives, or have the distinctive structure of narrative, then they must have endings. On this view, we cannot be immortal (insofar as our lives are narratives or have narrative value), if our lives are indeed narratives. To imagine immortal human life is to imagine human life devoid of an essential or at least very important characteristic: having narrative structure and thus a distinctive dimension of value.

I think that, strictly speaking, this is correct. If a narrative must have an ending, then it is clear that our lives cannot have the sort of meaning that involves taking a retrospective perspective on its totality, as it were, and assigning a meaning that reflects the overall arc of the lifestory. But an immortal life could have something very much like narrative meaning, strictly conceived; or, perhaps better, the relevant temporal stages or parts could be explained in the distinctive and strict narrative manner, and they could have the signature features of narrative value. Whereas the life as a whole could not be considered a narrative, the parts could be, and this would seem to render immortal life recognizably like our current human lives and also potentially desirable (in a distinctive way).[32] The literary analogue for such a life is not the novel, but perhaps a collection of short stories. Of course, the collection needs to be infinitely large, and the short stories need to be interconnected, with the same character appearing as the protagonist. Perhaps a better analogy would be a series of novels with the same protagonist, like a mystery series with the same detective. Over time the detective's character may change, but the changes can be organic; they need not be discontinuous.[33]

Another analogy would be a 'serial' novel or even a television series. Our lives may seem to be soap operas at times! Or perhaps they are 'sitcoms'; if so, mine is in certain respects (apart from pecuniary considerations) more like Larry David's on HBO's marvelous series, *Curb Your Enthusiasm*, than Ward Cleaver's on *Leave it to Beaver*. Now, of course, all sitcoms do eventually get cancelled—*Leave it to Beaver* can only be seen in syndicated reruns. But, as far as I can see, it is not part of their distinguishing features or essence that they be so (cruelly) terminated. A serial novel, a television series, a series of mystery novels with the same detective, a collection of short stories—they all have parts that can be explained and evaluated in the characteristic narrative fashion.[34]

If I consider an apparently possible immortal human life, I can see parts of it as having the distinctive features of narrative understanding and value. Parts of the life can be explained in such a way as to achieve emotional resonance and resolution. But since the life as a whole has no ending, there is no possibility of achieving distinctively narrative understanding of the whole life. And thus there is no final answer, as it were, giving the narrative value of the life as a whole. Whereas this is indeed the case, I do not think that it renders immortal life unintelligible or unrecognizably human; nor do I think it makes it impossible for a human being to find such a life valuable and desirable. (After all, to find such a life potentially desirable does not require rank-ordering it even ordinally against other such lives, or against finite human lives. And even in a finite life, there is the problem of combining the two irreducible dimensions of value into some overall value score—the cumulative measure of momentary well-being and the narrative dimension.)

Someone might say that there is a big difference—a big and crucial difference—between merely (!) very, very long life and *infinitely* long life. It might be suggested that, although we can 'get our minds around' long life, it is a mistake to suppose that infinitely long life is relevantly similar to merely very long, finite life. The infinite, it might be said, is just fundamentally different, and thus fundamentally mysterious (and not presumably amenable to evaluation in the relevant ways).

This raises difficult and obscure questions. Consider, first, the putative Divine Attributes, such as omnipotence, omniscience, moral perfection, and so forth. It is sometimes claimed that we cannot understand these properties, since they are fundamentally different from the bounded and finite analogues in human power, knowledge, and goodness. The standard reply, of course, is that the Divine Attributes, although different from their finite analogues, are to be understood along the lines of those attributes; the relationship between the infinite and finite here is one of analogy.

Similarly, the arithmetical rules that define certain operations, such as addition, subtraction, multiplication, and division are different for infinite and finite numbers. It is sometimes supposed that, because the arithmetics are different, there must be a difference in *kind* between finite and infinite magnitudes (and thus between finite and immortal lives). Given this difference in kind, it may not even be possible to grasp or comprehend an infinitely long human life. But, again, the reply should be that, although the rules pertaining to the relevant mathematical operations are different in finite and infinite numbers, they are not totally dissimilar. Indeed, there are sufficient similarities to suggest that the relationship between these sets of rules is one of *analogy.*

But Erich Reck has raised an interesting question here:

> …one can now start to play with other mathematical facts about the infinite to create some curious questions: Suppose, e.g., that every hundred years I have one bad day (for whatever reason). Then over the span of an infinite life (say a life that is omega days long—the smallest infinite), the number of bad days will still be infinite. In fact, the number of bad days overall will be the same as the number of good days (both omega). Or to modify the example a bit: suppose you have a bad day after ten days, then the next after 100 days, then the next after 1000 days; i.e., the intervals between bad days get longer and longer. Overall, there will still be infinitely many bad days, thus the same (infinite) number as the good days. Or to turn the example around: imagine that after ten days you have your first good day of your life, then the next good day after 100 days, then the next good day after 1000 days, etc. Overall you will still have the same (infinite) number of good and bad days. These kinds of examples are used in the literature on the infinite to illustrate how different it is from the finite.[35]

In my view, the difficulties to which Reck brings our attention pertain to any attempt to quantify and aggregate welfare in the way typically employed by the function that determines overall welfare, given information about momentary welfare. These phenomena need to be addressed. But they do not pertain to the second dimension of value, the narrative dimension, which is irreducible to the first. The narrative dimension of value has to do with the structural relationships among events; it does not involve any sort of addition or mere quantitative analysis of good and bad experiences, good and bad days, and so forth.

Here then is a way in which the narrative dimension of value is *better* able to address certain features of immortal life.

Similarly, consider a point raised by Borges in his short story, *The Immortal*, as described by Gustavo Llarull:

> ...the immortals are fundamentally devoted to intellectual pursuits; their physical needs are very easily satisfied (they can go without food for days) and sensual pleasures do not entice them. They are immersed in thought for entire weeks, and they barely talk to each other. In this context, Borges presents an interesting episode: one of the immortals falls from a cliff.
>
> Although the other immortals know about this accident, they go to his aid *months later*. Borges suggests that what from our finite view is surely deemed as cruelty or negligence may simply be the natural expression of attitudes that have changed in virtue of the correlative change in time patterns. In an average life span of 70 years, taking 15 minutes to help someone in need may be appropriate...Now, the same proportion, for a life span of 7,000 years, yields 25 hours! Needless to say, the idea of having to wait 25 hours, or more, to be aided by my fellow immortals, when they are fully aware that I am in need of help, sounds repulsive to say the least...[36]

As Llarull points out, Borges' description need not be the reality in an immortal life. Llarull says, '..."negative" or pain-related episodes, interactions or events would *not* lose their urgency [in an immortal life].'[37] It is clearly a mistake to think of immortal human life along the lines of an anatomical 'horizontal (or longitudinal) explosion' of ordinary, finite human life, keeping the temporal proportions fixed, as it were. Although there are perfectly good welfare-based reasons not to take the 'longitudinal explosion' model seriously, one can also invoke narrative relationships. Pain must be responded to as soon as possible, other things equal, and this fact would still obtain, in an immortal existence. It is a mistake to take a purely quantitative approach to envisaging and evaluating the relationships between finite and infinite human existence.[38]

IV. CONCLUSION

I have in a tentative way explored the interconnections among narrative explanation, narrative value, free will, and immortality. I have built on the fascinating and suggestive work of David Velleman. I have suggested that our acting freely is what gives our lives a distinctive kind of value—narrative value. Free Will, then, is connected to the capacity to lead a meaningful life in a quite specific way: it is the ingredient which, when added to others, endows us with a meaning over and above the cumulative value derived from adding together levels of momentary welfare. In acting freely, we are writing a sentence in the story of our lives, and the value of acting freely is thus a species of the value of artistic creativity or self-expression (understood appropriately). Finally, I have suggested that the fact that our lives are stories need not entail that they have endings, or that immortality would necessarily be unimaginable or essentially different from ordinary, finite human life. Yes, a certain sort of narrative understanding of our lives *as a whole* would be impossible in the context of immortality; but much of what we care about, and value, in our stories might remain.[39]

NOTES

1. It is well known that it is difficult to predict the future. A colleague of mine once pointed out that the situation is even worse with respect to the past: it is, he said, *impossible* to predict the past.

2. John Martin Fischer, 'Responsibility and Self-Expression,' *The Journal of Ethics*, Vol. 3, No. 4 (1999): 277–297.

3. John Martin Fischer, 'Epicureanism About Death and Immortality,' forthcoming, *The Journal of Ethics* (Chapter 7).

4. J. David Velleman, 'Well-Being and Time,' *Pacific Philosophical Quarterly* 72 (1991), pp. 48–77.

5. *Ibid.*

6. Cashiers in California have asked me, 'How's your day going so far?' Also, I've been implored to 'Have a great rest-of-your-day!' Of course, these sorts of thoughts, from people one does not really know, are superficial and slightly irritating. They can also reflect a mistaken view about value—or, perhaps, a focus on only one dimension of value.

China's Chairman Mao was asked what he thought of the French Revolution. He reportedly replied, 'It is too early to tell.' This clearly goes to the opposite extreme. Aristotle more moderately urged us 'to call no man happy, until that man is dead,' alluding to an old adage going back to Herodotus' tale about King Croesus. The adage was ubiquitous in the 5th century BCE, made especially so by Sophocles, whose play, *Women of Trachis*, begins, 'There is an old saying that no man is blessed until his final day.' (Heracles dies at the end of the play, after entering as hero at the start.)

7. J. David Velleman, 'Well-Being and Time, p. 51; the quotation is from Michael Slote, 'Goods and Lives,' in his *Goods and Virtues* (Oxford: Clarendon Press, 1983), pp. 23–24.

8. *Ibid.*, pp. 53–4.

9. *Ibid.*, pp. 54–5.

10. *Ibid.*, p. 55.

11. Whereas Velleman's contention here is appealing, it is tantalizingly underdeveloped. One problem is that there is a limited number of examples actually offered; also, as I point out in the text, Velleman does not offer any general formulaic explanation of narrative value. Perhaps not surprisingly, then, various philosophers have suggested to me that there are other potential explanations for our intuitions or judgments about various lives that are at least as plausible (as 'narrative value'). Thaddeus Metz has suggested to me that we can account for the judgments to which Velleman draws our attention

by keeping in mind that stretches of one's life (or activities in these stretches) can have *instrumental* value as well as intrinsic value; thus, even a utilitarian can account for the greater value of certain lives by pointing out that stretches in certain lives (but not others) can have instrumental value. (For a discussion, see Thaddeus Metz, 'Utilitarianism and the Meaning of Life,' *Utilitas* 15 (2003), pp. 50–70.) David Hershenov has suggested that the judgments can be explained not so much by invoking narrative value, but by the moral value of staying married, the desire for (or value of) moral self-improvement, and so forth. (A skeptic about the invocation of the notion of narrative value here, such as Hershenov, might then seek to construct examples of lives that lack the putatively relevant features—moral self-improvement, staying married, and so forth—to see if the relevant evaluations of the life stay the same.) Andrews Reath has suggested that what is significant about the cases under discussion is that they indicate that there are irreducibly *relational* goods; but this does not in itself entail anything about specifically 'narrative' value.

These matters require much more attention than I can give here. I should point out that I myself have some doubts about how to evaluate the various scenarios. For example, I do not think that it is somehow better or more valuable that a depressed individual pull out of his depression by pure strength of will, or a regimen of psychotherapy, or any other sort of extended and perhaps arduous set of activities and reflections, rather than by taking an antidepressant. Of course, if the chances of recurrence of the depression are greater if one simply takes the medication, then that counts against it. But I do not share the intuition that there is something less valuable—that it is somehow 'cheating'—to use the antidepressant (successfully). And it is not exactly clear to me how to distinguish this case, or class of cases, from those discussed by Velleman. I hope to turn to these issues in future work. Here I shall not press the worries, and take it, as a working hypothesis, that Velleman's intuitions or judgments about scenarios are plausible, and that his invocation of narrative value is explanatorily helpful.

12. J. David Velleman, 'Well-Being and Time,' p. 62.

13. This is not necessarily a criticism of Velleman, as it is unclear that he envisaged his account as providing guidance in all cases of potential physician-assisted suicide.

14. J. David Velleman, 'Well-Being and Time,' p. 71.

15. *Ibid.*, p. 71.

16. For skepticism about the necessity of this sort of capacity for the distinctive notion of 'valuing' (as opposed to merely preferring) and also for autonomy, see Agnieska Jaworska, 'Respecting the Margins of Agency: Alzheimer's Patients and the Capacity to Value,' *Philosophy and Public Affairs* 29 (1999), pp. 105–38.

17. I do not know how to prove my supposition, and I recognize that it would be good to have more to say here. I base the claim on consideration of contexts in which we would normally suppose that there is narrative value and thus the ability of the relevant agent to affect the meanings of past events, but in which it is explicitly understood that the agent is manipulated in such a way as not to be acting freely; in this range of thought experiments, my intuition is that the agent cannot affect the meanings of the past events, and that this is precisely because he does not act freely. I hope to be able to justify this intuition (at least to some extent) in future work. See Chapter 1 for further defense of my suggestion.

18. Of course, the past goods in question are not 'experiential' goods.

19. Carl Ginet, *On Action* (Cambridge, U.K.: Cambridge University Press, 1990). See, also, John Martin Fischer, *The Metaphysics of Free Will: An Essay on Control* (Cambridge, Mass.: Blackwell Publishers, 1994).

20. We now have available to us a kind of 'alternative' explanation—no doubt, not the intended explanation—of the putative fact alluded to in footnote 1 above—that it is impossible to predict the past. If we can go backward in narrative space-time by freely acting in the future, and this free action cannot be predicted, then we also cannot predict what the narrative past will have been.

21. J. David Velleman, 'Narrative Explanation,' *Philosophical Review* 112 (2003), pp. 1–26.

22. *Ibid.*, p. 1.

23. *Ibid.*, p. 1.

24. Louis Mink, 'Philosophical Analysis and Historical Understanding,' in Brian Fay, Eugene. O. Golob, and Richard T. Vann, eds., *Historical Understanding* (Ithaca: Cornell University Press, 1987), pp. 118–46; and E.B. Gallie, *Philosophy and the Historical Understanding* (London: Chatto and Windus, 1964).

25. J. David Velleman, 'Narrative Explanation,' p. 10.

26. *Ibid.*, p. 19.

27. *Ibid.*, p. 19.

28. *Ibid.*, p. 1.

29. To add just one dimension of complexity: note that a typical literary work or musical composition will not simply evoke one emotion, but many (sometimes colliding) emotions.

30. J. David Velleman, 'Narrative Explanation,' pp. 6–7.

31. I can only gesture briefly at an account of these matters here. Note that my sketch here may suggest an unintuitive 'relativization' of moral responsibility to a particular bit of story-telling. I do not know whether this is genuinely problematic; if so, one could define acting freely and moral responsibility in terms of the 'availability' (in some sense) of a story of the right sort.

32. It is a staple of 'postmodern' critiques of 'narrative' that they posit some sort of overarching or 'totalizing' meaning. On my account of the narrative structure of an immortal life, there is no single 'grand narrative' and thus no 'totalizing meaning'; and yet there remains much to which a postmodernist could object, given that the sub-parts of the immortal life are taken to have suitable meanings.

33. In Amanda Cross's (Carolyn Heilbrunn's) delightful series of academic mystery novels, Kate Fansler (English Professor and detective extraordinaire) changes noticeably but understandably over time. As she ages, Kate is no longer the hard-drinking detective who solved the murder of the first tenured woman professor at Harvard in *Death in A Tenured Position*. In the later works, she worries about her excessive indulgence in alcohol, and seeks moderation in this and other pleasures.

The story of Heilbrun's own life, as opposed to that of her fictional professor/detective, ended rather abruptly. The *Los Angeles Times* obituary (October 15, 2003), says:

> Carolyn G. Heilbrun, a distinguished feminist scholar who illuminated the female experience through erudite reinterpretations of classic English literature and in literate mystery novels written under the name Amanda Cross, was found dead in her New York City apartment Friday after an apparent suicide. She was 77.

The pioneering feminist critic had decided years earlier that she would end her life by the age of 70 to avoid the inevitable deterioration of age, but she later explained that she had let the deadline pass when her 60s proved deeply satisfying.

In *The Last Gift of Time: Life Beyond Sixty*, a book published the year she turned 71, she said she would decide each day whether to keep on living. Her son Robert told the New York Times last week that she had not been ill when she decided to kill herself.

It is almost as if Heilbrun always knew the end of her life-story, but she couldn't wait for the organic development of the plot. In any case, the details of her reasons for choosing to commit suicide when she did may remain (not inappropriately) a mystery.

34. In his classic essay, 'The Makropulos Case: Reflections on the Tedium of Immortality,' Bernard Williams argues that an immortal life would be essentially meaningless and unattractive: Bernard Williams, *Problems of the Self* (Cambridge, U.K.: Cambridge University Press, 1973), pp. 82–100, reprinted in John Martin Fischer, ed., *The Metaphysics of Death* (Stanford: Stanford University Press, 1993), pp. 73–92. In chapter 6, I argue against Williams' view. I suggest that the sort of immortality suggested in the text of the current essay—along the lines of a character in a series of novels or a continuing television series—could be appealing.

35. Erich Reck, personal correspondence.

36. Gustavo Llarull, 'The Problem of Immortality: A Response to Williams,' unpublished manuscript, University of California, Riverside department of philosophy.

37. *Ibid.*

38. The mistake of ignoring the crucial narrative structure of life, even infinite life, is also found in this passage from Victor Frankl: 'What would our lives be like if they were not finite in time, but infinite? If we were immortal, we could legitimately postpone every action forever. It would be of no consequence whether or not we did a thing now; every act might just as well be done tomorrow or the day after or a year from now or ten years hence. But in the face of death as absolute *finis* to our future and boundary to our possibilities, we are under the imperative of utilizing our lifetimes to the utmost, not letting the singular opportunities—whose "finite" sum constitutes the whole of life—pass by unused.' (*The Doctor and the Soul* [New York: Alfred Knopf, 1957], p. 73.)

39. I am grateful for thoughtful comments by Erich Reck, Gustavo Llarull, David Hershenov, David Glidden, Ward Jones, and Thaddeus Metz. I thank Gustavo Llarull for permission to cite his unpublished work. I have presented versions of this essay at the Winter Colloquium of the Department of Comparative Languages and Literatures, University of California, Riverside (2005), and the Free Will Workshop at the University of California, Riverside (2005). On these occasions many people gave me very insightful comments, including: Gary Watson, Andrews Reath, Nathan Placencia, Chris Yeomens, Neal Tognazzini, Thomas Scanlon, and Lisa Raphals.

10

Stories and the Meaning of Life

John Martin Fischer

I. INTRODUCTION: A FRAMEWORK
FOR MORAL RESPONSIBILITY

In various places, I (sometimes in collaboration with Mark Ravizza) have sought to present the elements of a theoretical "framework for moral responsibility."[1] Here I shall begin by sketching the framework in order to give the background for a more detailed development of the idea that the value of acting so as to be morally responsible is the value of a certain distinctive kind of self-expression.

The overall framework for moral responsibility includes (at least) the following elements: a distinction between the concept of moral responsibility and its conditions of application; a distinction between "regulative" and "guidance" control; an argument that guidance control, and not regulative control, is the "freedom-relevant" condition linked to moral responsibility; an account of guidance control in terms of mechanism ownership and moderate reasons-responsiveness; an argument that guidance control, so construed, is compatible with causal determinism; and an account of the value of moral responsibility (in terms of self-expression).

There are various plausible ways of specifying the concept of moral responsibility, including the "moral ledger view," the "fittingness-of-providing an explanation" view, and the "Strawsonian view," which involves aptness for the "reactive attitudes" (resentment, indignation, gratitude, love, and so forth). I do not take an official stand as to the proper analysis of our concept of moral responsibility; perhaps there is no single correct answer here, and our concept involves elements of the various suggestions. Even so, I find it helpful and instructive to take as a working hypothesis some version of the Strawsonian account of the concept of moral responsibility.

But under what conditions does the concept apply? I here follow Aristotle: an agent must meet both some sort of "epistemic" condition and a "freedom-relevant" condition. This tracks Aristotle's claim that an agent fails to act voluntarily to the extent that he acts from ignorance or force. My primary focus has been on the freedom-relevant condition.

I offer plausibility arguments for the contention that "acting freely" (an "actual-sequence" sort of freedom) plays the role of the freedom-relevant condition; put in other words, guidance control, and not regulative control, is the freedom-relevant condition associated with moral responsibility. On my view, then, an agent may be morally responsible but never have had genuine metaphysical access to alternative possibilities—he may never have had "freedom to do otherwise." These plausibility arguments employ the thought-experiments that originated with John Locke and have been dubbed, "Frankfurt-Style Examples," after Harry Frankfurt. Frankfurt has argued that such cases—involving a signature sort of pre-emptive overdetermination—imply the falsity of the Principle of Alternative Possibilities (the principle that states that freedom to do otherwise is a necessary condition of moral responsibility).

In my view, the moral of the Frankfurt Stories—and it is interesting that these hypothetical examples are frequently referred to as "stories"—is that acting freely (and being morally responsible) is a matter of how the actual sequence unfolds, *not* whether the agent has genuine metaphysical access to alternative sequences. Although I find the thought-experiments instructive and illuminating, I believe that there are other dialectical routes to the same conclusion, and that the thought-experiments should form part of an overall strategy of argumentation.[2] Even if one doesn't find the Frankfurt-Examples convincing, this should not in itself issue in a rejection of the basic conclusion about the relationship between moral responsibility and freedom to do otherwise. This point resonates with my general methodological approach, according to which stories play a key role, but not the sole or exclusive role in analysis of various phenomena. Thus, the role of Frankfurt-stories is like the role of hypothetical examples in ethics.

Especially with my co-author, Mark Ravizza, I have sought to sketch an account of guidance control. On our approach, guidance control involves two chief elements: mechanism ownership and reasons-responsiveness. An agent exhibits guidance control of an action insofar as the action issues from the agent's own, "moderately reasons-responsive" mechanism. Our more detailed accounts of both elements have elicited worries and objections; particularly contentious have been the claim that mechanism ownership involves a certain sort of "subjective" condition, and that reactivity to reasons is "all-of-a-piece." I have sought to defend the fundamental ideas where possible. Also, in recent work I have pointed out that the basic elements of the framework for moral responsibility can be preserved while adjusting the specific details; I have argued that I can still accomplish everything I had hoped to accomplish by offering a framework for moral responsibility even without a commitment to a strong subjectivity or to the contention that "reactivity-is-all-of-a piece."[3] That is, I can accept slightly adjusted accounts of the fundamental elements of the framework while still maintaining that moral responsibility does not require regulative control, that it is fundamentally a historical notion, and that it is compatible with causal determinism. This is important because some philosophers have apparently dismissed the view because they have found the specific subjective view or the view that reactivity is all-of-a piece troubling.

Finally, I have suggested that the value placed on acting freely and being such as to be held morally accountable is the value of a certain distinctive kind of self-expression. When we act freely, we express ourselves in a way that is perhaps a form of artistic creativity (or akin to such self-expression). What matters is not that we make a difference to the world, but that we make a certain kind of statement. In acting freely, we make it the case that our lives have a narrative dimension of value; thus, acting freely is the ingredient which, when added to other features, endows our lives with a meaning beyond the simple addition of momentary episodes of welfare, or even the addition of such episodes, weighted for their temporal location. Unlike mere non-human animals, our lives are stories in a strict sense, and they can have a distinctive kind of meaning—narrative meaning.[4]

II. FREEDOM AND THE VARIETIES OF VALUE: A PROPOSAL

I believe that we do indeed value self-expression, and that the value of acting freely (and thus being morally responsible agents) is a species of the value of self-expression. I am inclined to think of this as a sort of "artistic" self-expression, but if it is, it may be a context, which is unique or sui generis (in a way I shall explain below). Why exactly do we value this sort of self-expression? This is a hard question. I think it is connected to questions about the meaning of our lives.

As I said above, our lives are stories, whereas the lives of rats and even cats are not. Certainly, one can tell the "story" (speaking loosely) of a rock or a rat or a cat, but these accounts are not "stories" in a strict sense. They are not narratives. Of course, it is an interesting and vexed question just what has to be added to a mere account or chronicle of events to get to a "story" (strictly speaking) or a narrative; I am inclined to accept the bare bones at least of the suggestion of David Velleman that the necessary additional ingredient is some distinctive sort of *understanding* provided by the account.[5] Further, insofar as we act freely our lives have a narrative dimension of value. Along this dimension, one does not simply add together momentary levels of well-being, and the meanings or values of events depend on certain distinctive relationships with other events. Velleman calls these "dramatic" or "narrative" relationships.

When I act freely, I write a sentence in the story of my life; that is, the account of my life is strictly speaking a story (rather than a mere chronicle of events), and my life has a narrative dimension of value. Insofar as a story or narrative is by definition a work of art, I am an artist, when I act freely, and I am inclined to say that the value of my free action is the value of artistic self-expression.[6] Note that it does *not* follow from the fact that the value of our free action is a species of the value of artistic self-expression that it is a kind of *aesthetic value*; rather, the point is that the value of our free action is a species of the value of artistic self-expression, *whatever that value is*. I take it that artistic self-expression has value from the perspective of human flourishing or "doing well"; in a broad sense (that encompasses "goodness" as well as "rightness)," this is arguably a moral value.

Thus, when I act freely, I am by definition engaging in artistic or aes-thetic activity, and this activity can have value for us—a value that is distinct from the value of the product. For example, we might plausibly think that it is valuable—from the perspective of living well or flour-ishing—to engage in artistic activity; this value is conceptually distinct from any sort of evaluation (aesthetic or even moral) of the product— the sculpture or painting or novel. Similarly, on my view, the activity of my acting freely is a species of artistic activity, and thus it has whatever value we place on this sort of activity. Of course, it does not follow from the fact that my acting freely is a species of artistic activity that the value of the product—the life or perhaps life-story—is solely or primar-ily aesthetic. (It would be natural to suppose that, because the activity is by its nature aesthetic, the value we place on the product must be a spe-cies of aesthetic value; but this is a mistake.) My activity in acting freely is a kind of artistic self-expression, and it thus has the value we place on such aesthetic activity. But the product—my life or life-story—typically is evaluated primarily from the perspective of prudence and morality, although it can also be evaluated from the aesthetic perspective.

Of course, a work of art such as a sculpture can be evaluated along various dimensions, including both aesthetic and moral. (Here I am talking about the product of artistic activity—the sculpture.) Surely, evaluation is purpose-dependent, and we might have various purposes in evaluating a particular sculpture. We might, for example, want to know whether it is composed of materials that are environmentally sensitive or scarce, or that could only be procured by exploiting people, and so forth; such purposes would give rise to a moral evaluation of the sculpture. But perhaps typically we would want to know whether the sculpture is aesthetically pleasing, and thus our "primary" way of evaluating it would be aesthetic. That is, given the range of human purposes, perhaps the "typical" or "primary" sort of evaluation of a sculpture would be in terms of aesthetic dimensions. Here it might be said that there is a "match" between the sort of activity that issues in the product—artistic or aesthetic activity—and the "typical" or "primary" mode of evaluation of the product.

A life, or a life-story, can be evaluated along different dimensions, including aesthetic, moral, prudential, and so forth. A life or life-story—considered as a product of artistic self-expression—can certainly be evaluated aesthetically. It is perhaps most natural to think about stretches of a life or parts of a life here. For example, athletes are sometimes thought to retire too late; this seems especially prevalent in boxing, and it tends to tarnish or diminish the athlete's entire career. I also believe that certain athletes and coaches have retired "too early"—before reaching the heights they could have reached, or perhaps cutting off a string of accomplishments before its "natural" or "optimum" conclusion. (I believe that the great coach of the San Francisco 49ers, Bill Walsh, retired too early—and I believe he thought this too in retrospect.) No doubt, certain academics—even philosophers—have retired too early; but surely none—especially no philosophers—have retired too late!

I take it that these considerations are essentially "aesthetic," although they surely are related to (or perhaps involve) moral dimensions. They have to do with the trajectory or arc of one's career. Obviously, we can evaluate the trajectory of several of one's projects in addition to one's career, and we also are deeply concerned with the arc of one's relationships with others. Sometimes a relationship maintains its integrity, whereas in other cases a relationship might end abruptly or slowly unravel in an unlovely way.

Although we certainly engage in aesthetic evaluation of aspects or phases of our lives as well as our lives as a whole, I think it is undeniable that the typical" or "primary" modes of evaluation (given the standard human purposes and interests) are prudential and moral. Thus I suggest that if acting freely is indeed a species of artistic self-expression, this context is *sui generis*: it involves a kind of activity—artistic or aesthetic activity—whose product is not typically or primarily evaluated aesthetically. That is, when we act freely, we tell a story that is most naturally—given the intrinsic nature of human activity and a broad range of human purposes—evaluated in terms of moral and prudential considerations, even though the nature of the activity is artistic. Here then we have perhaps identified what is special and unique about the context of free action: whereas there is a match between the nature of artistic activity and the primary mode of evaluation of (say) a sculpture, there is a striking discrepancy between the nature of free human activity (arstistic) and the value of the activity; whereas its nature is a species of aesthetic activity, the typical or primary modes of evaluating the product are prudential and moral.

It is perhaps not surprising that the two elements of this idea about the value of acting freely correspond in some rough way to the two components of the analysis of guidance control. The value of acting freely, on the account I have sketched, is the value (whatever kind of

value that is) of artistic self-expression whose product is typically evaluated in terms of prudence and morality. Guidance control is analyzed
in terms of two components: ownership and reasons-responsiveness.
Ownership posits a special relationship to the self, and this corresponds
to the value of artistic self-expression. And reasons-responsiveness pertains to the salient dimensions of assessment of human lives in terms
of morality and prudence. Although the relationships here are perhaps
less tight than one might like, it is appropriate that there be echoes of
the elements of the account of the *value* of acting freely in the *analysis* of
acting freely. This is one way in which parts of the overall framework
for moral responsibility form a unified, cohesive whole.

III. IMPLICATIONS AND REFINEMENTS

III.1. Historical Narratives

I have contended that our exercising our capacity for acting freely transforms our lives into genuine stories and endows us with the narrative
dimension of value. Eric Schwitzgebel has pointed out however that
one can write "narratives" that are not most appropriately thought of
as works of art. If, say, one writes the history of a family or region, this
sort of "narrative" may seem to have the characteristics I have pointed
to (including the non-additive dimension of value), but we would not
typically say that such a narrative is a piece of art, that writing it is
a species of aesthetic activity, and that its value is a kind of aesthetic
value. One might then worry that simply having the characteristics of
being a narrative and having the narrative dimension of value doesn't
make our lives "works of art" in the relevant sense, or our free actions
a species of artistic self-expression, and so forth.[7]

Note however that such narratives—the history of a region or family—do not *themselves* possess the narrative dimension of value. That
is, we would presumably judge them by their accuracy in depicting the
events in question; it would not be a further virtue of such an *account*
that it depicted (perhaps falsely) individuals learning from prior mistakes, flourishing as a result of prior efforts (rather than mere luck),
and so forth. Certainly, these features would endow the *lives depicted*
with additional value—narrative value, but they would not endow the
narrative itself with such value. Similarly, although the lives depicted
would have the additional dimension of value, we would certainly not
attribute greater value to the creator of the (perhaps false) narrative!
So family narratives would typically not be works of art, but this does
not in any way diminish the plausibility of the claim that we are engaging in artistic activity in freely writing the stories of our lives, and that
such free activity helps to endow our life-stories with the distinctive
features of certain works of art. And, of course, as I emphasized above,

the fact that our activity in creating our life-stories is properly considered a species of aesthetic creativity does not in itself rule out the possibility that the typical or primary modes of evaluation of the *product* is not aesthetic.[8]

III.2. The Aesthetic Fallacy

My point is that it does not *follow* from the fact that one's free activity is a species of artistic self-expression, that the only or primary or typical mode of evaluation of the *product* be aesthetic. Of course, I have not argued for or *established* that the nature of the activity and the value of the product can pull apart in the way I have suggested. My point here is rather more modest; I wish simply to insist that, insofar as we distinguish between the activity and its product, there is no *entailment* between the nature of the activity and the mode of evaluation of the product. Given that evaluation is purpose-driven, it is not surprising that there are various perfectly reasonable modes of evaluation of the products of artistic activity, and thus that we cannot simply "read off" the (appropriate) mode of evaluation from the nature of the activity.

I have sought to carve out a space between the aesthetic nature of our free activity of writing our life-stories and the appropriate modes of evaluation of those stories. On this picture, it would be a fallacy to infer from the fact that the essential nature of our free activity is aesthetic to the proposition that our lives (or life-stories) should be evaluated exclusively or primarily in terms of aesthetic criteria. I suggest that we call this problematic move, "The Aesthetic Fallacy." Some have attributed to Nietzsche the view that our lives should be evaluated primarily along aesthetic—specifically, literary—dimensions.[9] Philosophers such as Nehamas emphasize Nietzsche's "aestheticism" and his view of "life as literature." The details of Nietzsche's view—and even the broad contours of it—are in dispute, and I am certainly not qualified to enter into exegetical debates. I simply wish to point out that it would be fallacious to suppose that it follows from the fact that our freely writing the books of our lives is a species of aesthetic activity that the books themselves should be evaluated *primarily* aesthetically.

I am not stating that Nietzsche himself or any of his commentators are guilty of this sort of fallacy; after all, they might think that it is helpful or illuminating or true to say that the primary mode of evaluation of lives is aesthetic, but not because it *follows* from the fact that our free activity exemplifies aesthetic value. I simply want to identify the Aesthetic Fallacy as such; it highlights a problematic *route* to the conclusion that our lives are to be evaluated primarily as works of art—a conclusion I do not in any case endorse. Perhaps someone could argue convincingly that it does indeed follow from the relevant activity's having a certain nature to the product's primarily having that same sort of value, or that it follows from the relevant activity's having this specific nature—aesthetic—that its product must primarily be evaluated aesthetically. In this case what I have called "The Aesthetic Fallacy" would not in fact be a fallacy. But I am not sanguine about the prospects for such an argument, especially given the purpose-driven nature of evaluation, and our multifarious purposes.

III.3. Constraining the Plausible Stories

The purpose-relativity of explanation, together with the multiplicity of human purposes, results in a challenge to the notion that there is some single "fixed meaning" to our lives—some master narrative that is, as it were, "given." Rather, on my account, one's life-story is evaluated along different dimensions, given different purposes. But there is an even more basic way in which I would contest the notion that there is a single, fixed, or given meaning to our lives. The claim that in acting freely, we write a sentence in the narrative of our lives suggests that there is a single story of our lives—a given narrative to which we add sentences. But of course this is an unreasonable picture. Rather, our bodily movements and behavior are subject to different interpretations from different perspectives; although we try to tell our own stories, and we do our best to offer our interpretations, we do not always get to tell our own stories. That is, at least in certain contexts, our stories are told by others—our behavior is at least in significant respects interpreted by others (and in ways contrary to our own understanding and preferences).[10]

Just as I do not suppose that there is a purpose-independent notion of evaluation or a "fundamental" or "privileged" purpose (or set of purposes), I do not suppose that there is a hegemonic perspective from which our stories get told. Thus, I would qualify my somewhat oversimplified formulation, according to which in acting freely, we write a sentence in the narrative of our lives. More carefully, perhaps, in acting freely we constrain the plausible stories of our lives. Whereas various defensible interpretations will still be possible, our behavior can significantly constrain the plausibility of some of these interpretations, thus limiting the range of reasonable life-stories.

Now perhaps this is somewhat deflating. You had perhaps thought of yourself as triumphantly writing the sentences in the book of your life, but now you are merely constraining the admissible stories—certainly a comedown! This picture seems to diminish an agent's control, and, after all, control is supposed to be the basis of moral responsibility (on my approach). I admit that the simpler formulation is snappier and a bit more attractive, but the more refined formulation is after all both humbler and more realistic. Guidance control is indeed the "freedom-relevant" basis of moral responsibility, and, as such, it is a significant and robust sort of control. In exercising guidance control, we determine certain aspects of the unfolding story of the universe; but it would be manifestly ludicrous to demand that we can determine *everything* about this story. I have also argued that it is unreasonable to aspire for what I have called "Total Control," the desire for which I have attributed to "metaphysical megalomania."[11] The realization that we don't (always) get to tell our own story—that there are multiple perspectives from which different interpretations of our behavior are offered, none of which is privileged "in advance" or "apart from specific contexts"—is parallel to a humbler, more realistic conception of the sort of control that grounds our moral responsibility (guidance control).

III.4. Life and Works of Art

I have argued that there is a sense in which our lives can be understood as stories. But why not think of our lives as poems, or plays, or other sorts of works of art? I think the question is interesting, and the answer may help to sharpen the view I am defending. Of course, a poem or a play—or, for that matter, a piece of music—can tell a story or determine a narrative, just as much as a novel or short story can. Clearly, the epic poems of Homer tell rich and detailed stories. I would say that the various literary and artistic forms—poems, short stories, novels, plays, even pieces of music—can be thought of as various ways of telling stories—various "vehicles" for storytelling or the determination of narrative content. Our lives, then, considered as a sequence of behaviors or even bodily movements, could be thought of as a way of telling a story—a certain sort of vehicle of narrative content (relative, presumably, to a perspective with a given set of purposes). Strictly speaking, then, our lives are not stories, but ways of telling stories, or, perhaps more carefully, ways of constraining admissible narrative content. They are—as with poems or plays or novels—the vehicles of content, rather than the content itself.

This point is similar to the notion that a sentence (or perhaps a sentence in a context) is the vehicle for content (say, a proposition that is expressed by the sentence in the context). It is illuminating to distinguish the properties of the vehicles of expression of content from those of content itself; for instance, some philosophers hold that the vehicles of content are structured linguistically, whereas the propositions expressed—the content itself—is not structured at all or at least not linguistically structured. Of course, this particular claim is contentious; for our purposes it is enough simply to mark the distinction between the properties of the vehicles of content and the properties of content.

I suggested above that when I act freely, I write a sentence in the book of my life. Perhaps this was closer to the truth than I had imagined, since sentences—or their utterance or presentation—are good candidates for the vehicles of content, rather than content itself—just as our behavior is the vehicle for telling our stories. (In the more refined formulation, our behavior would be the vehicle for constraining the plausible stories—a way of limiting the admissible narrative contents.)

Even if we say that our lives are (simply put) ways of getting to narratives—or vehicles for telling stories—we might also say that the vehicles themselves share some interesting properties with (say) poems. Now of course it is difficult to specify exactly what the defining characteristics of poetry are. One idea would be to specify poetry in terms of a given set of forms; but this would leave out much contemporary, free-form poetry. Another idea would be to define poetry in terms of the dominance or hegemony of a particular trope: metaphor. Again, this would seem problematic, insofar as much poetry does not seem to use metaphor as the hegemonic trope, and many other literary forms make heavy use of metaphor. Whereas it is very difficult to give the essence of poetry, I believe it has to do with *economy of expression*. On this way of thinking of poetry, certain lives could certainly be thought to be similar to poems insofar as they embody a kind of elegance.

IV. CONCLUSION

Perhaps following Nietzsche, various philosophers have accepted some version of "aestheticism" or the idea that life should be modeled (in some way) on art. Of course, I have interpreted this idea in a quite specific way, eschewing some of the more extravagant versions of the doctrine. I have suggested that the value we place on acting freely is connected in certain ways to the meaning of our lives. One way in which this is true is that acting freely renders us artists in the sense adumbrated above; in virtue of acting freely, our lives can be stories and can have narrative value. We care about acting freely, then, to the extent that we value engaging in artistic self-expression. Additionally, our free actions are artistic activity of a specific kind, whereas the products of this aesthetic activity are typically (although not exclusively) evaluated in moral and prudential ways; our free action is thus a special sort of aesthetic activity. It may be that we *especially* care about the sort of artistic self-expression whose product is typically evaluated in moral and prudential terms: although I cannot here argue for this claim, it seems plausible to me that the aesthetic activity in creating a product with deep prudential and moral value is particularly important to us. I would further suggest that we care especially about products that are assessed prudentially and morally that *come from this particular avenue—artistic self-expression*. So the value of the artistic self-expression is enhanced by issuing in a product that is typically evaluated morally and prudentially, and the value of such a product is enhanced in virtue of coming from a distinctive sort of artistic activity. It might be said that what makes our lives or life-stories so uniquely special and valuable is that they are in the realm of the moral and prudential, but *arrived at via the aesthetic*. The meaning of life, then, occurs at the *intersection* of the aesthetic, moral, and prudential.

I think there is an additional feature of this sort of self-expression (connected to the meaning of our lives) in virtue of which we deem it valuable. In Richard Taylor's fascinating essay, "The Meaning of Human Life," he argues that a crucial element in our lives' having the distinctive sort of meaning they possess is our power of *creativity*.[12] He says:

> If you were to learn that the rest of your life would be spent digging an enormous hole, then it would perhaps be a reassurance of sorts to be told that you were actually going to enjoy doing it. If, further, you were born with, or at any early age conditioned to, a strong desire to do this, then you would not need to have such a task assigned to you—you would go to great lengths to gain the opportunity and consider yourself lucky if you got it. And you would someday view the great hole you had dug with a deep sense of fulfillment. And therein does each of us find, in varying degrees, the very picture of his or her own life.[13]

Taylor goes on to say that what transforms our lives into *meaningful* lives is *creativity*:

> That one word ["creative"] sums it up, and, if really understood, discloses entirely what is missing, not only in all the animate and inanimate existence that surrounds us but in the lives of the vast majority of human beings. It is also what philosophers have always sought as godlike or what makes man, in the ancient metaphor, the image of God. For what is godlike is not blind power, or aimless knowledge, or unguided reason, but simply creative power. It is the primary attribute in the very conception of God.[14]

Roderick Chisholm thought of the agent as a kind of Godlike first cause. Perhaps we are indeed the images of God, but not in virtue of having the power to create ex nihilo or to transcend the network of natural causation or even to make a certain kind of difference to the world. Perhaps it is simply in virtue of our power of artistic self-expression that we are creative in a way that renders us images of God, even if pale images.[15]

NOTES

1. See, for example: *The Metaphysics of Free Will: An Essay on Control* (Oxford: Blackwell Publishers, 1994); (with Mark Ravizza, S.J.) *Responsibility and Control: A Theory of Moral Responsibility* (Cambridge, U.K.: Cambridge University Press, 1998); *My Way: Essays on Moral Responsibility* (New York: Oxford University Press, 2006); and (with D. Pereboom, R. Kane, and M. Vargas), *Four Views on Free Will* (Oxford: Blackwell Publishers, 2007).

2. For other strategies, see R. Jay Wallace, *Responsibility and the Moral Sentiments* (Cambridge, Mass.: Harvard University Press, 1994), and Daniel C. Dennett, *Freedom Evolves* (New York: Viking, 2003).

3. John Martin Fischer, "Reply: The Free Will Revolution," part of a book symposium on John Martin Fischer and Mark Ravizza, *Responsibility and Control: A Theory of Moral Responsibility*, *Philosophical Explorations* Vol. 8, No. 2 (June 2005): 145–56; and "The Free Will Revolution (Continued)," *Journal of Ethics* 10 (2006), pp. 315–345.

4. John Martin Fischer, "Responsibility and Self-Expression," *The Journal of Ethics*, Vol. 3, No. 4 (1999): 277–97, reprinted in *My Way*, pp. 106–23; and chapter 9.

5. David Velleman, "Narrative Explanation," *Philosophical Review* 112 (2003), pp. 1–26.

6. In my essay, "Responsibility and Self-Expression," I contended that the value of free action is identical to the value of a kind of self-expression, but not necessarily artistic self-expression: p. 117. My view in the text thus represents a change.

7. See note 6 above. In "Responsibility and Self-Expression," this worry prompted me to propose that the value of our free action is the value of self-expression, but not necessarily artistic self-expression. It is interesting to consider whether such a view is importantly different from the view I defend here, that the value of our free action is indeed a species of the value of artistic self-expression.

8. Note that, on my terminology, it is lives, but not narratives, that have "narrative value." Of course, narratives (and the novels, plays, and so forth that express these narratives) can have aesthetic value (and can be evaluated along other dimensions, including the moral dimension—but narratives (as opposed to the lives they depict) themselves would not have "narrative value."

9. Alexander Nehamas, *Nietzsche: Life as Literature* (Cambridge, Mass.: Harvard University Press, 1985).

10. Different interpretations of behavior issue from different perspectives; thus, I may see my behavior as having a certain meaning, as being embedded in a certain narrative, whereas a third party may interpret it quite differently. (Obviously, individuals occupying various different perspectives might see my behavior as being parts of various different narratives.) These claims are about the interpretation of the behavior and the associated content of the story. The idea that from my perspective my behavior has a particular meaning has nothing essential to do with *how I experience my life*. That is, various versions of what Galen Strawson has called the Narrativity Thesis—a thesis about experience —are entirely orthogonal to my contentions here in the text, as well as to my contention that in acting freely, we endow our lives with "narrative value":

> There is widespread agreement that human beings typically see or live or experience their lives as a narrative or story of some sort, or at least as a collection of stories. I'll call this the *psychological Narrativity thesis*, using the word "Narrative" with a capital letter to denote a specifically psychological property or outlook. The psychological Narrativity thesis is a straightforwardly empirical, despriptive thesis about the way ordinary human beings actually experience their lives. This is how we are, it says, this is our nature.
>
> The psychological Narrativity thesis is often coupled with a normative thesis, which I'll call the *ethical Narrativity thesis*. This states that experiencing or conceiving one's life as a narrative is a good thing; a richly Narrative outlook is essential to a well-lived life, to true or full personhood. (Galen Strawson, "Against Narrativity," *Ratio* XVII (4) (2004), pp. 428–52, esp. p. 428.

My theses are about the structure and etiology of value, whereas Strawson's theses are about experience.

11. John Martin Fischer, "The Cards That Are Dealt You," *Journal of Ethics* (special issue in honor of Joel Feinberg) Vol. 10, Nos. 1–2 (2006): 107–29; also, see Fischer et al., 2007.

12. Richard Taylor. 1981. "The Meaning of Human Existence," in Burton M. Leiser, ed.,*Values in Conflict: Life, Liberty, and the Rule of Law*. New York: MacMillan Publishing. pp. 3–27

13. *Ibid*, pp. 23–4.

14. *Ibid*, p. 24.

15. This essay is a substantially revised version of: John Martin Fischer, "A Reply to Pereboom, Zimmerman, and Smith," part of a book symposium on John Martin Fischer, *My Way: Essays on Moral Responsibility, Philosophical Books* Vol. 47, No. 3 (2006): 235–44. In her insightful contribution, Angela Smith encouraged me to acknowledge more explicitly the social dimensions of moral responsibility. I concede that my development of the account of moral responsibility might suggest an overly individualistic picture, but I do not believe that, in the end, I am committed to a problematic sort of atomism. I certainly grant that the statements we care about (in acting freely) are *typically* parts of "conversations." In making such statements, we make connections—connections with other people and even causes "larger than ourselves" that are valuable parts of meaningful lives. I am inclined to accept the idea that we care about writing sentences in the books (stories) of our lives (on the simpler formulation), where these sentences are typically parts of conversations with others we care about. In thus making a statement, I make a connection. In writing my story, I help to write our story. My way becomes a part of our way.

I am grateful to Neal Tognazzini for thoughtful comments on a previous version of this essay. Also, I have learned from conversations with Howard Wettstein on the topics treated here.

The seminar is nearly over. The video monitors are bland and the surgeons are cleaning up and filing out into the hallway. Marilena replaces the white cloth on her cadaver's face; about half the surgeons do this. She is conscientiously respectful. When I asked her why the eyes of the dead woman had no pupils, she did not answer, but reached up and closed the eye-lids. As she slides back her chair, she looks down at the benapkined form and says, 'May she rest in peace.' I hear it as 'pieces,' but that's just me. (Mary Roach, Stiff: The Curious Lives of Human Cadavers)

Index

LaVergne, TN USA
28 November 2010
206551LV00001B/5/P